NONGRADED
SCHOOLS
IN ACTION

Bold New Venture

ALREADY PUBLISHED IN THE

Bold New Venture *Series*

TEAM TEACHING
INDEPENDENT STUDY
FLEXIBLE SCHEDULING
NONGRADED SCHOOLS IN ACTION

NONGRADED SCHOOLS IN ACTION

IN ACTION

Bold New Venture

EDITED BY

DAVID W. BEGGS, III

AND

EDWARD G. BUFFIE

INDIANA UNIVERSITY PRESS

BLOOMINGTON AND LONDON

Harold G. Shane—Teacher, Scholar, Friend

Preface

Bold New Venture Series

American education is emerging as a new frontier. Staggering challenges brought about by the contemporary demand for quality education for a bulging and diverse student population must be met. Old solutions for new problems will not suffice.

Pioneer educators are testing promising new programs and practices to effect fundamental improvement in the schools. Healthy dissatisfactions have led to the belief that if the schools are to be significantly better, they will have to be substantially different. Both the substance and the form of instruction are undergoing searching reappraisal. Exciting innovations have been instituted in schools scattered throughout the country. The *Bold New Venture* series is designed to inform educators and the interested public about these new developments and to assist in their evaluation.

The books in this series differ from much of the professional literature in education. The contributors, for the most part, are practitioners. Admittedly they are partial to their topics. Nevertheless, pitfalls are exposed and candid treatment is given to the issues. Emphasis has been put on reporting *how* as well as *why* new practices and programs were inaugurated. The volumes in this series are intended to be a stimulus to the conversation which must take place if fresh methods of teaching are to find their way into the schools.

Topics included in the *Bold New Venture* series include team teaching, flexible scheduling, independent study, the nongraded school, instructional materials centers, data processing, small group instruction, and technological aids.

While journalists criticize, scholars theorize about, and philosophers analyze education, the teachers of America must act. Educators must leap from theory to practice in individualizing instruction. More responsibility must be given and accepted by youngsters for their own learning. Intellectual inquiry must become full-time, leisure-time, and life-time pursuits.

Progress in education does not always come by the process of addition with more teachers, more books, more courses, and more money. Real improvement can come from original uses of scarce human talent, precious time, and new methods.

Because it is intended primarily for teachers and administrators, the *Bold New Venture* series focuses on the practical problems of teaching. What has been operationally successful for some teachers may have application for other teachers. If new practices or programs result from these books, then the series will have fulfilled its aim, for the *Bold New Venture* books are calls and guides to action.

BLOOMINGTON, INDIANA   D. W. B.

                                                 E. G. B.

Contents

Introduction   xi

PART I   THE DISCUSSION

1   A Historical Perspective   *by Edward G. Buffie*   3
2   The Nongraded School: A Dynamic Concept
                                     by Maurie Hillson   28
3   The Nongraded High School   *by David W. Beggs, III*   53
4   A Strategy for the Development of Nongraded Schools
                                    by Roy A. Larmee   77
5   Research and Evaluation of the Nongraded School
                                    by Robert J. Garvue   95
6   The Future of Nongraded Schools
                                    by Stuart E. Dean   107

PART II   NONGRADED SCHOOLS IN ACTION

7   Bellevue, Washington, Moves Toward
     Nongraded Schools   *by Roy Patrick Wahle*   127
8   Continuous Progress in Appleton, Wisconsin
                by Royce E. Kurtz and James N. Retson   135
9   Chicago Schools Design a Continuous
     Development Program
            by Evelyn F. Carlson and Jerome H. Gilbert   144
10   The Southern Humboldt Story from Northern California
            by Clara Shumaker and Warren Linville   154
11   Continuous Plan of Pupil Progress in Cabool, Missouri
                by Neal Neff and D. A. Ferguson   159
12   The Monteith Plan   *by Marshall C. Jameson*   166

13 The Peter Boscow Primary School, Hillsboro, Oregon
                 by Richard H. Hart and Alton O. Smedstad   174

14 The Torrance, California, Approach   *by John H. Hull*   184

15 The Cedar Falls, Iowa, Story
                 by Verna Sponsler and Marvin Zieman   191

16 Breaking Grade Level Barriers at the Webster School,
     Pontiac, Michigan   *by Edith Roach Snyder*   199

17 The Nova Nongraded High School,
     Fort Lauderdale, Florida   *by Arthur B. Wolfe*   207

18 The Middletown Project: A Nongraded
     Secondary School   *by Joseph H. Gaudet*   217

19 A Continuous Progress Plan at Brigham Young
     University, Provo, Utah   *by Edwin A. Read*   226

     Appendices   239

     Selected Bibliography   247

     Notes   259

     Index   263

Introduction

Some important changes have been brought about in education. But *some* changes are not enough. If the elementary and secondary schools of the United States are to be improved significantly, they must be substantially different.

The schools must provide quality education for every youngster. To offer quality instruction, the instructional program must be personal, flexible, and without artificial limits. Personal intellectual needs and interests must be accounted for in designing instruction on an individual basis for each learner. Standards, policies, and programs must be flexible to be appropriate for the individual requirements of a widely diverse school population. No limits must be set by administrative policies or organizational arrangements to restrict the maximum development of the able and ambitious learner or to frustrate the slow and disadvantaged learner. The schools of today must leap from theory to practice in individualizing instruction. New methods must replace old traditions of school organization. Thus, the nongraded school concept is proposed as a practical means of improving teaching and learning.

Monumental effort has been expended to bring about improvement in the programs of studies in both elementary and secondary schools. Scholars of the highest stature have given attention to the content of science, mathematics, and modern foreign language courses. English and social studies are undergoing searching reappraisals. Curriculum reform is in the air. But valuable as improved course content is, alone it is not enough to provide quality education for all youth. There is a need for a new organization for learning to make individual methods of instruction a standard mode of operation.

The Teacher's Role

Teaching is more than talking. Learning is more than listening. The teaching–learning process requires a diagnosis of the individual student by the teacher and a high degree of personal involvement by the learner. Effective teaching requires close observation of the student by the teacher. Ample time must be provided for students to work individually, sometimes with and other times without the teacher at hand. Careful prescriptions by the teacher of appropriate learning activities need to be given to every child. Teachers must be able to meet with students on an individual basis to make particular study recommendations. The school's organization should make this possible. Students need to be able to work at their own rate on subjects they are best able to handle. Thus, the school's program of studies should have both breadth and depth.

Even when instruction is given in groups, learning is an individual enterprise. Group membership often puts a burden on the learner. Group progress is sometimes too rapid; other times it is too slow. In either case, the individual is disadvantaged. The focus of the group will nearly always be only in the shadows of interest or understanding for some individuals. Thus, the school's organization for instruction must be reformed so that personal attention to learners takes the place of group teaching practices.

A promise for progress in education is proposed through the nongraded school organization. Such an organization for learning values highly and places profound faith in the professional competencies of teachers. Also, the nongraded organization implies that each individual has unique instructional needs.

This Book

The first part of this book attempts to present a discussion of the nongraded concept. The rationale and the historical development of school organization are discussed in the first two chapters by Edward Buffie and Maurice Hillson. In the third chapter David Beggs gives a theoretical description of a nongraded secondary school. Emphasis has been given to the procedures and problems of establishing nongraded schools in the elementary and secondary schools by Roy Larmee in the fourth chapter. Research and evaluation of nongraded programs are discussed in the fifth chapter by Robert Garvue. Stuart Dean assesses the development of nongraded schools to date and comments on the future of this form of school organization in the sixth chapter.

To institute a nongraded program is indeed a bold new venture. The second part of the book presents reports of individual schools which use varying forms of nongraded organization. The unity in these reports lies in a healthy dissatisfaction with graded school organization and with the belief that youngsters should be thought of as individuals, not as members of a particular group. Some of the program descriptions may cause the reader to conclude that it is easier to discuss the concept than to implement it. Other descriptions clearly show that progress has been made in instituting quality-centered and flexible school programs.

There is wide range in the characteristics of the schools included in this report. The account of the small school in Cabool, Missouri, is contrasted with the story of the steps toward nongradedness taken by the huge Chicago, Illinois, school system. The affluent suburban school districts are represented by the Monteith School from Grosse Pointe, Michigan.

Nongraded secondary schools in Fort Lauderdale, Florida, and Middletown, Rhode Island, are described. There are fewer nongraded secondary schools in operation in the country and fewer reports of high schools included in the book. Interest of secondary school educators in the concept, nevertheless, is high.

The program of the laboratory school at Brigham Young University tells how one school under a university's influence operates. Accounts from Hillsboro, Oregon, and Pontiac, Michigan, describe how public schools have moved into various types of nongraded organizations through their own efforts.

Individual Not Group Focus

The promise of progress in education is proposed through the nongraded school. Such a school organization ignores group classifications with their attendant individual transgressions. Instead, focus is put on nurturing each human being, regardless of his contrasts with the accomplishments of others of similar years on earth.

The establishment of the nongraded school implies no radical departure from the accepted educational objectives of the American schools. But the nongraded organization does help teachers and students meet those objectives more easily and with new and personal advantage. The nongraded school gives considered attention to human variability. The goal of quality education for every student is the foundation of such a school. However, for some teachers, nongradedness does demand new approaches to instruction and requires a vastly different mind-set about how the schools are to be ordered, as the program descriptions in this book reveal.

The nongraded school offers advantages to teachers as well as to students. For students, the nongraded school offers freedom from the unreasonable assumption that one lesson, one course, and one set of requirements suit all. For teachers, the nongraded school organization offers the opportunity to exercise personal judgment, give skillful service, and receive increased professional satisfaction. In the nongraded school, the teacher makes a diagnosis, gives a prescription, and sometimes even works as a therapist while learning takes place. Teaching takes on a new meaning as an intimate, strong relationship is built between student and teacher.

The Pace of Adoption

The spread of nongraded schools has been both alarmingly slow and surprisingly rapid. Contrasted with the increased introduction of new programs in science, mathematics, and foreign language, the nongraded movement has been slow in development. But there are no federal funds to sponsor institutes, prepare guides, and concentrate on development for the nongraded school, as there have been for the content revisions. Also, the introduction of the nongraded concept implies widespread faculty participation in this innovation. In changes of course content, only the particular teachers of the subject field are called upon to alter their programs. In spite of these factors, the nongraded organization has increased in use in recent years at an unusual rate, considering the adoption of this concept implies the rejection of the traditional way teachers were taught to teach.

National study groups can develop grand statements of purpose. Scholars can follow scholars in developing new materials. But in the final analysis, teachers and administrators in the elementary and secondary schools are the ones who must make the decisions about how and what youngsters will be taught. The faculty in each school has great potential for improving instruction. Some ignore this potential by refusing to search for more effective ways to teach. But others—and happily the number is increasing—are actively seeking better solutions for educational problems.

If this book helps teachers critically examine the instructional arrangements in their schools, it will have satisfied one of its purposes. If this book is any help to schools in introducing a nongraded program, it will have achieved its ultimate purpose.

Acknowledgments

Without the sterling cooperation and interest of countless educators, this book would not have been possible. Some helped by informal discussions of the need for this kind of book on the nongraded school. Others assisted in recommending contributors and in evaluating the raw manuscript. Still others interrupted their busy schedules to write chapters for the book.

A single author would be hard pressed to present the range of ideas expressed herein. This book is intended as a guide to action as well as a discussion of certain educational theories. As such, it represents much of the experience the contributors have had in their schools. Therefore, any credit which is due should be due the contributors. However, if the book has faults, these are the editors' responsibility. The editors made the final selection of what is and what is not reported.

Special mention must be given to our colleagues both in the public schools and at Indiana University. With their questions and assertions, and through our association with them, our convictions about the nongraded school were formulated and cemented. Particular debt is due Dr. Robert H. Anderson, Harvard University professor, and to Dr. J. Lloyd Trump, National Association of Secondary School Principals Associate Executive Secretary, for their professional inspiration.

Bloomington, Indiana   EDWARD G. BUFFIE
                                                        DAVID W. BEGGS, III

PART I

THE DISCUSSION

CHAPTER 1

A Historical Perspective

by

EDWARD G. BUFFIE

Throughout his professional career, Dr. Buffie has been associated with innovations in education. First as an elementary school teacher and later as an administrator in Park Forest, Illinois, one of the communities to pioneer the use of the nongraded organization, Dr. Buffie has had intimate association with the concept of the nongraded school. At Indiana University, Dr. Buffie has served as curriculum coordinator, principal, and consultant to the University Laboratory School.

In addition to his work at the University School, Dr. Buffie is an associate coordinator of the INSITE Program, which involves a new design for teacher education at Indiana University.

T HE MOST widely accepted plan of school organization today is the graded school plan in which each grade level represents a predetermined year of work, and subject content for all the pupils is approximately the same. Despite numerous attempts to change this basic organizational structure, the schools in our country, with few exceptions, have maintained this traditional graded structure for well over a century. The time has come to reconsider and revise the school's organization to make it serve the educational demands of these times. Today, there is little consolation in Alexander Pope's comment: "Not to go back is somewhat to advance."

Historical Development of Elementary School Organization

The development of public education in the United States is something of which this nation has every right to be proud. The United States was one of the first nations in the world to develop an educational system designed to provide free public education for all its people. Evolving as the result of a combination of social and economic factors present in the early development of its democracy, this system also owed much of its organization and philosophy to the European countries from which the colonists emigrated.

As each wave of colonization brought people from different countries to the New World, a variety of European traditions were transplanted. And so it was that the dame school, the district school, the writing school, the Latin grammar school, and the college were each based almost completely on counterparts found at that time in England, France, and Spain. The greatest scholastic influence, however, came from England.

The schools were not always graded in the colonies; the seventeenth-century dame schools and the eighteenth-century district schools disregarded grade classification. In the dame school children ranging in ages from three to ten met together for instruction and usually youngsters received twenty minutes or so of individualized help twice a day. The rest of the time they either worked on written lessons or listened to the older students.

Children attended the district schools only when the teacher and school came to their particular district. The teacher simply picked up where he had left off at the end of the last trip. In that situation, teaching was of necessity on an individualized basis, at least as much of the time as possible.

Each district school was organized for a specific academic purpose and followed similar practices in terms of accepting children of various ages and abilities. In the district school, the pupils met together in a single room and worked under the direction of a single teacher, primarily on an individual basis. Identification of pupils by grade levels generally was unknown and promotion came only after students had mastered enough of the fundamentals to succeed at the Latin school or in college.

By the beginning of the eighteenth century, the dame schools were well established. Together, the writing school and the dame school provided all the reading and writing instruction considered essential in that era. These lower schools were terminal for the masses and promotion to higher schools, especially for girls, was rare indeed. But in these times, for most people, to be educated was to be able to read and handle simple arithmetic processes.

Soon, however, educational leaders began to envision a unified system of education publicly controlled and supported and open to all in order to meet the needs of the emerging democratic society. Long before the beginning of the national period, elementary education began to assume the character of the one-room schoolhouse, long to be a familiar part of the American scene. This type of district school achieved a certain permanency, was ungraded, and accepted pupils of any age. Small, one-room schools soon dotted the landscape. Due to their small enrollments, more than any other reason, these schools were ungraded.

During the ensuing years, the development of the first graded schools took place. The Quincy Grammar School, founded in 1848, is a typical example. The organization of this school was the expected result of the many movements toward grading which were clearly in evidence during the preceding century. Goodlad and Anderson[1] have given a telling description of the major developments which ultimately resulted in the creation of the graded school. The first of these has already been mentioned: the movement toward public, state-supported education, which manifested a predilection for a rigid order of instruction. It came to be expected that arithmetic would be learned at a certain age, writing at another age, and each grade would have as its goal some particular set of accomplishments for all youth at the grade level.

After the graded system came the monitorial system, which put the older and, hopefully, the more able student in the role of teacher's helper. The school master would teach a lesson to the more apt of his students, and they, in turn, would attempt to teach what they had learned to their immediate subordinates. The responsibility of these monitors extended even to examining and promoting the pupils for whom they were responsible.

Samuel Hall, in 1823, and James G. Carter, in 1827, opened the first normal schools in the United States, fashioning them after German examples. Thus, the establishment of the teacher-training institution in this country was on its way. The last half of the nineteenth century saw these institutions contribute to the spread of the graded structure. As they trained teachers, they instilled in them a belief in a precise order for instruction and promoted a common educational practice based on the graded school system.

Another development which had considerable impact upon the movement toward the graded structure was the appearance of the graded textbook. The phenomenal acceptance of the 1836 edition of the *McGuffey Eclectic Reader,* which was graded through six levels, was enough to encourage others to produce graded textbooks. And soon, textbook series—available first in reading and arithmetic— were on the market for all areas of the curriculum.

Finally, the influence of European educational thought and policy was once again felt as leading American educators who had traveled to Europe returned to extol the virtues of foreign schools. Horace Mann was particularly impressed with his visit to the graded schools in Prussia, and he returned to urge the adoption of a similar system in this country during the 1840's.

All of these developments, in addition to the increase of thousands of children flocking to the schools and new state laws lengthening school terms and extending the number of years of schooling, emerged as influences which ultimately led to a system of classifying pupils according to a predetermined criterion based solely on age. Even as early as 1799, in Middlesex County, Connecticut, and 1800, in Providence, Rhode Island, school districts were calling for some kind of pupil classification. The desire of educators to classify pupils into instructional groups is deep in the professional grain.

While there is disagreement as to the exact origin of the graded school, the Quincy Grammar School, established in 1848, is generally recognized as the first graded structure in the United States. The merits of the graded plan, particularly its administrative convenience, caused it to take hold quickly, and wherever it was applicable, the system spread. By 1870, our present-day system of graded schools, graded textbooks, and grade-oriented teachers was already firmly established.

The development of the graded elementary school in the nineteenth century was a significant creative effort appropriate for its time. Goodlad and Anderson state:

> It permitted the convenient classification of unprecedented numbers of pupils pouring into the schools during the second half of the century. It encouraged the division of knowledge into segments to be taught at the various grade levels. Consequently, it simplified the task of preparing needed teachers quickly; teachers were simply taught what they were themselves to teach in a given grade. Man's zeal for efficiency was challenged and he met the challenge vigorously. Soon an enterprise of gigantic proportions was functioning with amazing efficiency while continuing to expand at an astonishing rate. That so many people agreed so quickly and so generally on distinct learning tasks for each grade level is truly amazing.[2]

Within a short period of approximately twenty years the graded elementary school organization had spanned the nation. But soon a few rumblings were heard, and it became clear that not all educators agreed completely on its merits. The same educational system which gloried in its new-found efficiency also gave rise to an inhibiting form of regimentation. The pendulum had swung from no system to nothing but system. Heavy pupil dropout, resulting from too much rigidity in teaching methods and an unbending method of annual promotion, was viewed by some educators with dismay. Educators began to speak out against the graded system as one which demanded mass conformity. To the critics, it seemed as if the uniqueness of each individual was being overlooked in the schools' organization. Consequently, innovations in school organization began to appear in American education designed to correct some of the more obvious defects of the early graded schools.

Early Innovations

Not long after the graded concept claimed popularity in this country, the first attempts to modify that basic, rigid pattern were formulated. These early attempts, as well as those that followed throughout the remainder of the nineteenth and into the early decades of the twentieth century, were usually efforts to vary the instructional program within the framework of the graded school. Educators sought to modify instructional practice within, rather than to break down, the existing graded structure. Thus, the interest of the post-Sputnik days in special classes for gifted students was not new.

The galaxy of plans and approaches which emerged were all variations on the graded regimentation. Some attempted to temper the adverse effects of grading, particularly failing; others tried to provide more realistically for the differences in groups of children progressing through school; others were designed to provide opportunities for individuals to progress at varying rates through the curriculum. Still another plan examined the teacher's position and how his strengths might best be employed.

The graded structure has long been a concern of thoughtful educators. But, adaptations of the graded structure, rather than departures from it, were the means used to attempt to compensate for its weaknesses.

Problems of Failure

Not too many years after the graded movement began to be popular, one of its less fortunate by-products became apparent, pupil failure. "I failed first grade" became an horrendous phrase heard much too often. This problem of children failing grades reached its awesome peak in the 1920's, when some of our large eastern cities were reporting failure rates for first grade pupils as high as 40 per cent.[3]

Several school systems created plans wherein it was hoped more frequent promotion would tend to offset failure. In the Elizabeth (New Jersey) Plan, for example, there was promotion three times a year. If a student failed in this plan, it was not quite so bad as if he failed in a community which had only annual promotion. The best known of these attempts was the St. Louis (Missouri) Plan. Even though St. Louis had formally adopted the graded plan of organization in 1857, by 1862 a new course of study was in operation in which some of the recognized disadvantages of graded organization, particularly with regard to promotion and retention, could be lessened if not eliminated. The year's work was divided into four ten-week units and promotions were made every ten weeks. Quarterly promotion was a unique variation in comparison to what was then in vogue. Reports do not clearly indicate exactly how successful this experiment was within its own sphere of influence. However, the quarterly plan had very little impact on the national level and was not generally adopted.

Focus on Groups

Most of the early innovations based on the first graded schools were concerned with the lock-step pace in which all children proceeded through the schools. Although grade programs did not vary, the children did vary widely in many ways. Thus, educators began to vary the curriculum to cope with these extreme differences. However, the programs were still little changed except for the fact that the children were being placed in ability groups and, thus, the length of time each group spent on any particular phase of the curriculum could vary. Still, individuals were treated as members of a group of 30 students or more most of the time.

The Cambridge (Massachusetts) Plan and the Portland (Oregon) Plan are good examples of attempts to provide for individual differences within the terms of group organization. In Cambridge, in 1895, a plan was devised wherein all pupils would take the same work during the first three years of a nine-year elementary course. However, the work of the last six years was arranged in two parallel courses. The regular course for average students took the full six years to complete, while a special advanced course for brighter pupils required only four years. By 1910, in Cambridge, the elementary curriculum had been reduced to eight years, and the double-track system extended down to the first grade.

In Portland, Oregon, in 1900, a nine-grade course of study was divided into 54 units. The average children covered six units each year; the bright children were placed in a separate division, permitted to take eight units each year, and thus complete elementary school in seven years. Elements of this plan have been found in various other plans, but inadequate data make it difficult to determine the extent to which it was adopted by other schools.

At Batavia, New York, special provision was made for slow-learning pupils. Interestingly, the emphasis here was on the slow student rather than on the average or bright student. At this time, classes were large, consisting of 80 or more students, and two teachers worked with each class—the direct instruction teacher and an assistant. The slow children received special instruction from the assistant teacher in the back of the room, and this extra help was expected to aid such children in coming up to standard. Used in Batavia and elsewhere in various forms, this plan was in effect for approximately 30 years. Certain phases of the plan can be recognized in the various special classes in existence today, such as remedial reading, which are designed specifically to bolster achievement of particular youngsters.

Other attempts were made to vary not only the rate of progress but also the content. The North Denver (Colorado) Plan was just the reverse of the Batavia Plan. Here the bright children were singled out for additional instruction. Classroom organization remained the same with all pupils covering certain minimum requirements or assignments. However, enriched work was provided for the brighter students, and each classroom was provided with 50 to 75 carefully selected library books for their use.

The Santa Barbara (California) Concentric Plan, devised by Frederick Burk, called for the division of pupils into three groups designated A, B, and C. The C group did the basic work; B did a little more; and the A group did the most work. This plan also provided for promotion three times a year. After it had been in effect only a short time, it was reported that the plan had been discontinued because it was too impractical and difficult to administer. It can be assumed the benefits to students were less telling than the work involved for educators.

Undaunted, Frederick Burk then moved to the San Francisco Normal School and extended the Pueblo Plan developed earlier by Preston W. Search. Grades were still retained, but the curriculum was organized into various units. Successful test performance completed the work of a given unit in a subject. There were no grade failures and children simply moved forward on an irregular front, subject by subject, according to the number of units completed.

Focus on Individuals

Even as interest in providing challenge within the curriculum for groups of varying abilities continued to grow and gain impetus, another interest posed a new question: What about the development of the individual?

Preston W. Search, superintendent of schools in Pueblo, Colorado, from 1888 to 1894, has been given credit for being the first American educator to voice loud protests against the class lock-step method of teaching and to argue for complete individual progress for each pupil. His idea was put into practical application during his tenure in Pueblo and later in Los Angeles, where he was superintendent in 1895. This was one of the first attempts to bring about a radical change at the high school level.

Essentially, this plan consisted of a program in which the work of each high school subject was outlined in such a way that each child could progress at his own rate in each subject. All units in each course were studied by every student but at varying rates. No marks were given, the concept of nonpromotion was eliminated, and teachers' records simply indicated the number of units completed satisfactorily. Emphasis was upon individual work and progress as opposed to group work and group progress. While this plan was applied most extensively in high school, Search believed that it could be used in the elementary school.

Again, how extensively the basic principles of this plan were utilized and adopted in other cities is difficult to assess. Although the term *Pueblo Plan* has been obscured through the years, there is evidence that its influence was strongly felt and that it had considerable impact upon the programs and thinking found in subsequent deviations from group-centered educational practices. In his own writings, Search gives many illustrations of school practices which embodied certain elements of his Pueblo Plan. A close look at the work done a little later by Morrison at the University of Chicago High School, the programs developed under the name of the Dalton Plan, and the elementary plans developed by Frederick Burk in San Francisco and Carleton Washburne at Winnetka, Illinois, reveals many interesting parallels to the pioneer enterprise of Preston Search.

Although both the Dalton Plan and the Pueblo Plan place great emphasis upon the individual, the former was mostly concerned with the individual's performance in group situations. The Dalton Plan was first introduced in 1919 by Helen Parkhurst in an ungraded school for crippled children. The next year it was adopted by a high school in Dalton, Massachusetts, from which it took its name.

Essentially, this plan consisted of subjects of study being divided into academic and vocational groups. The academic subjects were organized sequentially, and students worked and progressed on an individual basis. The individual job-sheet-unit conference technique was employed. The work of each grade in each of the academic subjects was laid out by a series of related jobs or contracts, each of these consisting of a number of smaller units. The learning tasks were thus identified for each child, and he was permitted to progress to the completion of his requirements, which were determined through a checking conference with his teacher. The nonacademic part of the curriculum was taught by class or group methods. There were specialized teachers and facilities, and students were grouped on a nongraded basis. Pupils had considerable freedom of choice regarding the units of work they undertook. While each pupil was free to determine his own pace, each was required to complete the corresponding grade-level units for a subject before moving on to advanced work in a single subject matter area.

The Winnetka Plan was very closely related to the Dalton Plan and perhaps better known. It derived its name from the work of Carleton Washburne in Winnetka, Illinois, where he carried on the ideas introduced by Frederick Burk in California. As in the Dalton Plan, the individualized task approach was emphasized. Extensive development of this idea was also pioneered in Chicago, Illinois, by James E. McDade and in Bronxville, New York, by Willard W. Beatty.

In Winnetka the course of study was divided into two parts. One half in the morning and one half in the afternoon were devoted to two types of activity. First came "common essentials" which consisted of the so-called basic subjects—knowledge and skills which, presumably, everyone was expected to master. In this phase of the program, pupils worked on individual assignments, each at his own rate. Tests were administered at appropriate times to measure academic achievement. Established standards had to be met before successive units of work could be undertaken. The second part of the program dealt with the "group and creative activities." Included in this category were literature, music, art, physical education, and manual arts. Self-expression and the individual development of interests and abilities were stressed and there were no specific standards to be met.

The quality of the Winnetka program has been recognized for several decades. However, the program has undergone several

modifications since its original introduction, and for a more up-to-
date treatment of the situation as it exists today, the reader is
referred to Washburne's recent writings.[4]

Innovation and Role Change

Some innovations have had a much greater impact upon the role of
the teacher than have others. The plans described previously, while
changing group composition and the time spans, did not greatly
alter the one-to-one relationship between the teacher and the class.
However, modifications to this arrangement have also been considered.

The earliest plan for changing the one-class-per-teacher arrangement, was the Platoon System, first established in Bluffton, Indiana,
in 1900 by William A. Wirt, when he was superintendent in that
small midwestern community. By 1908, Wirt had moved to Gary,
Indiana, and put the plan into operation there. Sometimes referred
to as the "work-study-play" program, it called for the division of
students into two groups. Instruction in the fundamental subjects
was provided by the homeroom teacher for one group while opportunities for activity were available to the other group. Activities
included such things as manual arts, physical education, art, music,
auditorium, library, nature study, and home economics, most of
which required special facilities or laboratories. These areas were
taught by specialists on a departmental basis. Oftentimes, some sort
of special grouping by ability or I.Q. was made. Except for auditorium and gymnasium periods, the grade-level structure was maintained. By limiting the number of areas in which a teacher would
give instruction, it was assumed that his proficiency in the areas of
concentration would grow, and consequently, the educational program would be improved.

Departmentalization, an outgrowth of the Platoon System, gained
widespread acceptance, during the 1920's and 1930's, particularly at
the high school level. To date, departmentalization has had a more
lasting impact on education than any other organizational innovation other than the basic graded plan. Departmentalization in junior
and senior high school is often taken for granted. Today, there is a

trend in the direction of departmentalization at the intermediate level (grades four, five, and six).

In 1930, along with the growth of departmentalization, there was an early attempt at team teaching. The Cooperative Group Plan, as it was named, was simply an attempt to have groups of teachers, each a subject-matter specialist with a classroom designed for his specialty, work cooperatively to coordinate their efforts in planning and evaluating the work of students. The plan's primary purpose was to provide for the individual differences of both the pupils and the teachers.

Pupils in a given group usually ranged across several grade levels, so that multi-age group instruction and some degree of continuous education were possible. Children often stayed with the same group of teachers for two or three years, and each teacher in a group (there were usually from three to six in a group) was expected to relate his work to the work of the others, so that the picture was one of general cooperation and unity of purpose, in which each teacher sought to capitalize on the strengths of the others. Too advanced for its time, the Cooperative Group Plan quickly disappeared and remained undercover until its vestiges were brought again to new life in the mid-1950's in the form of team teaching.

One of the most comprehensive and carefully designed grouping plans, the Dual Progress Plan, was developed by George D. Stoddard and his associates at New York University, in cooperation with the Long Beach and Ossining, New York, school systems. Based upon an elaborate cultural and learning-theory analysis, it represents a highly specialized and well-designed synthesis of many of the important features of earlier programs. The plan is creatively and sensitively handled to achieve an exciting approach to what has become the fundamental question in education today: How can we best provide for individual differences?

In the organization of this plan, a distinction is made between what the authors designate as cultural imperatives: English, social studies, health, and physical education; and cultural electives: mathematics, science, art, music, and foreign languages. The school day is divided into two halves: One half is devoted to the cultural imperatives under a single teacher who generally has an academic background in English and social studies and who functions as a homeroom teacher responsible for registration, counseling, and so forth. The other half of the day is devoted to the cultural electives taught by teachers who are subject-matter specialists and offer their subjects on a longitudinal basis.

The cultural imperatives are offered in grade units, and students are divided in sections at each grade level according to their ability. On the other hand, electives are nongraded and organized into systematic subject sequences. The students are then placed within each continuum according to their interests, ability, and performance. Scheduling is handled on a platoon basis. However, the specialist teachers must work together like a team in order to develop sequences and schedule pupils to best provide for their interests and abilities.

Many Attempts Over Many Years

The programs described above do not tell the entire story; many, many other attempts at improvement in school grading systems have been made throughout the country over the decades. But those mentioned are certainly among the better-known examples and represent a good cross section of those plans which have been described in the literature. It is evident that from the period of 1900 to the present considerable discussion and action relating to inadequacies of the graded pattern had resulted in little agreement regarding an improved structural framework for teaching and learning. Because the variety of attempts which had been made were all efforts to cope with the situation from the vantage point of a graded approach, they were, from the beginning, off to a wrong start. The evils of graded organization cannot be taken away if any form of the graded structure is preserved.

The graded school then, as now, simply is not in harmony with the basic purpose of American education; namely, that every child should have an opportunity to develop his talents to the fullest extent possible. If one recognizes that all children vary tremendously in past achievement, potential, interest, and socioeconomic background, and if one believes what many decades of painstaking study have taught regarding learning theory and child development, then it becomes obvious that graded schools, graded classrooms, graded textbooks, graded expectations, and graded instructors are all out of step with the goal of individualized teaching. With programs geared to the mythical average student, graded-school organization has, for the most part, simply ignored the variety in human capabilities by the very nature of its lock-step pattern and rigidity of structure.

None of the plans described in the preceding pages, with the exception of departmentalization, has withstood the test of time. Although traces of certain of the plans were to be found in one form or another, it has been quite apparent that the search for better ways to organize schools was to continue.

The restless search for improvement slowed down for a time; the depression and World War II did not further the cause of educational change. In the 1950's and early 1960's the search was renewed and finally the break came. Early innovations had paved the way for a massive attack on the strict gradation of the elementary school. The nongraded school was born.

Emergence of the Nongraded School

Like several of the innovations described in this chapter, the nongraded school is designed to implement a theory of continuous school progress. However, the nongraded plan differs very dramatically in one important aspect. It makes a complete break with the traditional graded-school organization of the past; it is not just a modification of that organizational structure. The organizational form thus complements, rather than hinders, the educational purpose of continuous progress for all pupils, who vary in all aspects of their development. Some pupil differences are great and cannot be substantially modified; therefore, it is the school structure which must be pliable enough to bend with the child. Nongrading works for, rather than against, the basic premise that each child is different. It encourages the efforts of all involved to treat this difference as a challenge, rather than an inconvenience to be sidestepped, and it does so by the very nature of its basic principles.

This is not to say that the philosophy which undergirds nongraded organization could not be implemented within a graded pattern of organization. But the truth seems to be that this simply does not happen. Admittedly, there are fine schools doing an outstanding job in curriculum planning and program development which are not nongraded, but, unfortunately, they remain, year after year, the exception, not the rule.

Similarly, there is no guarantee that a smashing curricular success will grow out of every organizational shake-up. But the likelihood of success is much improved when the organization for education that is adopted is consistent with the philosophy to which the plan's supporters subscribe.

The Beginnings

The 1930's mark the emergence of the nongraded movement. Although it is difficult to identify the exact beginning of this organizational operation, the development of a nongraded school at Western Springs, Illinois, seems to have been the first of its type. The method of organization was called the Flexible Progress Plan. It was initiated in 1934, and in September, 1935, grades one, two, and three were abolished. In the 1936–1937 school year, the program was extended to the intermediate grades. The only phase of the program in which there was actual differentiation in teaching procedures was in reading.

There were several other nongraded schools in the late 1930's. In 1936 a junior primary unit was first organized in Richmond, Virginia. This unit replaced kindergarten and first grade and is still utilized in many schools today. The College Avenue School in Athens, Georgia, has had a nongraded system called the Continuous Progress Plan in effect since 1939. At that time, a letter was sent home to all parents explaining why grade symbols were being abolished and replaced by the primary grade plan or organization. Also, it has been reported that some experimental work in this direction was done in Fond du Lac, Wisconsin, during the late thirties under the leadership of Lowell P. Goodrich.

The development of nongraded schools in the early 1940's was reported in Petoski, Michigan, Glencoe, Illinois, and Cleveland, Ohio. However, the plan begun in 1942 in Milwaukee, Wisconsin, under Lowell P. Goodrich, is generally recognized as the oldest nongraded school plan still in existence. Certainly, this was the first large school district to initiate such a plan on a wide scale and it represented a milestone in the nongraded school movement. Today, all but two of the Milwaukee schools have ungraded primary units. Though the development of the Ungraded Primary School at Milwaukee did much to focus attention upon this concept of elementary school organization, the movement remained more or less stagnant throughout the late forties.

That the modern nongraded school was born at the primary level has already been suggested, but proof of this came in the studies made by Goodlad in 1955.[5] Of sixteen nongraded centers identified by Goodlad at that time, ten were of the primary-unit pattern. While Goodlad had identified 16 such centers, Slater[6] reported that she had identified 28 primary school organizations.

After starting with a single school in 1942, Milwaukee was reported to have 78 primary schools functioning under this organization by 1955. As late as 1955, then, the nongraded movement was still developing at a very slow pace, though beginning to pick up momentum. Anderson wrote:

> Although I should like very much to regale you with accounts of numerous successful examples of the ungraded primary school, the distressing truth is that the movement is very young and has accelerated at the pace of the tortoise than the hare.[7]

By 1957 Austin[8] identified 31 centers with active nongraded units. Most of the centers identified by Goodlad and Austin were started between 1947 and 1950. Generally speaking, except for a few scattered efforts, the nongraded school has been in existence only since the end of World War II. There was a little flurry of action between the years 1947 and 1950, after which spread of the movement slowed down somewhat for a five-year period. From 1955 on, however, considerable momentum was gained as indicated in surveys compiled by Goodlad and Anderson in 1958 and 1960, by the United States Office of Education in 1960, and by the National Education Association Research Division in 1961. This interest is reflected in the frequency with which the professional journals and educational literature focused attention on nongraded schools.

In late 1958, Goodlad and Anderson,[9] recognized authorities in this area, reported in the findings of their questionnaire survey that as of 1957–1958, 44 of the 180 communities contacted operated one or more nongraded schools according to the definition they had devised. They defined the nongraded school as one in which grade labels were entirely removed from two or more grades. Thirty other communities were reportedly studying the nongraded organization at that time. The number of schools actually involved ran into the hundreds. Two years later, another survey conducted by the same two writers revealed that 89 communities or centers had nongraded schools and 550 were believed to be utilizing this method of organization.

In a very comprehensive and extensive survey carried on in 1958 and 1959 by the United States Office of Education, Stuart Dean reported that 18 per cent of the elementary schools in this country were using the primary unit. Regarding the inclusion of this type of organization in a survey of national practices, Dean remarked:

> A third area of Early Elementary Education investigated was the "primary unit." Variously, this is known as the ungraded school, the ungraded primary, the nongraded elementary school, the primary department, a continuous growth plan, the primary group and the primary unit. It was felt that it was pertinent and essential to the purposes of this survey to discover national practices and trends in this new and timely aspect of elementary school organization and administration. Increasingly public schools have been reporting the adoption of this administrative and instructional practice and the volume of educational literature has been building up markedly on this topic.[10]

A random sampling of all cities of over 2,500 population was made (555 cities out of a possible total of 4,307). Projections indicated that 776 urban places were using the primary unit at that time, and 473 others were considering future adoption of this type of organization.

The findings reported by Dean are unusually high, particularly when compared with the 1960 Goodlad and Anderson survey and a National Education Association Research Division survey of 1961. This is understandable when one examines the definition used in Dean's study: "Primary unit means an administrative device by which children are grouped to permit continuous progress during a period of two or more consecutive years. The teacher may remain with the same group for more than one year."[11] Nevertheless, this survey provides some idea of the extent of influence of the continuous progress philosophy with which the nongraded school is most closely associated and identified.

In a survey made the following year, the National Education Association Research Division sent out questionnaires to 1,495 urban school districts regarding the extent to which nongraded plans were in use. Out of 819 replies, 71 reported the use of a nongraded plan. Using weighted estimates based on the sample of replies, it was determined that about 6.3 per cent of all urban school districts (about 230 systems) were using an ungraded primary block plan either for the entire system or on an experimental basis in just a few schools.[12]

Most of the growth realized up to the late 1950's was at the elementary school level. But the high schools were also moving toward nongrading. The Staff Utilization Studies directed by J. Lloyd Trump and the team teaching emphasis have given considerable push to the development of the nongraded high school. The interest with which B. Frank Brown's *The Nongraded High School,* the first full-length book describing in detail the inception and operation of a nongraded high school, was received gives strong indication of the educational climate of the moment.[13] Today, many nongraded high schools are in the blueprint stage, particularly in California. A description of two such examples is given in Chapter 7 in the description of the high school at Middletown, Rhode Island, and the Nova High School at Fort Lauderdale, Florida.

Interest continues to mount. This is particularly evident in professional publications released since 1961. The first of these papers is rather innocently entitled, *Elementary School Organization: Purposes, Patterns, and Perspectives* (The National Elementary Principal Department, NEA, December, 1961). This little book, which reveals the thinking of this normally conservative group, leaves little doubt that for them nongraded schools are very much in the future. The next year a study reported by another NEA group revealed a prediction that some sort of nongrading would appear in twenty-six per cent of the schools by 1966. And in 1963 the National Education Association Project on Instruction, through its *Planning and Organizing for Teaching* report, made firm recommendations regarding the exploration of nongrading and multi-grading, both of which can claim a basic emphasis on the concept of continuous progress.

A Point in Time

Today we have come to a point in time where the vast majority of nongraded programs are in the cocoon stage. In most instances, the nongrading which exists, stretches, unfortunately, only far enough to cover one area of the curriculum—reading. There are exceptions, however, in which we find significant strides being made in other areas as well. These are identified and discussed in the last chapters of this book.

Strangely enough, the high schools which have taken the plunge have done much more than just get their feet wet, they have almost all made across-the-board changes. But there just are not enough high schools using this form of organization to conclude there is a widespread trend toward nongradedness at this level.

What Is a Nongraded School?

A good question. A nongraded school is a school which denies the limitations of grade structure and is organized so that the individual student may develop his academic and creative talents as rapidly or as slowly as his abilities permit. Instead of 16 grades, one might well envision a program such as the following:

	PRIMARY	INTER-	JUNIOR	SENIOR	
An educational continuum		MEDIATE	HIGH	HIGH	
	SCHOOL	SCHOOL	SCHOOL	SCHOOL	

Before entering the primary school, which would be, roughly, the equivalent of work traditionally covered in grades one, two, and three, there would be ideally the opportunity for a pupil to spend one, two, or three years in a pre-primary school. We already have kindergarten programs which represent the nucleus of such a program. And as concern for the education of the culturally disadvantaged child grows, there is good chance that a real pre-school (or pre-primary) movement may be on its way. Operation Head Start is a solid move in this direction.

Pupils would spend two, three, or four years in each school, three being the average. Progress in each academic area would be continuous, as illustrated in the following example:

THE NONGRADED PRIMARY SCHOOL
Progress of three pupils through an ungraded primary reading program

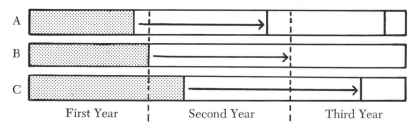

That the program for the various schools would overlap becomes obvious when we understand that a pupil may very well be considerably ahead in one area and not in another. This should create no particular problem if the content program is set up on a continuum. Each teacher would simply continue the program of instruction for each child at the point where the pupil discontinued work in the previous school.

The pupil who is able to move ahead rapidly in all areas and whose overall maturity seems to indicate his readiness may move on to the next school block, of course. And it is this pupil who would, conceivably, complete the average three-year program in only two years.

In the case of a youngster who is advanced academically, but shows other indications that his needs would be better met within his peer group, the accelerated move to the next school would probably not be wise. Here again, however, a flexible curricular program would allow him to pursue advanced academic work, even though he would remain with his chronological peers. Advanced placement programs at the high school level are applications of this same idea.

The less-able pupil, too, benefits from the flexibility nongrading provides. He might spend four years, for example (consider the very young six-year-old, who just makes the first-grade deadline), in primary school and, through this added year and a somewhat less intense approach to his early learning, find every ensuing year a welcome experience rather than a hurdle. The older, physically more mature primary student, still academically slow, might be moved on to the next (intermediate) level so that he remains with his peers, but every attention would be given to keeping his program at a level consistent with his abilities.

Let us be clear. One of the most unfortunate misconceptions about nongrading has been that it serves only the "gifted" child and that the other 99 per cent of pupils in the educable stream is left to paddle along in the same old way. This is not correct. The whole idea of nongrading is bastardized if only one segment of the student population is served.

For the skeptic who chides, "impossible," just stop for a moment and think. We all know that every primary teacher worth her salt already provides for the beginning reader's differences in ability. And, of course, pupils at the secondary level have been scheduled in band, orchestra, and art classes on the basis of ability and interest, rather than by chronology or years in school, for years. Almost every extracurricular activity you can name cuts across grade lines. Look at your community; swimming lessons, tennis lessons, Little League, even summer school offerings pay little attention to anything but interest and ability. Why should there be any less effort put into the child's total academic program?

Nongraded Schools and Their Justification

The development of a nongraded school program is not a simple task. Any time people turn their attention and energy to innovations which represent a marked departure from the status quo, their reasons and justifications for doing so must be well grounded. The development of the nongraded school will be seen as a completely natural advance if one but realistically examines the basic educational philosophy in our nation and the accumulated knowledge regarding child development and learning. The issues involved will be dealt with throughout this book.

It has been said time and time again that the role of the school is to help each child develop his potential to whatever degree his abilities permit. Few educators would argue that point. But the means selected to achieve this end are open to debate. Typically, graded schools simply are not designed to individualize instruction or they are not able to do so. A careful look at the programs in most schools would seem to imply that all children should be subjected to the *same* content at the *same* time and at the *same* rate simply because they are in the *same* grade and are approximately the *same* chronological age. Focus is upon the content to be covered rather than upon the individual to be taught. Within such a rigid framework, it is virtually impossible to visualize how the pupil's personal potential is ever individually considered.

For hundreds of years, physical differences have been quite naturally accepted and understood. Not so with academic differences. It has been only within the last thirty years or so that we have really had valid and reliable data on the pupils we teach. In a typical first grade class, it is not unusual to find pupils whose mental age spans a range of four years, or whose I.Q. scores vary as much as 60 points. And it does not take too many years before those differences in potential are reflected as differences in academic achievement, as evidenced in the table below with data taken from a typical fourth-grade class in Bloomington, Indiana, in 1965.

TYPICAL ACHIEVEMENT DATA FROM
A FOURTH-GRADE CLASS

	Reading	Language	Arithmetic
High	8.7	7.9	4.9
75%	6.4	6.6	4.3
Median	4.7	4.6	3.9
25%	3.9	4.0	3.7
Low	2.9	2.7	2.8

These test scores are from a standardized test battery. For each of the above areas the average score would be 4.1. This class is slightly above average in reading and language but somewhat below average in arithmetic. Notice the wide range of scores in every area.

As another example, the following data is from three fourth-grade classes in three different schools in the same community:

I.Q. DATA FOR THREE FOURTH-GRADE CLASSES

	Group I	Group II	Group III
High	122	145	129
75%	109	125	103
Median	104	117	92
25%	100	106	82
Low	91	96	70

Classes were located in three different schools all within the same community.

Recently a diagnostic reading test was administered in September to a group of six-, seven-, and eight-year-olds in a nongraded primary school in Bloomington, Indiana. The following results were obtained:

READING TEST RESULTS OF 166 PUPILS IN A
NONGRADED PRIMARY SCHOOL

Level	Number of pupils	8 years old	7 years old	6 years old
8.5	2	1	1	—
7.5	7	6	1	—
6.5	10	7	2	1
5.5	8	5	2	1
4.5	18	8	10	—
3.8	10	4	4	—
3.3	12	5	1	—
2.8	11	3	6	1
2.3	16	5	10	1
1.8	4	—	4	—
1.6	9	1	5	3
1.3	1	—	1	—
Beginners	58	—	4	54
T =	166	47	58	61

Tests were administered in September. Most 6-year-olds had just completed one year of kindergarten.

These data are shown simply to reinforce the thesis that pupils vary greatly in terms of potential and achievement. Since there are these academic extremes, to say nothing of social and emotional differences, the implication is that not all pupils should begin or end their formal education at precisely the same place, nor will they progress in school at the same rate.

It all boils down to a need for two elements in the school: (1) an organization for instruction which encourages flexibility and (2)—

and this is a big need—teachers with the training and ability to determine what are their pupils' individual strengths and weaknesses and plan a program of instruction accordingly. If this last element seems to be the stumbling block, remember that no one has said it would be easy, but teachers need to do these tasks. We will probably see a good deal more cooperative planning and teaching in the future than we have ever seen in the past as the nongraded school continues to be developed.

"But," comes a cry of dismay, "how many teachers can boast of even the most minimal diagnostic skill?" Perhaps only a few today, but effective in-service programs, more research, and increased experience will add to knowledge and give guides for the teacher's role in diagnosis of individual student's learning problems and potentials. Years ago, few teachers could make claim to even a smattering of child psychology, philosophy or, for that matter, even a four-year degree. But progress has been made in these areas. It is not fair to say teachers cannot make changes in their instruction. Look at the new science and modern mathematics programs if it is reinforcement in the belief that teachers can adjust and grow that you are seeking.

We must have confidence not only in the teacher's ability to learn, but also in his judgment regarding decisions to be made when diagnostic data has been gathered. Today's teacher is a professional with a minimum of four years' college work and five years in many cases. Many states already require a master's degree for teacher certification. In addition, today's teacher is expected to continue his education, formally or informally, for years. We can surely look for such persons to have what it takes in planning and implementing programs of continuous instruction and optimum academic growth.

A Climate For Change

As is often true during periods of rapid expansion of new educational practices, there is little in the way of statistical or experiential descriptive data to support nongraded programs. Nor are all the new programs being researched or evaluated with much objective consistency. This is understandable as program development calls for a staff's full attention. However, it must be realized that changing an organizational structure only provides the opportunity for bringing about significant educational improvement. The real heart of the educative process is to be found in the influences of curriculum and instruction of youngsters. In all too many cases, labels have been changed, but the basic school program has remained unaffected. To create the climate for change, to establish an organization which provides the means for a substantial breakthrough in program development, and then to fall short of individualizing instruction is to discredit seriously the nongraded movement.

CHAPTER 2

The Nongraded School:
A Dynamic Concept

by

MAURIE HILLSON

Dr. Hillson has been a provocative and frequent con-
tributor to the professional conversation about the
nongraded school concept. Among his publications is
Innovation and Change in Elementary School Organization: A Book of Readings, *an important piece of the*
contemporary professional literature.

Dr. Hillson, a former elementary teacher, is pres-
ently a professor of education at the Graduate School
of Education, Rutgers, the State University of New
Jersey. Also, he has been on the faculties of Bucknell
University, Harvard University, the State University of
New York, and Fairleigh Dickinson University.

E VEN a cursory glance at the history of both graded and nongraded education in America leads to the conclusion that circumventions of the graded structure are attempts to eliminate the restrictions which such an organization insinuates about its users. In the activities which aim at eliminating the graded school structure, the desire to deal more effectively with individual differences is central to almost every attempt.

At this moment in the short history of the nongraded movement, limitations of another kind are seen in some plans. These plans bring demurrers from the spokesmen on the educational scene. What Frazier observed about problems of nongrading, the "Criterion of progress combines quantity and rate to carry the old conception of the curriculum to a new point of impoverishment,"[1] is not very much different from the protestations made by some enlightened educators of the late 1800's concerning the graded school.

Philosophy of Nongraded Schools

The philosophy of nongraded schools is one born in the heat of reaction. It is pragmatic and inextricably bound up in the great scientific and child-centered movements of the past three decades. The wholesome desire to deal with the individual and his needs, and the empirical evidence offered by an increasingly sophisticated scientific age indicating how to obtain better learning results, combined to form a framework in which the administration of programs for satisfying these needs could take place.

Nongraded schools represent an attempt at organizational plans which embrace the scientific findings about the learner and how he learns. They are attempts to deal with the problem of inflexibility in the education of the child. The nongraded school gears the school's administrative structure to the intellectual development of the child. It is a practical means for making it possible for teachers to personalize instruction for every youngster.

Educational Tenets

Several basic educational tenets suggest the essential need for rethinking and recasting the present educational-organizational scheme of the schools. These tenets are drawn from a vast number of fragmented studies. The findings frequently repudiated the wisdom of the graded school as it is traditionally organized and they also reject the features of teaching, grouping, and advancement which are indigenous to such an organization. By necessity these findings lead to a different kind of organizational format. They help to establish, in some measure, a philosophical framework for the creation of a different type of school. These several tenets do not make up an exhaustive list. A much more comprehensive treatment of the basic idea that these tenets propound was done by the late William H. Burton.[2] His perceptive analysis inescapably leads to the conclusion that a new school organization is needed, not just a tinkering with established and sacred practices. Six tenets drawn from the literature may serve to clarify nongraded education in its philosophical context.

Tenet one contends that there exists in every group of learners, without exception, wide differences in quality, desire, and intent concerning learning. One of the better articles dealing with this tenet, written by Edgar A. Doll, observed that, in reality, four I.Q.'s must be recognized as factors which operate in achievement. These four I.Q.'s—"the intelligence quotient," "the inner quest," "the ideal qualities," and "the innate quirks"—may be operative in any individual at any given time.[3] This alone could create an impetus to find a concept of organization quite different from the traditional grade school, where consideration is usually limited to the intelligence quotient.

Tenet two indicates that certain undesirable growth characteristics, unrealistic school programs, and poor progress in school are all closely associated with nonpromoted children more frequently than with slow-learning promoted children. Also, the slow-learning children who have been promoted usually do make better progress and indicate better mental health habits and adjustment than do their peers who have been retained. Many studies exist which support this tenet. The knowledge that repeating a grade yields very slight, if any, advantage relegates nonpromotion as an academic practice to a vestigial position in educational growth and progress. Retention and failure with all of the attendant frustrations and social stigma still are widely practiced in the graded schools of America. Yet of all the evidence for or against these tenets, the collection of empirical evidence which indicates that nonpromotion as an educational practice is unequivocally indefensible is by far the most consistent and impressive. If progress through the graded school is primarily based on subject matter mastery over a given period of time, then it becomes clear that failure, retention, or nonpromotion are basic by-products of such a system. Conversely, acceptance of the basic tenet stated above which precisely rejects the concept of nonpromotion must lead to a divergent type of school organization.

Tenet three restates that bold philosophy of education which calls for instruction to meet the needs of all of the children of all of the people. It makes the assumption that every pupil in both the elementary and secondary school should be judged by the best which he can do. If a child works to capacity, makes strides in learning according to his intellectual growth pattern, and becomes in essence an ultimate learner, in a personal sense he has accomplished a full measure of existence in this area of his living.

Tenet four moves sharply away from a graded school philosophy. It states that no child should be judged by the median performance of a nonselected group. Ample evidence supports this. For instance, every book on the teaching of reading importunes its readers to group reflectively according to the various ranges which result due to nonselective assignments and grouping. Ponder what Goodlad felt to be the case when he "once found himself in a teaching situation which offered promise of considerable homogeneity. The institution was a specialized one in that it received only boys committed for delinquent acts. The pupils were relatively homogeneous on a criterion supposedly related to learning in that almost all of them fell in low I.Q. range of 70 to 110, with a mean of 85." It did not take long for the obvious to happen. In six weeks Goodlad reports that he "found himself wishing for a 'special' specialized school down the road that might receive those who deviated most markedly from the others on various significant traits."[4]

Tenet five states that no child should be judged solely on the basis of his chronological age. That such a premise is valid follows, if one accepts the previous tenet that the judgment of progress should not be based on a median performance of a nonselect group. This should be the case even though chronological age plays a large part in many endeavors during our daily life. Everyone knows people over twenty-one years of age who never should be allowed to exercise a franchise because they are essentially immature in every aspect of the requirements needed to make a sound and rational judgment. Cronbach contends that "age-grading is inconsistent with the facts about pupil differences, and allocating pupils to grades according to their over-all ability in one subject does little to improve the situation."[5] Age-grading is inconsistent with the evidence amassed in the studies of educational psychologists.

Tenet six, reciprocally, is an adjunct to the concept that any assessment and placement based on chronological age only is invalid. This tenet asserts that no child should be judged on a grade standard which is clearly indefensible and which cannot be defined in realistic terms related to the research on child growth and development. Grade standards, as a matter of fact and as matter of measurement in educational progress, become very untenable in light of the studies of intuition, cognition, and mental age. Bruner hypothesized "that any subject can be taught effectively in some intellectually honest form to any child at any stage of development. . . . No evidence exists to contradict it; considerable evidence is being amassed that supports it."[6] Thirty years ago and without the sophisticated techniques presently being used, Luella Cole observed that individual differences must be coped with even though these differences exist in every grade.[7]

For many years educational literature has been replete with similar ideas. Some are based on the perceptions of day-to-day educational practitioners. Others are carefully documented by controlled studies. The late William S. Gray, discussing this area of education, summed up the conclusions found in the vast body of research. He wrote: "Research has shown conclusively that children differ widely in capacity to learn and other basic characteristics. The need is urgent, therefore, of organizing instruction to provide adequately for the needs of all."[8]

A New Position

These tenets are current in the field of education and lead to a philosophical position concerning the organization of the public school at all levels from the first through the twelfth year. This position provides varying levels of instruction which are set up to meet the needs of the wide differences found in learners and in their rates and capacities to learn. It calls for an organization which takes into consideration the millions of retentions found yearly in the primary and intermediate grades and the host of failures given in secondary schools. At the same time, it is a plan that considers progress within the realm of reality and replaces frustration, fear, and failure by continuous growth. It considers the variations in learning, the aspects of cognition, the timing for the presentation of materials, and the spurts and lags which typify the process of learning. Most importantly, it considers the factors of readiness and embraces the concept enunciated in Cronbach that "under a nongraded plan, learning activities are determined by readiness, not by seniority."[9]

Basic reactions to graded school education as being the type of education which is inimical to learning as it should be leads to a philosophical realization that a different organizational scheme is necessary. Also, it leads to the thought that what is needed is a dynamic structure, not a static form. The nongraded school may be that dynamic structure.

The term *nongraded* is a reactive one. It means the absence of, or the reverse of grades. Armed with the scientific findings on learning, bolstered by the historical attempts to get around the grades, and encouraged by a Space Age public's growing receptivity to change, the educational movement of nongraded schools is a bold new venture on the educational scene. Nongraded schools are no longer academic exercises. They exist throughout the country in all kinds and all types of school districts; they are viewed as one of the valuable organizational ideas for education in slum areas and have vital use in affluent school areas. Nongraded schools are to be found more often at the elementary school level, but this kind of organization is as valid in secondary school years. The tenets set forth above, and research on child growth, development, mental health, and learning find themselves in compatible balance within nongraded schools. The definition of nongraded schools and what their potentialities are, based on the notions expressed above, now require fuller investigation and exposition.

The Nongraded School Plan

The nongraded school is an organizational plan. It does not answer all of the problems which confront the schools. It is not a method of teaching *per se*. It is not an administrative or teaching panacea. But it does create a framework in which better methods can be used and in which fluidity and flexibility allow for the exploitation of various activities which further learning. As Goodlad and Anderson point out, "the nongraded school is not for those who would stop with a little organizational reshuffling. It is for those educators who would use present-day insights into individual differences, curriculum, and theories of personality, and who would commit themselves to a comprehensive revision of education."[10]

Because of the very decentralized nature of the American educational enterprise with all of its features of educational self-determination, various plans of nongrading exist. Before attempting to define and categorize with some precision what a nongraded school is, it might be wise to contemplate momentarily what the ultimate nongraded situation could be. The ultimate might be realized when each child is intrinsically motivated to work to his full capacity and is faced with problem-solving situations at his level of competence and capacity. It is necessary to deal with group situations in our massively populated school systems. Some framework for capitalizing on this child's commitment to his ultimate development must be thought out. The organization could be one in which collections of these youngsters, each of whom is a group unto himself, are set up so that these clusters are taught at the same time. They would be at nearly the same problem-solving level, in a particular substantive area relative to their ability, their desire, their intents, and their skill in learning. Any teacher will agree that this is devoutly to be wished and represents the ideal. This remains the ultimate nongrading ideal, however. Immediate nongrading of a different sort can be a practical reality. It can open ways for teachers so that steps toward the ideal come more readily and easily.

The present-day nongraded elementary schools, for the most part, rely on levels of accomplishment in reading as the bases for advancement and assignment in a program of vertical progression through the six years of the elementary school organization. Current nongraded plans, with some rare but exciting departures, accept the format of an attempted homogeneous grouping based on factors attendant to reading achievement.

Some thought has been given to groupings based on a total language arts constellation, and Weaver[11] has written about a nongraded sequence in elementary mathematics. Basically, however, assignments to classrooms based on reading accomplishment levels is the practice. Some school districts couple this practice with semi-departmentalized groupings based on arithmetic study.

Elementary school science still remains in an area of curricular heterogeneity. Whether or not this should continue as a practice is open to question. If the impressive evidence being built up in behalf of nongraded schools is correct, and since present controlled experimental studies are indicating that nongrading significantly improves reading achievement, then in this scientific age it seems very plausible that within a different type of organization a significant advance in the learning of science during the elementary school could be made.[12]

As an educational movement, the nongraded schools developed as basic organizational attempts for dealing with the problem of inflexibility in the education of the child. These schools have plans that call for continuous academic progress. As noted above, this progress is usually based on the accomplishment of reading levels. Grades are replaced by these levels, which are attained by the child at his own speed. These levels of clearly described experiences serve as guides. The child or groups of children move through them at their own comfortable learning rates. Imprecise and unrealistic year-end norms are eliminated. Just because the winter snows have passed into the warmth of June of the year, a child does not by some magical experience turn from a first-grader into a second-grader.

Promotion and nonpromotion and the attendant fears of both are eliminated. How can there be failure if the child works to his ultimate capacity? The fear of encroachment on material reserved for the next higher grade becomes a thing of the past. A competency in the levels is attained, and readiness is indicated for more difficult material; the child moves ahead regardless of the number of stars, circles, or lines boldly imprinted on the binding of the books indicating a certain grade level. This movement allows for a realistic recognition of the various rates of learning which exist in a normal school population. These nearly chronologically similar pupils work at academically different levels at different rates in keeping with their ability, desire, intent, and readiness to learn.

The nongraded elementary school allows for a concentration on the individual pupil and his needs. It usually consists of a three-year program (primary nongraded) or a six-year program (elementary nongraded). During these years, the activities, grouping, teaching, and learning more nearly reflect the research on human growth and development. The collocation is one in which a fruitful educative experience is realized. This concept of grouping, based on reading or on language factors, and its success, based on pupil growth in this area, assumes the existence of what could be called a pole of intellectuality. Such a pole of intellectuality does exist for mathematics, and it would seem from the current discussions in the educational literature that a third pole of intellectuality exists in the field of science. However, in the nongraded programs which now exist, levels of sequential reading content are most often the first organizational stepping stones to nongradedness.

In nongraded programs which could be created, sequential science content could be another organizational stepping stone as could mathematics or any other desirable content area. Under the present nongraded schemes based on reading levels, the attempt may be to achieve unlimited aims with limited means. A more precise assessment of the polarities which offer themselves as bases for various groupings, and a clearer and more concentrated research activity concerning these polarities (i.e., the content itself) are now in order. Add to this still other bases for grouping (teaming, collaboration, etc.), and one can begin to sense that the distance traveled thus far is slight.

But with the realization that nongrading offers limitless possibilities to the perceptive and enthusiastic educator and that within the movement there exist some amorphous nongraded plans, a traditional plan of nongrading must be within some greater depth. Nongraded plans based on reading levels and considerations about grouping, progress, and grade remotion should have a pandemic rather than an esoteric application.

A Nongraded Reading Plan

The nongraded reading levels plan is one in which continuous academic progress is based on the accomplishment of clearly described reading levels. The number of levels to be accomplished by the child varies from plan to plan. One well-known nongraded levels program uses twenty levels in its system of grouping elementary school children for reading. The children start at level one, which is an "extended readiness" level, and progress through to level twenty, with a traditional sixth-grade reading book. The levels are either odd numbered or even numbered. The even-numbered levels employ basic books of a basal reading series required of all children, and the odd-numbered levels employ supplementary books of a co-basal reading series. The odd-numbered levels are used to sustain and reinforce the work of the immediately preceding even-numbered level.

The actual nongraded reading levels plan starts at level three because all of the children are involved in the basic readiness levels of one and two. By moving through a series of small steps, each even level being bolstered by a lateral movement to the odd level, a child progresses upward. It should be noted at this point that schools using programs of "individualized reading" lend themselves very neatly to this kind of progressive arrangement.

The self-selection of trade books, those drawn from the lists of publishers of children's books within the suggested guidelines of clearly described levels, allows for healthy progress. The child may be more intensely motivated because of his interest in the story quality, a quality sometimes absent in stories of the usual basal reading series. Even though a basal book represents one level and a co-basal represents one level, most nongraded reading levels plans include other representative "back-up" books at each level drawn from various other reading series of the same level of difficulty. If a child needs reinforcing work over a longer period of time and of a more intense nature so as to achieve the essential competencies, it is reasonable to have available those necessary reading materials.

During his experience with school systems, the author worked in this type of program and was able to do two things which seem to complement each other. In the first instance, he set up the levels program using the basal and co-basal idea described above. He made a careful analysis of the trade books and from this analysis he listed the core books, which are basic in terms of the difficulty and content of the materials suggested for a level, of each of the levels. These books sustain, bolster, or clinch the competencies called for in the description of the level. Skills acquisition and story enjoyment complemented one another in an expanding program of reading accomplishment unhampered by grade-level promotion, retention, and pressure. Figure One might represent the levels XII, XIII, XIV, and XV of such a program.

The amount of time that it takes a child to accomplish these levels varies. Generally, the average child does it in one school year. The

LEVEL XII   Basal Reader III[1]
  LEVEL XIII   Co-Basal Reader III[1] and Several Trade Core
          Books
    LEVEL XIV   Basal Reader III[2]
      LEVEL XV   Co-Basal Reader III[2] and Several Trade Core
              Books

FIGURE ONE

slower child who needs more work at level XII does not fail. He is advanced to the next level, level XIII, where he has materials of the same difficulty to reinforce or fix the competencies called for at that reading level. Another dimension offered by this type of plan is the opportunity to help children who are having specific difficulties. The odd level gives support to the child who needs help in making the next step. If a child is absent or enters school from another district, the viability of this type of organization allows for reinforcement or reorientation without going backwards. With several groupings at different levels operating in a school, the child can come back and take up where he left off, albeit in another group. Thus, the nongraded elementary school could be defined as a school which groups children for instruction using criteria other than academic attainment or chronological age. Many of the present-day non-graded programs are based on a reading levels progression. Lest this last statement seem contradictory in terms of the definition stated above, it might be wise to discuss some of the criteria for grouping in our definition of the reading levels program of the nongraded elementary schools. The same principles have application in the secondary school, although the reading program would not be the content vehicle.

Grouping Considerations in Elementary Schools

In the nongraded reading levels program, youngsters are grouped after consideration is given to the many factors concerning the ways they learn. This does not mean that they are grouped according to I.Q. score. This does not mean that they move unalterably in the same group forever. It means that for various reasons people learn or have the desire to learn or are ready to learn at different times and at different rates, and appropriate decisions are made about their instructional prescriptions consistent with these learning differences. To facilitate learning, the extremes of the ranges of a whole host of abilities found in any given classroom need to be narrowed. The narrowing of the range in any one area by careful grouping creates a matrix in which a child with an able teacher has a better opportunity to achieve up to his capacity. In many nongraded rooms, one can find a whole range of I.Q. scores. I.Q. scores are not the single determinant for success in learning. Desire, motivation, obstacles to learning, maturity, physical well-being, and social adaptation are all considered in a nongraded school's organization.

These things are related to success in reading and, therefore, are necessarily considered in grouping. This is especially the case at the earliest reading levels. It should be the case in the later levels as well. The natural result of this kind of grouping would lead to a nongraded school running from at least the kindergarten through what is now the sixth grade.

Increased sophistication in grouping practices and the adoption of the obvious new approaches of team teaching, cooperative teaching, pupil-team learning, and various methods of nongrading cannot help but lead to programs of continuous growth with realistic rates of learning being a prime consideration. It means that a child completing six years of elementary school, or seven years including kindergarten, does not need to move into a rigid kind of departmentalization which is frequently characterized by some junior and senior high schools. It could mean a closer and more realistic articulation between the elementary and junior and senior high schools. It could mean that eventually each child could reach that stage of being a group unto himself and the hoped for genuine attention to individualized learning would be attained.

A Survey Report

The author made a survey of one hundred and seven nongraded programs to ascertain what criteria were employed in grouping. These programs represent, for the most part, the nongraded reading levels plan. A few school systems established nongrading on a broader base such as competency in the language arts. In general, however, the responses can be grouped into eight basic categories. It seems safe to say that ideally the following items should be considered in grouping in the nongraded school. These items are not ranked in order of importance. The survey did not indicate the single most important criterion used in grouping. The categories are:

1. Chronological Age (with special note of behavioral activities)
2. Achievement Test Results (with special note of reading ability)
3. I.Q. Test Results (with special note of the Mental Age)
4. Social Maturity (with special note of relations with others)
5. Reading Ability (with special note of readiness at that stage)
6. Interest (with special note of desire or motivation to achieve)
7. Needs (with special note of school and family background)
8. Physical Set (with special note of physical maturation in terms of motor skills)

The administrators of a nongraded school district that has been in successful operation since September, 1953, in a recent bulletin explaining their program indicated the way they did their initial grouping. They administered a battery of tests in the spring of the year to all of the students in grades one through six. They then set up conferences which included the teachers, principal, school psychologist, and supervisors. Armed with the test results, they then discussed the mental and emotional maturity, health, and family background of each child. The result of every discussion led to an assessment which allowed them to place each child in the level most suited to his particular needs and abilities, regardless of his chronological age. The ten-year evaluation of this nongraded program showed that there was a marked decrease in behavior problems normally encountered under the old graded system, plus a marked increase in achievement in all areas of the curriculum. This is convincing evidence of the value of the nongraded school over a period of ten years.

This all-at-once grouping described above is an atypical practice rather than common practice in the nongraded movement. For the most part, nongrading is done on an emerging basis. That is, after the kindergarten program the child moves into the first year of a nongraded program. Each successive year he moves upward through the levels into the second and third year of nongraded classes and beyond.

There are recurring questions concerning how, when, and in what ways determinations are made about this succession from initial assignments through to progress, movement, and transfer of pupils in the nongraded schools. Any full definition of nongraded schools by necessity must attempt to answer these questions. It must be understood that they are not simply answered because of the basic commitment to individuality which characterizes nongrading. It is readily apparent that it becomes difficult to establish an operable yet consistent set of circumstances which apply to all aspects attendant to pupil assignment. Some guidelines can be drawn from the experiences of others. When carefully appraised, these lines can be adhered to or departed from, as any particular situation dictates.

Initial Assignment to Levels

Initial assignments to nongraded levels are made on a tentative basis at the end of the kindergarten experience. This is done by creating a profile of each youngster. Various factors are used. Basically, reading readiness and an assessment of characteristics which indicate readiness (emotional development, social readiness, and physical set

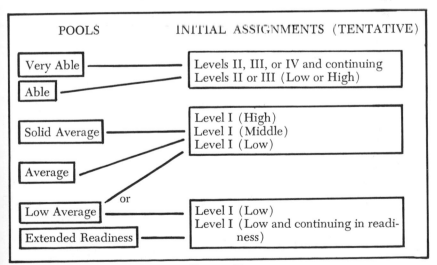

FIGURE TWO

for learning) are studied and evaluated so that a precise profile is ascertained. The first step following this is to assign the youngsters to "pools." These are used to draw on for assignments to more specific levels. Figure Two indicates a schematic picture of this procedure.

Early First Year Levels Adjustments

In the first two or three weeks of the first year of the nongraded program, especially during the reading readiness program, careful assessments of each child's placement are made so as to catch over-estimations or under-estimations or results of changes from summer growth and experiences. The presence of any of these may indicate a needed transfer or different assignment. If the original or initial grouping was carefully done, these changes do not account for more than approximately one or two per cent. As learning spurts and lags are noted throughout the year, additional changes may be made.

Levels Adjustments at End of First and Second Years

At the end of the first as well as at the end of the second year, levels assignments are done on the basis of the achievements of the child, as well as on the other factors mentioned previously that are necessary for fruitful learning. Growth spurts and lags, rate of learning, and motivational aspects of growth are noted. The rate of the previous advancement is noted and studied prior to making assignments to the levels which are operable. Assignments to levels should become more sophisticated; the result is a greater narrowing of the range or spread within any nongraded classroom. Teacher assessment, service tests allied with the basal reading series in use, and a selected set of standardized tests are used. Other criteria suggested by teachers' observations can also be established to help in arriving at a comprehensive inventory of the child.

Adjustments of Assignments for Various Types of Learners

The slow mover in a nongraded school can benefit to a much greater extent than is the case in a graded school. An attempt at an early prognosis of his educational advance is desirable. He may take four years to complete what others do in three. The first place where this is noticed is in the extended readiness program. Preparation for this four-year program, barring a learning spurt which obviates the necessity for the extra year, is continuous and progressive. It is done through transfers to other rooms where the child can exercise leadership in a level and where his continuous progress, albeit slow, is studied, understood, and capitalized upon.

The fast mover is also one who benefits under this plan. The decision about whether to enrich or advance the child who finishes three years in two is a basic one which involves many variables such as age, size, intellect, and flexibility, plus a host of other social and psychological aspects concerning the child's life situation. If he was held up because of a school entrance-date conflict, it may be wise to advance him. If he is immature, it may be wiser to place him in a level in another room for reading and enrich him in other areas while he works with his own group.

Some General Thoughts Concerning Levels Assignments

When sufficient numbers of varying cases are dealt with, a heightened sophistication in the whole process in grouping will be achieved. A good rule of thumb is to under-assess the child's capabilities in assigning him to a level. This will assure making future assignments or transfers upward rather than having them become a series of adjustments which may result in putting the child into lower levels.

The schematic design, Figure Three, which follows the progress of a levels plan and the movements through it, indicates some possibilities. The figure is intended to represent a primary nongraded school with ten reading levels.

The nongraded reading levels program provides for various rates of growth and learning. The levels are not geared to any one kind of learner. They serve the fast, average, and slow learner. The teacher can benefit because of the reduced ranges in reading levels and is able to deal more directly with individual differences. The teacher of the first year generally will be teaching beginning learners. The second-year teacher generally will be teaching youngsters who are

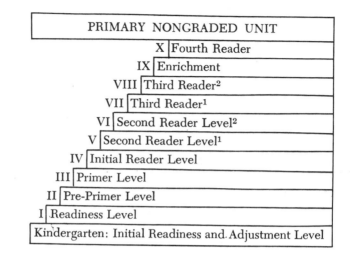

PRIMARY NONGRADED UNIT	
X	Fourth Reader
IX	Enrichment
VIII	Third Reader[2]
VII	Third Reader[1]
VI	Second Reader Level[2]
V	Second Reader Level[1]
IV	Initial Reader Level
III	Primer Level
II	Pre-Primer Level
I	Readiness Level
Kindergarten: Initial Readiness and Adjustment Level	

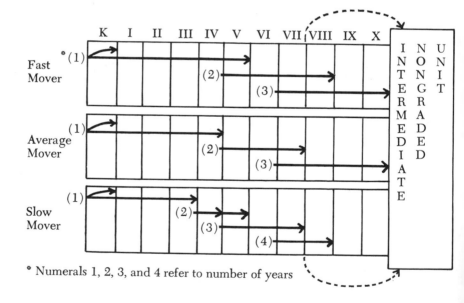

* Numerals 1, 2, 3, and 4 refer to number of years

FIGURE THREE

in their second year of school. The third-year teacher generally will be dealing with youngsters in their third year of school, and so on. Both teachers and youngsters will be working within a flexible framework in which youngsters of the same chronological age may be together but still be challenged at levels commensurate with their academic ability.

These reading levels and the philosophy which supports both the operation and the spirit of teaching them will allow for continuous growth. Teacher efficiency will be improved if the child is taken when he is best ready to learn, carried by good teaching to a place that he can comfortably achieve, and then regrouped with other youngsters and another teacher who picks him up at that place and continues to carry him forward progressively at each stage of his development. When the program is organized into reading levels, each teacher can realistically do this. The slower child can move slowly, and the rapid learner can move rapidly. The grouping of the children and the narrowing of the ranges within the groupings will allow the teacher to maximize his teaching impact based on the principles of child growth and development from which the teacher derives his methodology.

Briefly, then, many of the present nongraded schools are ones in which grades are replaced by levels which a child accomplishes at his own speed. No grade designators are used. These levels of experience are clearly described and without the fear of retention or, conversely, without the fear of encroachment upon material reserved for a next higher grade, the child progresses through them as competency is achieved. He is not pressed into achieving some prescribed year-end norm regardless of his ability. The rapid learner may accomplish a three-year nongraded program in two years. In the graded school, where he usually faced lassitude or boredom because of his rapid assimilation, he could very likely become a problem. In the nongraded school he either moves into the intermediate nongraded unit or has his program enriched in depth. He has the competency and skill to delve more deeply into the substantive areas as well as the skills areas of the curriculum. The slow learner may take four years to accomplish three. He does not have to repeat a whole year as is the case in the graded school. Instead, he takes up where he was when he left school for the summer. This is not retention nor does it carry the stigma of retention.

The nongraded school is a realistic attempt to recognize the various ways and rates of learning which exist in any normal school population. It is an attempt to create a methodological approach to teaching and learning. It is an attempt to create flexibility so that pupil progress is better, tensions lessen, attempts at unrealistic accomplishments are eliminated, individual adequacy replaces personal rivalry, and higher levels of general academic performance are achieved. The collected research to date indicates this is the case as it concerns nongraded schools.

A Nongraded Mathematics Program

Some schools are beginning to pioneer in the development of nongraded mathematics programs. As in reading, efforts have been made to identify a continuum in terms of skills or understandings to be mastered. As one might suspect, the initial attempts correlate closely with the levels approach used in reading. Again, as with reading, these early innovators have almost all used a basal textbook series in the continuum planning. There is logic in this since most textbook series in mathematics are written with the idea of moving from simple to complex in skill development and in their approach to understandings.

For the elementary school, a mathematics levels plan might look like this:

Level 1	Level 2	Level 3	Level 4
Readi-ness	Book 1	Book 2	Book 3

FIGURE FOUR

Level 1	Level 2	Level 3	Level 4	Level 5	Level 6	Level 7	Level 8
Readi-ness	Book I Ch 1–5	Book I Ch 6–10	Book II Ch 1–5	Book II Ch 6–10	Book III Ch 1–5	Book III Ch 6–10	Book III Ch 11–15

FIGURE FIVE

Using book tests (end-of-chapter and/or semester), and standardized tests, one can develop a fairly accurate picture of the computational skills possessed by any group of students. Finding equivalent measures of mathematical understandings is another thing. At the present time we know of no standardized instruments which are adequate to this purpose.

When the data you have available is accumulated, a picture like Figure Six will probably unfold.

MATHEMATICS DATA (AND I.Q.) FROM A
TYPICAL FIFTH-GRADE CLASS

		Arithmetic	
			Problem
	I.Q.	Computation	Solving
High	130	7.5	7.9
75%	118	6.0	6.8
Medium	111	5.6	6.0
25%	104	5.4	5.5
Low	87	4.2	3.4

FIGURE SIX

Refer also to Figure Two in which one can see that the range in reading is limited not only to a wide range within a single chronological age period, but actually spans several years. Once the data accumulated has made obvious the range of difference, the point of concern again becomes how to provide for differences through a continuous or nongraded program.

There are several ways to go about curriculum planning to provide for continuous education. It is possible to provide for individual or group differences within the self-contained classroom. The other alternative is to create a means of providing for these differences which involves a change in class or group structure and makes use of cooperative teacher planning (team teaching) and/or large- and small-group instruction.

Providing Differences Within the Classroom

Assuming now that within a given group of students, all are functioning at approximately the same level of performance, several alternatives have become available. In Plan No. 1, which follows, the basic unit of study may be a chapter in a book or a skill or an understanding to be developed. All pupils will have the same basic introduction to the new concept. As soon as differences in mastery or

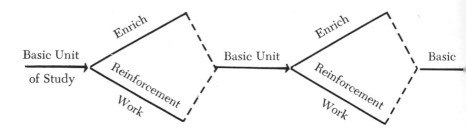

understanding become apparent, the better students move on to enrichment which might involve group instruction of the same topic or skill in depth, exploration of new topics, or independent study using programed materials. Other pupils would be helped through further instruction based upon a diagnosis of their respective problems, so that they would be assured of a firm grasp of the new concept before going on to more advanced work. Again, group or individual instruction would play a part depending on the need.

In Plan No. 2, the design is a little different.

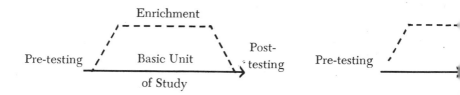

Before moving into a basic unit of instruction, pupils are tested to find out what skills and understandings they already possess. After an introduction for all pupils, the more able branch off and participate in enrichment work. As discussed previously, this may be group- or individual-oriented. The class is brought together from time to time for various purposes: introduction of a unit, testing, or whenever the need dictates (as indicated by the converging dotted lines).

Should a teacher have more than one level in a classroom, and this is very possible depending upon how the continuum is organized, it may be necessary to work with two groups—as in reading—for basic instruction. Enrichment activities may be woven into the program at appropriate times. Some basic concepts, such as problem solving or measurement, which permeate the many skill activities and do not necessarily fit into any special niche in a mathematics continuum, may be taught to all pupils regardless of their general level of achievement.

No matter which plan of action is decided upon, focus must be upon the use of diagnostic tools, identification of a pupil's approximate position within the mathematics continuum, and then provision for group and/or individual differences. The emphasis will be upon the individual's uninterrupted and secure growth in his math learning, rather than upon an occasional stab at "catching up" activity for the slower learner or a "fill-in" type enrichment activity, too often simply repeat practice for the student who is, in reality, ready for a depth study of an already assimilated concept or to move ahead to a new and more advanced area.

Providing for Differences Through Specialized Grouping Plans

For years, junior and senior high schools have attempted to provide for group differences by using track plans of various types. Based upon mathematics tests, grades, and teacher recommendations, pupils are placed in one of several different courses. For example, practical mathematics or ninth grade algebra might comprise one division. Little attempt is made, however, to provide for the wide range of differences inherent within these groups.

The nongraded school, while very possibly beginning with a similar pattern, would go on to some valuable extensions. In these schools, the mathematics continuum must be developed very carefully. After testing, the pupil would be placed at his level or in his position on the continuum. More variety of instruction should be provided within each level. Pupils would be given the opportunity at any time in the year to move from one level to the next as growth in achievement permits. Individual differences will be provided for within each general level of instruction. Flexibility will be the keynote and pupils will progress from one level to the next whenever their abilities permit.

As emphasis grows upon the "modern mathematics" and its related drive for increased understanding of basic concepts, pupils will gain in their mathematical abilities. The classroom teacher, armed with a better understanding himself of mathematics through in-service programs, institutes, and conferences, and greater emphasis in his training upon understanding, problem solving, and technique, should be able to provide a much better program for students. However, increased mathematical understanding, better materials, and more effective techniques may still be aimed at the same classes that were taught previously. The real breakthrough will not come until more effective organization for instruction is sought —an organization which recognizes the great differences in human abilities and makes its plan accordingly.

Whether the mathematics program be traditional or modern in content, whether the basic design is the self-contained classroom or some type of special cross-class grouping plan, the emphasis must be on the individual and his continuous learning.

Nongrading and Secondary Schools

Someone once observed that from grade four on, the number on the door indicating the grade level was also the minimal number of years of spread found in the achievement levels of the pupils of that grade. If this is generally so, then it follows that those pupils who make up the junior and senior high school populations are more apt to be irrationally grouped for instruction under a traditional plan than their peers in the traditional elementary school which to a much larger degree makes some use of intra-class grouping. As a matter of fact, the literature clearly supports the contention that first-grade children in their readiness to learn span a range of as much as five years in terms of the range of materials of a typical first-grade program. By the end of the sixth grade, this range doubles as it concerns the ability to learn. If you add to this the differences in learning found in the various areas of the curriculum, it can be readily seen why Wiles and Patterson[13] and Grambs et al.[14] call for "planned individually" high school programs and ungraded junior high schools.

One of the spokesmen for the program of nongrading at the high school level is B. Frank Brown. In his book he has set down in some detail what a nongraded high school is, and how it should be organized, staffed, and operated. His concept of nongrading at the secondary level is to recast the traditional courses into phases that reflect the student's ability at a given moment, as well as the intensity needed in order to learn particular materials. When readiness for the next phase is shown by the student's willingness to advance, he is encouraged to move to the next phase. Dr. Brown's ungraded program at Melbourne High School has five phases in four basic intellectual disciplines: English, history, mathematics, and science. Phase one is a remedial one for those who need intense help. Phase two is for those who would benefit from work which emphasized the skills of the basic subject area. Phase three is for those who indicate readiness to deal with the material of the subject involved. Phase four is for those who can go into a depth treatment of the subject matter. Phase five is one of independent work which is reserved for the learner who can, with the supervision of a teacher, benefit by assuming responsibility for pursuing his own work. All of the courses of the curriculum have been adapted to fit the different phase levels of this program. Now freed from the structures of the traditional curriculum, with a library as "large as a gymnasium," and a new intellectual atmosphere, the students at Melbourne High School work in the "flexibility of the nongraded structure" which in turn "gives a new image to both the learning process and the educational establishment."[15]

Chapter four of Dr. Brown's book gives detailed attention to the nongraded program at the secondary level. Case studies of secondary schools are included in chapter three.

A Summary and Some Conclusions

It is not within the purview of this chapter to support the nongraded school movement by adducing what now seems to be unequivocal evidence in its favor. Both the descriptive and empirical research indicate very strongly that youngsters in nongraded programs perform significantly better in all measures of school achievement than do their counterparts in randomly assigned or paired regular graded classrooms. The author conducted a study in which he found that certain gains were revealed in the betterment of attitudes and social and mental adjustments as a result of nongrading. A by-product of that study pointed to a common agreement among teachers on a whole list of values which accrued to them and to the school administration because of nongrading. The literature of education with its discussions about the organization for instruction has turned the nongraded school movement into a ubiquitous one. This type of change in educational organization cannot be sustained by mere enthusiasm. By necessity it must rest on the evidence which clearly indicates it to be a better way of doing things, and everything points to this being the case.

In summing up the impact, direction, and intensity of this bold new venture classified as nongraded schools, one must understand that the graded school is a static organizational reference being imposed on a dynamic evolving process. School organization must emanate from and, in turn, serve the needs which are experimentally shown as those worthy and germane to the vast educational endeavor. To accept the graded school organization as the environment for this endeavor is much like accepting as a fact the idea that the roads and highways of 1910 to 1920 are sufficient to carry the vehicles, the traffic, and the aspirations of the American people today. It would seem from our knowledge that the nongraded schools fit our space-age needs more realistically. At this moment in history, they represent a better organizational design for carrying forward the intellectual traffic which must travel through our schools.

CHAPTER 3

The Nongraded High School

by

DAVID W. BEGGS, III

*David W. Beggs writes about the nongraded school
after experience as a teacher, principal and curriculum
consultant. He is on the faculty of the School of
Education at Indiana University, associated with the
Division of School Administration and Field Services.*

*In addition to consulting work, Dr. Beggs is author
of* The Decatur-Lakeview High School: A Practical
Application of the Trump Plan.

M ODERN NONGRADED secondary schools, whether junior or senior
high schools, look like traditional graded schools from the outside.
Both are fashioned from mortar and steel. Each requires an equivalent amount of space. However, inside there are significant, dis-
tinguishing characteristics which set the nongraded secondary
school apart from the graded secondary school. These fundamental
differences often consist of what students are learning and more
often are related to how they go about their learning. Corre-
spondingly, teachers in the nongraded secondary school approach
the teaching tasks in distinctly different ways from teachers in the
graded school. This contention about changed methods of instruction has more validity for the nongraded secondary school than for
the nongraded elementary school. Historically, it seems that good
elementary school teachers have placed more emphasis on indi-

53

vidual, as opposed to group, teaching techniques than have secondary school teachers. The nongraded plan nearly always puts emphasis on individual teaching techniques.

In this chapter, a model of a nongraded high school is given. While this model may be only a basis for professional conversation for some, hopefully it will be a guide to action for others. This model is, of course, derived partly from actual educational innovations, as described in Chapter One, and partly from the author's firsthand confrontations with the graded secondary school as a teacher, principal, and friend. The nongraded organization is a logical consequence of systematic, school-wide team teaching— flexible schedule programs. The introduction of the nongraded organization into a school using team teaching and flexible scheduling gives the teachers more latitude in making decisions for individual students. At the same time, nongradedness is the next developmental step from flexible-scheduled schools.

In the traditional school, students are found most often in groups. Depending on what grade-level group adolescents are in, the principal puts them in one class or another. Teachers think of students as group members—one without distinction from the other—when instruction is planned and even when it is executed. The rate and the depth of the content of instruction in any class is geared to group accomplishment. Individual learning prescriptions are seldom made, as the same dose of instruction is given to all students in the class.

Everyone knows that in June, and not ever before, a telling judgment will be made. Either the student will leap to the next grade level for study with another group or he will repeat all of the year's work with still another group. Both the content of the courses and the learning activities are usually organized by the school on a yearly basis. Actually, some students may have completed the year's work well before the semester's conclusion; others may need more time than the semester provides to study the course content. However, the magic date for moving to new content consideration with another class group is that last day of school in June.

Sometimes students are admonished not to study advanced subject matter for fear the next year's teacher will have his thunder stolen. Instructional activities are cast too often into rigid molds to suit a casually developed curriculum guide or an all-things-to-all-people textbook, rather than to satisfy an individual student's thirst for new knowledge. The rate of study can be so slow and deadening that what is casually learned at one point is easily forgotten by the time the student is called upon to use this knowledge.

Students necessarily are locked into rigid groups in the graded secondary school. Their individual learning abilities and interests are supposed to be woven by the teacher into an instructional fabric that is to cover everyone. One topic, one assignment, and one content consideration, usually from one textbook, are supposed to serve all the students. While some instructional variations are made in a few classrooms, these usually are not differences in depth or breadth of learning activities but in the sheer volume of work students are asked to do.

Educators know that individuals vary in both ability and interest. The dogma of the profession says that the school should provide for these human variations. So special classes are formed. The gifted and the dull learners are put into separate groups. All others find their seats in rooms with other "regular" students. Special texts are sought for the gifted and for the slow learners. Thus, the critical difference in these special ability groups is related to what text is used. Little substantive difference in methods of instruction exists for either the slow or gifted students. It is either more or less of the same diet, sometimes diluted and at other times dehydrated.

Often the device a teacher uses in these time-worn school organizations to signify the individual differences of students is the letter grade. A low but passing grade can be given to the poor student to move him ahead, thus making a stab at compensating for his individual disability. Equally unfortunate is the practice of giving an able learner either a low grade, which sometimes is intended to motivate him, or an undeserved high grade, which often reflects natural ability without personal accomplishment.

Few fundamental distinctions exist between what the bright and the less able youngsters study in high school. But the differences in the quantity of work the gifted and less able students study are marked. Bright students have ten problems rather than five. It is as if bright youngsters had to pay a penalty for ability. A two-page theme, rather than a one-page paper, often is required of the gifted student in the graded school in the name of individualizing instruction.

Accepted by generations of use and continued because of an absence of alternate organizational options, the graded school continues to treat unequal abilities and potentials of students as equals. While public education in the United States has come a long way in school district reorganization, little progress has been made in fundamental instructional reorganization since the Quincy Grammar School was organized in 1848. Scattered small schools have been combined into larger units, but the same procedure of one teacher working with a fixed group of students has been unalterably maintained. Students are classified into age groups, sorted by subject groups, and arranged by ability groups. The goal of individualizing instruction will be thwarted forever until each student's education is considered on an individual basis. Unique abilities and interests require unique instructional programs. Practices of mass production used in industrial manufacturing cannot meet modern educational requirements. The educational demand in this era is quality. Real quality means getting the best from each young adult and, at the same time, giving him a hunger for more knowledge. The nongraded secondary school is a means to allow teachers to individualize instruction.

Teachers in high school too often complain that their students come to them ill prepared for the teachers' predetermined educational expectations. Unfortunately these wailing teachers never generate a professional conversation with other teachers on what really is a mutual problem. The graded school builds barriers between teachers which are seldom overcome. This is to the disadvantage of both students and teachers. On the other hand, the nongraded organization stimulates professional conversations between all teachers in the instructional network.

Learning in the Nongraded School

The nongraded high school offers an escape from organizational shackles which inhibit individual development and personal progress. A student in the nongraded school can have a tailor-made instructional program shaped to his unique needs. Group teaching is replaced by personal teaching in the nongraded school. A student is neither classified by his years in school nor instructed only as a member of this or that group. Instead, the student is free to move through an unending sequence of study which has infinite variations of content. Although students spend some time in activity groups, most of the day is organized around individual learning activities.

Instructional goals are set for each content area and each student may approach these in a different way and to varying degrees of depth. Content objectives, process objectives, and behavioral outcomes are necessarily established in each content area for the individual student. Thus, the companion requirements for a nongraded secondary school for the faculty are a clear conception of instructional purposes and intimate knowledge of every student.

The rate of a youngster's progress is his rate of accomplishment. The depth of study is his depth of understanding. The breadth of consideration is his breadth of interest. When a student has developed one skill or mastered one concept, he is free to move to the next, regardless of the progress of others or the time of the year. Movement through a varied instructional program is continuous. Success in the mastery of one subject breeds interest in the mastery of another subject.

A simple comparison is shown in Figure One. In the graded school, students in each grade work from step to step together. In the nongraded school, progress is an individual matter, independent of all other students. A student may progress more rapidly in some subjects than in others. Also, the depth study given to a subject can vary widely among students.

In the nongraded high school, students spend a large portion of their day in independent study. Another part of the day is spent in small discussion groups. Some time, although less than in either independent study or small inquiry discussions, is spent in large-group presentations. Students meet in groups as a supplement to their individual learning. In the traditional graded school, the converse is likely to be the case. The nongraded school is organized in such a way that there is time for students to meet with teachers and time for individual study. Group meetings and activities are an outgrowth of the personal confrontation of student with teacher, and of students with ideas and skills.

Teachers play a new and important role in the nongraded high school. They meet with students some of the time in the large groups and in some discussion groups, but most of their time is

Years of School	THE GRADED SCHOOL	THE NONGRADED SCHOOL
12th 11th 10th 9th 8th 7th	*Graduation* Students move from grade level to grade level together	*Graduation* Entry to School Students move up a progression at different rates and to different heights and breadths

Figure One

spent in individual conferences with students. Teaching becomes an intimate process of interaction as teachers get to know and understand the abilities and interests of each student. Group assignments give way to customized learning suggestions by the teacher.

The relationship between teacher and student is reversed. Instead of teachers asking most of the questions, the students question the teachers. Instead of teachers transmitting most of the ideas to students, the students reveal their understandings to teachers. After this, real teaching takes place as the pace of conversation between teacher and learner quickens.

In the nongraded school more responsibility is put on the learner for his own learning. Broad instructional goals are set for content areas but specific learning activities are suggested by the teacher to the student. Thus, youngsters take an active part in setting their own particular instructional goals and in carrying out their individual learning activities. The rewards for learning come from the self-gratification which results from successful learning itself. The praise of the teacher re-enforces the progress individuals make.

Students in the nongraded high school are encouraged to collect data before making decisions, to draw inferences from analogous relationships, and to use curiosity as a guide to investigation. Teaching in the nongraded school is best thought of as the stimulation of the will to understand. More emphasis is placed on the process than on specific products of learning. Figure Two attempts to give a general comparison of the graded and nongraded secondary schools.[1]

COMPARISONS	
Graded High Schools	*Nongraded High Schools*
Students	
1. Are classified by grades determined by years in school	1. Are not classified by grades determined by years in school
2. Spend most of their day in class groups	2. Spend most of their day in individual study
3. Are quasi-passive for much of the school day	3. Are active most of the school day
4. Are evaluated according to group norms	4. Are evaluated according to personal progress
5. Study four or five courses each year	5. Study unlimited numbers of subjects during the school year
6. Perform tasks selected by teachers	6. Perform learning tasks selected by themselves
Teachers	
1. Work mostly with groups of students	1. Work mostly with individual students
2. Spend a large portion of the school day explaining and directing	2. Spend a large portion of the school day listening and advising
3. Gear instruction to group interests and abilities	3. Gear instruction to individual student interest and ability
4. Work most often along with students	4. Work as a member of a teaching team
Content	
1. Is usually the same for all students	1. Is varied, depending on the student's ability and interests
2. Is determined essentially by the textbook	2. Is determined by faculty decisions

FIGURE TWO

Considering Change

The nongraded school will not emerge because of an administrative mandate or even by a total staff commitment to its rationale. Instead, it will be the result of serious thinking and hard work at a high level of professional competency. The development of the nongraded high school will take time and will come into operation gradually. However gradual the inauguration, it must be by careful design. Involuntary evolutionary processes will not lead to a nongraded secondary school. Instead, the transformation of a traditional school to a nongraded school will take place only as the attitudes and teaching performances of teachers develop.

Adjustments in content, in methods of teaching, and in the school's organization must be made if the nongraded theory is to get into practice. Only the academically competent and the professionally secure staff should attempt the total transformation from a traditional to a nongraded school. The difficulty in going to the nongraded organization does not come from circumstances after the transformation has been made. The barb is likely to be evident during the retooling process. Teachers, with all the attributes of humanity, find it difficult to adjust to a change in professional behavior. The past is too much with us. Teachers have to work, sometimes with evangelistic zeal, to teach in a way that is different, even if it promises to be better, from the way they were taught and have been teaching. The formidable nature of the change is no reason to shirk from it, but it is a challenge to the capable school administrator and teaching staff. As the school's instructional leader, the building principal must give dynamic leadership and careful attention to changes in the school's instructional program. The program will change only as the methods used by the teachers change.

Teachers thinking of moving into a nongraded organization might profitably begin with organizing teaching teams and using a flexible schedule. These are important elements of the nongraded high school organization, as will be noted again later. The successful use of these innovations related to techniques of teaching make it possible to structure real content adjustments and new teaching procedures. The focus of several teachers on a common instructional problem, evident in team teaching, is a necessity in a highly developed nongraded program.

Team teaching is the instructional procedure whereby several teachers share the responsibility and functions for instructing a given group of students in a defined content area. Teaming provides a structure in which teachers can arrange content into learning sequences for the nongraded school. Team teaching encourages cooperative teacher planning, decision-making, and evaluating. The flexible schedule organizes a school day in such a way that varying amounts of time can be spent on different subjects. The flexible schedule usually offers students large blocks of time for individual learning activities and calls for the use of small group instruction. Team teaching and flexible scheduling are priority items in the list of requirements for the nongraded secondary school.

Isolating Objectives

The first step in nongrading a high school is for the faculty to establish broad educational objectives for each content area. These should be quality objectives but, at the same time, they should be refined so they can be described in behavioral terms. Formulating only abstract objectives destroys the operational value of a statement of objectives. The school's statement of objectives is the reference point from which all decisions are made about teaching and learning.

It is helpful to consider objectives in two classifications, educational and instructional. The educational objectives may be thought of as the general aims which have universal application. While the instructional objectives may be narrower, they have individual application. Educational objectives should be thought of in terms of the total school population, while instructional objectives should be formulated for each student. Educational objectives are set by considerations of the student as a member of a modern democratic society. Instructional objectives most often are established to take the particular characteristics, the interests, and the needs of the individual into account. Every learning activity should be ordered to contribute to a specific instructional objective. Instead of having required courses, as in the traditional school, there should be required information and processes for students to master.

Once the broad objectives are selected, scholastic disciplines must be identified which will contribute to the achievement of these objectives. Then, each discipline must be divided into manageable learning units. A learning unit is a body of related information or cluster of ideas which leads to the development of a concept. For example, in mathematics, a learning unit may be concerned with the concept of probability. The study of this learning unit implies that the student already can handle computation, can discriminate between values, and understand numerical relationships. The probability study will introduce the student to idea choice, random sampling, and statistical inference. Of course, the probability theory is just one segment of the great world of mathematics which secondary school students will study.

Each content area will have a learning sequence. The learning sequence will be organized around a related concept or unitary skill. Each sequence will require students to move from simple to complex ideas, and, where possible, from related ideas or skills to other more complex and related ideas or skills. Some students will explore sequences that are quite different from those pursued by other students. The purpose of each sequence is to introduce students to concepts they can master and to order these concepts logically so that mastery of one will lead to an understanding of the next without meaningless repetition. Pupil-teacher planning, long thought of, but infrequently used, can become a reality in educational practice. The organization of the school can, unlike the day's organization in a traditional school schedule, accommodate pupil-teacher planning.

Each sequence within a discipline will have stated objectives, established study sequences of the basic understandings or skills to be mastered, and suggested varieties of learning activities. The teacher's assessment of the pupil will, along with the pupil's interests, determine what is an appropriate activity for each youngster in every course. There will be as many sequences in each subject as there are organizing notions, arranged from the simple to the complex. The purpose of structuring the learning sequences is to organize content into manageable form so that content can be prescribed by the teacher to students of varying abilities and interests. Student progress can be assessed with precision when personal mastery or achievement is measured at the end of each sequence. After one concept or skill is mastered, the student can move to another with facility. Also, a sense of satisfaction so essential to successful learning can be given to every youngster as he sees what he has mastered in each learning sequence. When one body of content or one sequence is conquered, ambition is instilled in students encouraging them to attack new knowledge or skills.

The content of education is important but it is, at best, only a means to an end. The nongraded school emphasizes content as a way to develop thinking, judging, and creating abilities. No scholastic discipline is properly studied for its own sake, but for the benefit it gives the student in sharpening thinking processes and in expanding his horizon of interest.

The secondary school program must have sufficient breadth to expose students to the full range of human knowledge. Therefore, high school students should become familiar with both the arts and sciences. Narrow specialization properly should be left to education beyond high school.

The specific determination of what a student will study should be a cooperative decision of the student and teacher. Tests, either written or performance, of ability to use ideas or skills can be available to assist students in assessing their potentials and teachers in making study recommendations. When a student has accomplished all he can in one sequence, the teacher recommends he move on to the next sequence. Within each study area there is room for wide variation in activities for different students. For example, some students of poetry may read only James Whitcomb Riley, while others will delve into the richness of Dylan Thomas.

An irregular sequence may be established in some disciplines in which one understanding does not necessarily build on another. A student may first study journalistic writing, then some aspects of rhetoric and later literature, perhaps the short story. A variety of short stories may be included in the sequence. The teacher advises the student as to which selections are appropriate to his abilities and related to his interests.

Selecting Content

The school's program of study is more important for what it does to students, than what it is itself. Therefore, each school program must be structured in light of the particular students for which it is intended. The educated man is characterized not so much by what he is able to recite as by how he is able to locate and evaluate information and to formulate judgments. Thus, content is important in what it contributes to a student's personal development. Of course, emphasis must be put on some basic information, understandings, and processes that all students must master.

The subject-matter content of the nongraded school does not assume one body of knowledge for all students to master. Instead, the content of the school is open-ended. That is, it is imperative that all students be introduced to the widest possible range of knowledge. Not only should science, mathematics, English, and social studies be investigated, but economics, art, music, sociology, and vocational fields need to be explored.

The nongraded school assumes that students seek satisfactory explanations to phenomena, not learn bodies of close-ended content. There are as many methods of learning as there are learners. Some students read more than others. Some write or construct or discuss more than others. Not only should the content of a youngster's education be tailor-made, but the methods of learning should be customized to his individual methods of thinking and learning. Each student should be encouraged to do what he can do best to develop individual understandings. Teachers should play on students' strengths in interests while encouraging them to strengthen their areas of process weakness.

Some disciplines will be studied by all the students, others will be explored on an election-agreement basis. The required studies will include those that are necessary for the liberally educated man. The elective-agreement studies used will be those that suit the specific aims of the individual, as settled on by teacher and student. Even within the required content considerations there is a range of breadth and depth possible. Some students may spend most of their high school career on the required studies while others can finish those early and move into the elective-agreement studies.

An elective-agreement study is in an area which a student elects and formulates in agreement with the teacher how he is to attack the subject. The agreement is developed cooperatively by the teacher and student. The student's individuality will be considered by teacher as the agreement is ordered. Students may be required to attend formal lectures and participate in scheduled group discussions or they may work on their own for most of the time.

Students probably will spend their day in formal classes for about 40 per cent of the time after the nongraded program is fully developed. Half of this time will be spent in large assembly groups and half in small inquiry groups. The remainder of the day will be consumed by independent study. Figure Three illustrates the distribution of a typical student's time for a week in the nongraded secondary school.[2]

The program of studies in the nongraded school will likely be the same as that of any good school today. However, all students will likely study in more disciplines than today's youth do. It will include basic and advanced courses in every content area. The time students

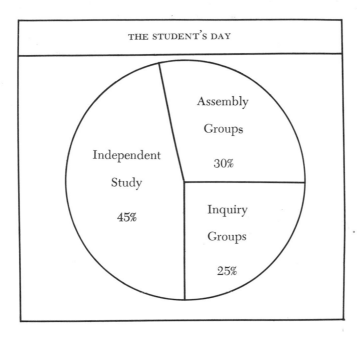

FIGURE THREE

spend on each course will vary, depending on their rate of progress and the modifications the teachers make in it for individual students. Teachers still vary the content, omitting some processes and knowledge for some students and enriching it for others. The emphasis in all subjects will be on application of concepts and skills. Activity will typify learning in the nongraded school.

The range of content of any high school program must be wide enough to accommodate the range of variations of the interests in a student population. Every student cannot learn all things easily and well. The notion that a student gifted in one subject is necessarily gifted in others should be rejected. Students with superior reading skills sometimes appear to be able to handle most subjects because of the information they muster. Conversely, poor readers can give the surface impression that all their abilities are limited when this is not actually the case. While this view is a solid argument for emphasizing reading programs in the high schools, it also implies that particular subjects can be studied successfully by other means than reading.

Using Many Resources

The school should make it possible for students to learn by listening to recordings and electronic tapes, in addition to individual conferences with teachers. The use of technological aids to instruction will come to the foreground in the nongraded school. Explanations, historical incidents, and literary productions can be put on recording devices and used over and over by different students. Teachers' time saved as a result of the use of technological aids may be most profitably used in working with individuals and small groups.

Some of the content of the program of studies may be available to students through teaching machines. By the use of these devices one student can study a topic at a time different from all other students. If there is need for repetition, the technological aid will patiently repeat its message. At the same time, if a student understands its content, he can quickly move on to another topic by the flip of a switch.

The school's program of studies should not follow any specific series of textbooks, anthologies, or workbooks. However, good materials appropriate to the learning sequence which are available in textbooks or paperbacks may be used where possible. If materials are not available in textbooks or inexpensive paperbacks, they may be prepared in mimeographed form. For example, a program for teaching basic sentence patterns to slow-learning youngsters may have to be prepared by the teacher.

Students sometimes will be given text materials after each learning sequence has been selected. For other studies the content will be wide in scope and diverse in direction. When appropriate, content will be from a single text, at other times study data will come from a variety of materials. Necessarily the school's instructional material resources must be rich. It is safe to predict the school's budget for instructional materials and supplies will double, if not triple, as the nongraded program takes hold.

Developing Learning Centers

All of the school's reference materials can be housed in an instructional materials center (hereafter referred to as an I.M.C.). The materials collection and personnel of the graded schools' library is one segment of the I.M.C. In addition, the I.M.C. may contain all of the teaching machines, the electronic recordings, and the other reference materials the school owns. The I.M.C. can cover a large area with particular spaces devoted to functionally specific activities. There would be a quiet zone for reading, writing, and individual study. Also, there might be a noise zone for typing, viewing films, listening to recordings, and holding student conferences. The instructional materials center will be the heart of the school. Both teachers and students will use it as a location to carry on much of the teaching-learning activity of the school.

The establishment of the I.M.C. will require additional space. This can be provided by a rearrangement of existing space. Less classroom space will be needed as students spend fewer hours in them and more time in the I.M.C. and in specialized learning laboratories which will be established within the school. These learning centers will be constructed throughout the school to facilitate study. There will be spaces divided for specialized learning activities or for study of particular subjects. Individual science laboratories, art studios, typing rooms, shop facilities, kitchens, and the like will be designed for independent study and small-group work. Some of the school's existing space will be converted to use for large-assembly group instruction.

Teachers' offices can be located adjoining the I.M.C. for teachers of English, mathematics, social studies, and foreign languages. Teachers of art, business education, industrial arts, homemaking, music, science, and physical education will have their offices adjoining the laboratories for their fields. There will be easy access to teachers by students as they work on their independent study projects and as they attack individual learning problems.

Assigning Responsibility

Responsibility for the development of a nongraded high school organization, or any other kind of program, must be put in the building principal's hands. While the principal probably will not make the decision to move toward the nongraded school alone or do all of the planning necessary, he is the pivot on which the program's inauguration will depend. As the person directly responsible for all that does or does not go on in a school, the building administrator is at the nerve center of the school. He controls some of the communications and most of the decision-making machinery of the school.

Of course, the building principal gets his authority from the superintendent of schools for program development. Superintendents necessarily must rely on the building principal to translate school-wide objectives into operational programs. The building administrator has the time, unique knowledge, and the potential for influencing the staff and, most important, he has the responsibility for the particular school's program development. A wise superintendent will clarify to the faculty, the board of education, and the community the role of building principal as the school's instructional leader.

Working With the Staff

If faculty meetings are concerned with routine management announcements which could be dispatched in bulletins, or if they fail to provide the opportunity for a conversation about the nongraded school, the shaping of such a program will be impossible. Before any innovation is introduced on a successful and widespread scale, pervasive communications among all the staff are vital. The communication systems in every school operate on both formal and informal levels. The formal system influences much informal communication. Formal communications take place in written bulletins, in faculty meetings, in department and department-head meetings, and in the special-interest meetings the principal arranges. The informal communications system often excludes the principal as a participant, but not necessarily what he says and does. As the nongraded concept is introduced into a school, the principal must take steps to get related discussion into the mainstream of both the formal and informal communication systems. Faculty discussion needs to include all of the implications of nongradedness. Attention must be given to the effects on students, on teachers, and on content. To ignore any of these interests is to do disservice to a full investigation of the concept.

Discussion, important as it is, is not enough in getting a nongraded program in operation. The building administration needs to identify the decision-making process within the school. Methods of making decisions about the curriculum vary among schools. No single method can be advocated over others. But with assurance it can be asserted that a principal who wants significant change to take place in a school must be clear in establishing the way decisions are to be made. Responsibility must be assigned to the entire faculty or to representative members of the group for various kinds of decisions. The extent to which decision-making groups can go must be clearly stated. Not only the maximum but the minimum limits must be understood. For example, if a group is charged with the responsibility of making a recommendation as to whether a nongraded organization shall be employed, it should be required that careful attention will be given to all of the implications. Decisions made without a full understanding of the facts may lead to future frustration, even unfortunate failures.

The building principal should be charged with the responsibility for an in-service program of professional study. This charge is not a biannual or periodic one, but a continuing demand. It is proper for each school faculty always to be engaged in study of the impact of its total program on students and its professional advantage to teachers. Such a study program is essential both to inaugurate and to maintain a nongraded program.

The teacher can affect instruction within the province of the classroom and influence, to a lesser extent, the department or the faculty. However, the principal can effect constructive change in the whole school. His influence often is not related so much to what he says and does as to what he encourages others to say and do. Effective principals provide vision, encourage the staff to become personally involved in program development, and, most often, ask provocative questions. Finding fault without offering constructive suggestions will not lead to the development of a nongraded school program. The principal makes the difference between progress in program planning and stagnant satisfaction with a senseless status quo.

Not only must the principal work with the faculty as a group or with subgroups, but he must be in tune with the attitudes and views of individual teachers. Personal attention to a teacher's nagging questions or personal reservations about moving to a nongraded

organization will go a long way in making the necessary transformation in such an individual's teaching behavior.

The nongraded program should not be thought of as the private
property or pet project of the principal. It must be owned by all the
staff and student body. Wide ownership will lead to the kind of
attention and care which will make the nongraded school organization fulfill its promise to both teachers and students. It is the
building principal's job to assign the deed to all of the school
community.

The organization of the school day should be such that teachers
will meet together during school hours to do the planning and
evaluating necessary for the nongraded program. Teacher conferences are necessary to precede student contact sessions. Both efficiency and productivity can be gained by cooperative teacher
planning and evaluating. Since the students will be in formal classes
much less than in the traditional school, time will be available for
these necessary professional meetings.

Securing Outside Consultation

There are those who hear of the nongraded high school and say that
it will never be a reality because of restrictions of state departments
of education and regional accrediting agencies. This contention is a
shallow one, for if the nongraded concept holds promise for the
improvement of education, state departments of instruction, and
regional accrediting agencies will not stand in the way of its development. Educators interested in the nongraded school organization should discuss their plans with both agencies before a program
is implemented. Usually, a public school administrator will find the
agencies are not only approving, but anxious to give assistance in
such a program's development. Hopefully, there will be funds available for educators to use in the development of nongraded schools.
There can be no question that a full array of resources, human and
financial, will be needed to develop a number of nongraded schools.

Requirements for class time, class size, and the like are set by
educators to help provide resources for education in schools. These
were never intended to be restrictions barring truly creative and
improved programs of teaching. Once the traditional organization of

the school is altered, the administrative requirements also must be changed. The intention of the state departments of instruction and the accrediting agencies is to help the schools in staffing and housing instructional programs. Therefore, these agencies will be careful to assess the intention of a school which deviates from the norm. No school district with inadequate financial support, with meager instructional materials, poor facilities, or with poorly prepared teachers has any business considering, or being approved to employ, a nongraded school organization. Few, if any, in this category will seriously consider it.

Aside from the help of the state department of instruction and universities, a school embarking on a nongraded program would be advised to locate a consultant who would work with the staff in developing the program. The cold objectivity and the experience of a qualified consultant can shed light on important considerations as the school program is developed.

Changing the Teaching Task

The nongraded secondary school will fade into oblivion if a change in the existing teaching methodology does not accompany its introduction. There is little reason to rearrange the school's organization for instruction without the introduction of new methods of teaching. The nongraded high school is not a redistribution of the traditional school's schedule, but it is an original design for new teaching-learning procedures. While those who write about the elementary nongraded school see little reason to call for new methodology, any serious observer of the secondary school sees the need for adjustments in the teachers' roles. Perhaps this is a call for secondary school teachers to adopt the methods of competent elementary school teachers.

In the traditional school, the teaching task may be considered to have three distinct but related features. These vary from grade level to grade level and also with the goals of instruction. First, the teacher determines work tasks for pupils. This is usually done on a group or class basis and is concerned with devising the ways students will occupy themselves. Second, the teacher has the task of evaluating student progress. More often than not this is done by some standard, either objective or subjective, based on group norms. It is assumed that some standard exists against which pupil progress is assessed. Third, as a consequence of the first two operations, the teacher performs the teaching act. That is, he attempts to bring student understanding or behavior up to the specific standard set by the instructional objectives. Skill in teaching is determined by how well the teacher can cause the student to close the gap between what he does or knows and what the teacher wants him to do or know. The worth of the selection of the instructional tasks is, to a large extent, dependent on how well the first two tasks are accomplished. Teaching, as viewed by this model, difficult as it is, is less complex than the teaching task implied in the nongraded high school. While the model is the same in the nongraded school, the three tasks must be done for each student and not for the groups of students.

In the traditional school, the instructional objectives are usually set by texts or by curriculum guides. The teaching tasks, then, are geared to these determinants which the individual teacher may or may not have had a hand in developing. In the nongraded school, the teacher is asked to set instructional objectives for each student, perhaps independent of textbooks or curriculum guides. Also, the teacher in the nongraded school is asked to set individual learning tasks for each pupil. Group considerations give way to individual priorities.

The teacher in the nongraded school must know his students personally. As important as what students have done in the past, knowledge of what they want and can do in the future is critical to teaching in the nongraded school. This kind of personal understanding can only be developed through intimate association. Thus, some teachers may work with a given student for several years in the study of a variety of topics. The school's testing program and the counselor's insights will play a significant part in the instruction of every student. It will be common practice for the counselor to meet with the teachers about the learning problems and progress of every youngster in the nongraded school. The knowledge counselors have of students is of little value if it is not shared with the teachers who work with the students.

Teachers in the nongraded schools will become diagnosticians. They will make a diagnosis of a student's instructional requirements, his potentials, and the activities appropriate for him to develop his abilities. In the nongraded school, then, teachers will shift from group judgments to personal assignment prescriptions.

Teaching will require more preparation and a different kind of preparation than in the traditional school. Teachers will work as members of a teaching team in bringing the judgments of several associates to focus on both the content offered and the individual requirements of each student. Instead of spending time making group tests, group work sheets, and the like, teachers will focus attention on specific recommendations for every student.

Two broad teaching functions can be isolated as appropriate to the nongraded school. First, the teachers must present subject matter and generalize about it. This activity will go on in the large assembly groups. Second, the teacher will make specific suggestions and prescribe particular work tasks. This will take place in individual conferences or at the end of small inquiry classes. The nongraded school will provide the organizational potential for teachers to know and assist students in an intimate and individual manner. The teachers' professional behavior will determine whenever the potentials are realized. The science of instruction takes on a new importance in the nongraded school. Not only must it be based on a solid learning theory, as discussed in Chapter Two, but it must be operated on a different concept of the teaching process. The emphasis is on the selection of particular learning subjects and on the prescription of specific learning activities for each student. This has long range implications for the profession of teaching and rather immediate demands for teacher preparation and instruction.

Like students, teachers in the nongraded school will spend less time in formal classes. They will operate most of the time in student-centered, small inquiry classes and in individual conferences with students and other teachers. The amount of preparation teachers will do for the large assembly classes will eclipse the preparation time teachers in a traditional school devote to this activity.

As a school implements the nongraded organization, there will necessarily be added attention given to the in-service program. Not only should meetings be required to make operational decisions, but there should be time given to practice-teaching sessions. In these, some teachers will present lessons as they would in a large group. Others will play electronic tapes of small inquiry groups. The total staff will react to these presentations. Together the school staff will develop the competencies required for the nongraded program.

Bringing the Community Along

It is necessary for the board of education and the professional staff to make the community a party to considerations and action programs of the secondary school. Whether introducing a nongraded program, or any other new practice, the community needs to be informed of the adjustments made in the school. It is significant to notice that most school patrons throughout the country react positively, sometimes even with unbridled jubilation, to new programs in the schools. This is an era of change. The citizens of nearly any community, if adequately informed, are likely to respond by giving added support to the school when attempts to improve the schools are visible and are originated by the professional staff.

Taking Out Insurance

Evaluation should be a continuous process. It takes on added importance as a nongraded program is instituted. Both those directly and indirectly associated with the nongraded school will want to know how well it is meeting its stated objectives. A careful evaluation design should be worked out to provide answers to the questions the patrons or participants in the new program may have. This amounts to an insurance-type safeguard. If the program does not meet its objectives, adjustments and refinements can be made based on the evaluation's conclusions. While this is discussed in detail in Chapter Six, it is important to stress the need for keeping an accurate record of what happens in a school and, more important, why it happens.

Where possible, the services of an outside agency, perhaps the services of a college research staff, should be utilized in carrying out the evaluation of the nongraded program. Both objectivity and detachment can be brought to the evaluation if it is the work of persons not closely associated with the program. Also, a staff immersed in operation of a new program has little time for detailed evaluation of the total program.

Summary

Figure Four summarizes the major steps in nongrading the high school. Although the process is shown in steps, it is important to note that one step does not necessarily end when another begins.

STEPS IN NONGRADING THE HIGH SCHOOL		
Step	*Task*	*Responsibility*
First	Encourage interest in program development and constructive change in school organization	Principal
Second	Gain an understanding of the philosophic and operational implications of a nongraded high school organization	Total Professional Staff
Third	Make a commitment to the nongraded school philosophy	Total Professional Staff
Fourth	Secure board of education policy support for nongraded program study	Superintendent
Fifth	Establish broad educational objectives	Professional Staff and Community
Sixth	Determine specific learning objectives for each content area	Department by Department
Seventh	Structure a learning sequence for each discipline in the curriculum	Individual Teachers
Eighth	Select an organization for instruction to complement the program of studies	Total Staff
Ninth	Assess abilities and interests of each youngster	Guidance Staff
Tenth	Communicate information about the school program's aims and procedures to the community	Superintendent and Principal
Eleventh	Begin program evaluation procedures with the inauguration of the nongraded program	College Research Staff or Other Evaluation Personnel
Twelfth	Examine instructional problems and institute an in-service education program	Principal

FIGURE FOUR

Like Robinson Crusoe when he met Friday on that solitary island, American education has come upon a new partner in the form of the nongraded school. There will need to be administrative adjustments, behavioral changes, and new professional practices introduced into the high schools of the country as the schools are confronted with the requirements of providing for individual differences and for education in the technological era. Nongrading a high school is not for the timid or for those who would only tinker with a school schedule. Instead, the nongraded concept is both a challenge and an opportunity for the secondary school educator to do an even better job in providing quality educational opportunities to all the youth who bring different backgrounds, diverse aspirations, and distinct potentials to the place called high school.

There are those who believe, as can be noted in Chapter Five, that the task is perhaps too great and the change too difficult for individual schools to attain nongradedness. Yet, as the case studies show, some have begun the journey. While the verdict on the enduring value of the nongraded secondary school awaits the test of time, thoughtful, hard-working educators need to be about the business of developing demonstration schools, both for the advantage of their own students and teachers and for the profession in general. A few must lead before many can follow.

CHAPTER 4

A Strategy for the Development of Nongraded Schools

by

Roy A. Larmee

Roy A. Larmee is an associate professor of education at The Ohio State University. He has served as the director of the University of Chicago Laboratory Schools and has been an elementary, junior high school, and senior high school principal.

THE CASUAL reader of the literature in the field of education could easily conclude that change has been a major concern of educators in America for a long period of time. An examination of the schools of 1900 and a comparison of them to the schools of today shows many changes in pupil population, in curriculum, in physical facilities, and even in methods of teaching, as well as some distinct similarities in basic organization and administrative structure. Even though literature in the field of education reflects considerable concern over change in American education, the writers reflect little understanding of both the processes and consequences of change. In fact, it is only very recently that serious consideration has been given to the idea of carefully planned change. Terms such as change agents, change mechanisms, inhibiting forces, and facilitating forces have been given some attention in rural sociology and in other fields, but carefully developed research on change in the field of education is only a very recent proposal. The availability of data which could be helpful to those wishing to inaugurate planned change in education is extremely limited.

Consideration of the whole process by which an educational organization makes and implements decisions, such as the nongrading of a school, is of utmost importance, particularly for educators contemplating the introduction of some change in school organization. The development of educational goals and the adoption of a plan to achieve these goals is necessarily a cooperative effort for the educator, whether he be teacher, principal, supervisor, superintendent, or any other member of the educational team. While it is not difficult to identify the concerns of the various professional education personnel in the nongrading of schools, it is a more formidable task to plan for the specific roles of each in the investigation, preplanning, decision-making, programming, implementation, and evaluation stages of the total undertaking.

Recognition of the Problem

The development of a carefully designed plan to nongrade a school or schools must be preceded by systematic investigation, study, and planning. Probably one of the best ways to initiate a study of the nongraded school is to consider a series of problems related to the operation of a graded school. This is not a difficult task, for educators have been wrestling with many of these problems for years.

Initiation or recognition of these problems may come from any point in the educational hierarchy. Concerns such as the following are not new, but viewed in the context of the nongraded school, they offer a new set of challenges as well as new points of attack for staff study.

1. How do we deal with the differences in readiness of children who are entering our schools each year?
2. In a graded school system, do we make any special provision for children who have had one or two years of nursery school prior to entering our school system?
3. Do the initial differences in the ability of children increase or decrease as they continue their formal education experience?
4. Is there a difference in a child's interest and achievement rate as he moves from one learning experience to another?

5. In what ways does the graded pattern of school organization restrict a student from a desirable, uninterrupted, sequential, educational experience?
6. Does homogeneous grouping of students for all educational experiences at a given age level provide a solution for some of the problems resident in a heterogeneous grouping arrangement?
7. How do we fit independent study programs into a graded or homogeneously grouped school organization?
8. Do these independent study programs present new problems within the graded structure of school organization?
9. How can our report to parents on pupil progress be made more meaningful?

This is not meant to be an exhaustive list of questions but merely illustrates problems which could easily lead to the discussion of the nongraded school concept. It is also relatively easy to recognize the variety of sources from which these questions might come. Teachers, counselors, supervisors, administrators, and parents have all raised the same kinds of concern.

A careful examination of any of these or other related questions can justifiably raise the question as to whether the formally graded school system offers the best organizational pattern for dealing with these problems. Are there other patterns that hold some promise for meeting these differences in ability, interest, and rate of learning? What are some of these new patterns? In addition to concerns with organizational patterns, such questions will probably quickly move to consideration of some fairly firm policy questions related to staffing, curriculum, promotion, parent-school-community relationships, independent study areas, instructional materials centers, and team teaching.

The pattern of questions may vary from school system to school system, but it would be a rare system indeed which has not considered a number of them. It is also possible at this point in defining the problem that the concept of the nongraded school might well be introduced because considerable experience with this type of school organization has now been reported in the professional educational literature. Many teachers and administrators have had some contact with the idea through attendance at professional workshops or meetings and through college and university courses. It is entirely possible that a proposal for the study of the nongraded school concept may emerge because of prior work of the staff on some of the problems noted above.

The Role of the Administrator as an Agent of Change

At this point in staff consideration of the nongraded school concept, the role of the administrator as an agent of change is crucial. In a recent study of the change process in New York, Brickell states that teachers alone can make only three types of instructional change in the absence of administrative initiative: (1) change in classroom practice, (2) relocation of existing curriculum content, and (3) introduction of single special courses at the high school level.[1] He also states:

> Instructional changes which call for significant new ways of using professional talent, drawing upon instructional resources, allocating physical facilities, scheduling instructional time or altering physical space—rearrangements of the structural elements of the institution—depend almost exclusively upon administrative initiative.[2]

Basic change such as nongrading a school has far-reaching implications for staff members at the investigation, decision making, programming, implementation, and evaluation levels. The administrator from his unique vantage point in the educational enterprise has a critical role to play as planner, decision maker, facilitator, allocator of resources, stimulator, and appraiser.

Administrators have been increasingly committed to the involvement of teachers in the decision-making process, but they have been unable to develop agreement on the specific form which this teacher involvement should take. Some have argued the desirability and feasibility of teachers sharing in the making of all decisions, while others argue that the area of effective teacher involvement in decision making is satisfaction and morale. In one of the most comprehensive investigations in this area, Chase found in a study involving over two thousand teachers in forty-three states that teachers who report opportunity to participate regularly and actively in making policies are much more likely to be enthusiastic about their school systems than those who report limited opportunity to participate.[3]

Consideration of the implementation of the nongraded organization provides an excellent opportunity to illustrate the role of the administrator as a change agent and the need to involve other members of the teaching staff in the study which might lead to the decision to inaugurate an experimental nongraded school program. It is desirable to include members of the teaching staff in the investigation of the problems concerned with the introduction of the nongraded school, in the examination of the alternate solutions possible, and in the making of a decision based on these investigations and examinations. Fortunately, many administrators have followed a staffing policy which has resulted in the recruitment and retention of a teaching staff with many abilities, skills, special preparations, and experiences which would be invaluable in the consideration of a program as broad as that of the nongraded school. An essential element of administrative leadership is identifying this wide divergence of talent and using this talent to provide meaningful working relationships. The administrator must couple this knowledge of staff with a careful assessment of the scope of the investigation being undertaken, and he must assign the resources necessary to carefully consider all alternatives so that a sound decision may be made about adopting a plan of action.

Provision of the Proper Climate for Decision Making

In the initial stages of the investigation many decisions will be made which will affect the final outcome of the study. The administrator must decide, first of all, whether the study can be undertaken within the regular framework of faculty meetings, curriculum studies, professional conferences, and workshops. The scope of the problem may demand a greater commitment of resources. There are a number of alternatives which might be considered, and these would undoubtedly vary from school system to school system. In some schools, a portion of the regular school day is allocated each week for studies and professional concerns of the staff. Team visitations to schools carrying out interesting new practices are also provided for in some schools. In other school systems, extended contracts are available for a limited number of teachers in the summer months to make careful studies and preparations for projects of potential benefit to the school system. In still other schools, a leave of absence is provided to release teachers for a continued year of uninterrupted study. Partial release from teaching responsibilities is another approach used by school systems to provide personnel resources commensurate with the task undertaken. An investigation of the scope involved in the nongrading of schools might well require consideration of one of these alternatives.

The mental outlook of the total staff is greatly influenced by the work that is done during the planning, investigating, and decision-making stages. Teachers will vary tremendously in their attitude toward an undertaking such as the nongraded school. Initially attitude will probably range from enthusiastic support to open opposition. Recognition of these varied attitudes is important in selecting those persons who will be most active in the investigation and planning stages; also, this recognition assures those raising serious objections that their concerns will be sincerely and conscientiously recognized and investigated. Those who offer serious objections can often provide appropriate dimensions to be included in the evaluation and appraisal phases which must be a part of the initial decision and of the plan which is inaugurated. It is important also to point out to these objectors that all possible alternatives will be investigated impartially.

There will be many discussions of the new plan in the informal organization of the school, and as the plan progresses, there will be many questions from students and from adult members of the community. Questions will not always be asked of persons best qualified to answer them. In these cases it is important that the attitude encountered by the questioning parent or student is one sympathetic to the project being undertaken. Administrators have learned from the National Science Foundation projects that parents are very willing to have their children participate in a project that is clearly labeled experimental, if they can be assured that it has been carefully planned by competent persons who will thoroughly appraise the results.

Some teachers will have fairly well-established opinions which may be in opposition to the total study being undertaken. These opinions are often more apparent at the initiation stages of the study. Here, again, the role of the administrator is important and difficult since he must be completely honest and straightforward in his presentation of the problem and of the proposal.

Staff members vary a great deal in their respect for the leadership ability of the administrator. One of the frequent causes for disappointment of a staff undertaking this type of project is the introduction of serious limitations to the investigation after the undertaking has been under way for some time. This is especially disastrous to morale, satisfaction, and productivity if it is discovered that these limitations have existed since the beginning of the study but have not been identified in the investigation, planning, and decision-making stages. For example, are there limitations in the undertaking in terms of budget provided? If so, have these been clearly specified? Is there a time limitation involved for the study because of reports which have been promised by the administrator to the board of education? Probably the most devastating of all possible developments is the discovery by the staff that, although the administrator has given assurance that all possible alternatives will be investigated and a decision made based on these investigations, the administrator had a proposal in mind from the very beginning and has bluntly manipulated the study to reach this outcome. The possibility of success for this kind of approach is seriously limited and the opportunities and probabilities for sabotage are great.

Involvement of the Board of Education and the Community at the Planning Stage

Initial investigations of problem areas and possible alternate solutions should be planned with the full knowledge of the board of education and the total administrative staff of the school system. This stage should not be confused with later stages in the process when carefully developed plans are ready for explanation and dissemination to the communication media and to the community. In the early study phase, the board of education should be made aware of the care, the total scope, and the thoroughness of the study to be undertaken; and those who make the presentation to the board should be careful not to make premature statements or implications of desired outcomes.

Also, the board of education should be made fully aware of the nature of the study, and plans should be made for periodic progress reports as the investigation progresses. Opportunities should be provided for members of the board to raise questions and also to offer constructive criticism of the proposed plan. Support of the board is crucial to any new plan devised by the professional school staff and this support can be best gained from an involved, informed, and sympathetic board of education. Basic board policies should make provision for this type of investigation and care should be exercised so that all programs of study are carried out in line with established board policies.

In some school systems, it has been found most desirable to include members of the lay community in the initial study groups. Active members of the Parent-Teacher Association often are sincerely interested in studies of this type, and they provide a parent's point of view which can be invaluable in developing and implementing a decision when it is finally reached. Community support can also often be gained by the involvement of persons from both public and private community agencies concerned with the health, education, and welfare of children. Their views are expressed from another vantage point, and they often provide suggestions which prove to be very effective in dealing with some of the most difficult problems. The role of the administrator is, again, a key one as are his contacts with the various agencies and groups in the community.

Consideration of Alternative Plans of Action

The study of the nongraded school may start anywhere, the logical place to be determined by the local school system personnel. Eventually, after the initial investigation has been completed and all alternatives closely examined, the decision must be made to try a single plan or a combination of approaches to nongrading. Typically, one of the first decisions made is the choice between system-wide experimentation or selection of one or two schools for limited experimentation. School systems have varied widely in their approach to this problem, and some problems are associated with each approach.

If a choice is made to inaugurate nongraded organization in one school, the original plan should include logical, carefully developed reasons for the choice of this school. In reaching the point of communicating this decision to parents and students, adequate explanation must be given for the limited choice. This is now a much easier task than it was in years past because schools have undertaken limited experimentation in many other areas such as educational television, team teaching, and programmed instruction. Parents have learned to respect carefully planned experimentation if it is thoroughly evaluated and if the results of this evaluation are included in further expansion of the innovation throughout the school system.

System-wide introduction of an innovation such as the nongraded school should be done only after a complete assessment of the personnel and material resources available in the school system, since carefully planned introduction of any new idea is usually more expensive in its initial year even if proper provision is made for evaluation and modification of the idea as it is put into practice. However, many of these costs associated with initial introduction will disappear as the experimentation is perfected, in-service training programs completed, and consultant services dispensed with.

Making the initial introduction of the nongraded concept in a single school or in a small number of schools provides many advantages. Initially, teachers may vary considerably in their attitude toward the nongraded school and in their knowledge and understanding of the concept. It is important that those who will carry out the initial introduction be thoroughly familiar with the idea and willing to give it an objective and fair trial. These staff members should be rigorously selected and then given the advantages of a thorough in-service training program staffed by persons who are familiar with the concept and experienced in the use of the plan. Reading the literature on the nongraded school and carefully discussing it is not enough. The teachers must thoroughly understand the change in order to deal adequately with some of the new learning situations. However, in the initial planning stages it is extremely important to think beyond the original introductory situation. If the nongraded concept is introduced in one or two schools, or if the decision is made to nongrade only parts of a school such as the first, second, or third grade, consideration must certainly be given to the situation that will exist following the experimental period, assuming, of course, that the experimentation will be a successful one even though modified in some ways as a result of the appraisal process. A group or groups of boys and girls will have had a completely new and, hopefully, a largely successful experience.

Are they to be returned to the traditional type of graded organization? If so, some fairly knotty problems must be dealt with in terms of pupil, parent, and teacher reactions. Plans for this eventuality cannot await the completion of the experimental period. These plans must be made at the time the original investigation is undertaken. There may well be modifications at the end of the experimental period, but basic planning should have been included in the original master plan for the innovation.

Some schools have experimented with very limited introduction of the nongraded concept. This decision, too, is greatly dependent on each local school situation. Sometimes the introduction is in a specific curriculum area such as reading or arithmetic. Again, the assessment of local personnel resources is important. If the school system has some highly motivated, well-prepared teachers in their areas who have been thoroughly familiarized and trained to introduce nongrading in these limited curriculum areas, this might be the best initial point of entry. Such a type of nongrading, if successfully carried out, may well provide the needed stimulation to encourage a wider use of the idea in other areas of the curriculum. It is one of the most convincing types of demonstration, and the original plan for this kind of a nongraded program can be studied and observed at close range by teachers responsible for other phases of the learning program.

Closely associated with the possible alternative plans of action for the introduction of the nongraded plan of school organization, and directly related to the curriculum used by the school, is the question of student progress within the established pattern of organization. The nongraded form of school organization offers great flexibility when viewed in the light of recent revisions of curriculum materials in a number of learning fields. A great deal of attention has been given to the structure of content in the various learning areas. Consideration has also been given to the method of inquiry peculiar to each of the fields involved. Many of the new curriculum materials have been designed in such a way that pupils expand their knowledge of the field in the same way that new knowledge in the field is discovered. The rate of discovery for each pupil will be dependent on the ability, interest, and motivation of each child; however, this rate can also be restricted or increased by the organizational structure of the school system. When programmed instructional materials or independent study programs are utilized by a graded school system, the graded organizational structure offers some serious limitations. When these materials are used for program enrichment or for individualized acceleration patterns in the various fields of learning, the nongraded form of organization offers many new possibilities.

Programming the Change

Immediately following the major decision to attempt some form of nongrading in a school system, a series of implementing decisions must be made so that adequate resources are available to give the new undertaking a fair trial. Visitation to other schools using the new plan may need to be scheduled. In-service programs for the faculty will need to be developed, staffed, and carried out. The whole area of a faculty for the new program will require consideration. Careful position descriptions outlining the duties and responsibilities should be developed for each staff position, and these descriptions should be used in turn to determine the qualifications necessary for the person who is to fill each of the positions. If the present staff does not include persons with the necessary qualifications, additional staff may need to be recruited or additional training provided for persons presently on the staff.

Attention should also be given to adequate housing of the new program. One of the desirable by-products of the accelerated school building program which has been underway for almost two decades is a recognition of the magnitude of the school building and equipment market by manufacturers and product designers. Through the efforts of both public and private agencies, many new products have been specifically designed from carefully developed educational specifications rather than adapted from materials used for other markets not associated with the educational enterprise. New, adequate, flexible partitions, acoustical treatment of classrooms, specially designed furniture, technical communication systems, data processing programs, climate control systems, and many other new products have helped to remove material handicaps which have existed in the past. These new materials and techniques have created unique classroom arrangements, improved instructional possibilities, and led to new plans for better utilization of the teaching staff. In addition to changing and enriching instructional possibilities, in many cases, initial construction and continued maintenance costs have been reduced by these carefully engineered changes.

Programming the decision to nongrade a school must also be reflected in the budget of the school system. A number of references have already been made to costs associated with the planning and decision-making stages of the process—costs such as released time for staff planning, consultant service, travel, and in-service training, as well as costs associated with the appraisal of the new program. Many of the expenditures are not of a continuing nature and therefore will disappear as the initial experiment is completed. However, it is important that these funds to be used for personnel, materials, and equipment are available at the time and place and in the amounts that are needed to insure adequate resources for a fair trial of the new plan.

The programming step should also include a basic time allocation for scheduling the various stages in the master plan. While a time budget is certainly desirable, care should be exercised to make time allocations adequate and flexible. Movement into any new or unknown area is usually accompanied by some unforeseen problems regardless of how much care is exercised in devising the initial plan. Time provision should be made to allow for readjustments in the master plan as the experimental period progresses and as the evaluation processes reveal changes that need to be included.

The Role of the Administrator
as Stimulator and Coordinator

A crucial point in the introduction of a new innovation is often reached after the initial major decision to inaugurate the change has been made. After the first implementing decisions have been carried out and personnel and material resources have been allocated, the role of the administrator again becomes a critical one. Much stimulation of staff is usually accomplished during the investigation, planning, and decision-making stages of the project. A great deal of this inspiration will be carried forward to the experimental period.

Occasionally, however, it is necessary for the administrator to assist during difficult or trying periods with a word of encouragement or with the addition of resources not perceived as necessary during the planning period. In some cases, the administrator must remind some members of the staff of commitments which they have made and of their importance to the success of the entire undertaking. A face-to-face contact is usually most desirable for maximum stimulation. In relatively isolated cases, it may even be necessary for the administrator to exert pressure upon individuals to gain the desired results. If careful staffing procedures and planned involvement have been followed during the planning stages, the necessity for this kind of inspiration on the part of the administrator should be quite limited.

Closely associated with the administrator's role as a stimulator is his responsibility for coordination of the entire undertaking. In programming the master plan, he has made provision for budget, personnel, and material resources, as well as establishing a time schedule for carrying out the total experimentation. As the coordinator, he must make certain that all of the resources are brought together in a meaningful and effective relationship. The resources must be provided, and they must be provided at the time and place at which they are needed. The unique vantage point of the administrator affords him an excellent opportunity to observe how well the entire plan is moving toward the objectives established during the planning and decision-making periods. If the immediate goals of the project and the institutional goals of the school system are to be kept in proper perspective, the administrator will need to maintain an objective attitude toward the findings revealed in the periodic progress report and in the interim appraisal results. The administrator may find it necessary to point to the need for reorientation of the project in order to accomplish the agreed-upon goals of the undertaking and of the institution as a whole.

Appraisal of Innovation or Change

Probably the most frequent reason for failure of an experimental program is the failure to provide for its adequate appraisal. Provision for appraisal must be a part of all planning activities from the very outset of the undertaking, and it must be included in all phases of the project as it moves from investigation on through the experimental testing period. Appraisal programs, devices, and techniques, too, must be related to the goals of the school system and to the goals of the immediate project which is being undertaken. It is most discouraging to review an experimental project and learn that the only specific appraisal information available is that "the children feel very good about it," or "the experiment has been of real value to the staff," or "our parents are most enthusiastic and are encouraging us to continue our efforts." These are healthy outcomes, but they do not provide the specific information needed to appraise the undertaking, to revise and improve it, or to respond to the critics who are often present in any new undertaking. A proposal such as the nongrading of a school system has a direct relationship to the goals of an educational enterprise. Any plan which is considered must be examined in the light of these goals. Are we modifying them in any way? If we are, it is extremely important that these modifications are recognized and that those responsible for the operation of the school system are aware of these modifications and that they support them.

In the planning stages of the project, intermediate objectives will be established for the specific nongraded project which is chosen. These objectives may be based on specifically documented facts, or values, or assumptions; but in any event, they must be explicitly stated. The philosophy of the school system will usually provide the general framework for the selection of specific objectives. However, the learning experiences which are chosen to attain these objectives must be carefully examined. As each new experience is included in the program, it must be examined in terms of the school philosophy and in terms of its suitability for the age level at which it is to be introduced. It must, in other words, be sifted through both a philosophical and a psychological screen.

Once the experience has been termed a sound one as it relates to the school's philosophy and identified as a reasonable one in terms of the group of children who will experience it, provision must be made to determine ways of measuring the degree to which the pupil attains the objective for which the experience was selected. In this connection, a number of the new National Science Foundation Course Content Improvement Programs sought the assistance of a major national testing agency to determine whether the new programs were "better" than the traditional programs being used by most schools. In each case, the testing agency indicated that this is not a question which tests can answer. However, they were able to offer assistance in determining whether certain experiences and objectives were suitable for children of specified age groups. And they were able to assist in the preparation of achievement tests to determine how well-established objectives for the new program were being attained.[4]

The selection of procedures, tests, and other devices to be used in appraising the objectives of the new program is an integral part of the investigation, planning, and decision-making stages of the project. In many cases, testing programs appropriate for use in the project are readily available. Alternate testing programs should be carefully examined to determine their suitability for the experimental program which has been planned. Standardized testing programs are valuable tools for use in appraising a project, but other devices must also be developed in line with the objectives of the school and of the immediate project being undertaken. School communities differ in their composition and in the goals which they have set for themselves. Appraisal devices and techniques must be chosen to reflect these differences. Paper and pencil tests, case studies, anecdotal records, interview schedules, as well as skilled observations by qualified consultants are additional evaluation devices which may be used to assist in the appraisal of the new program. As each of the objectives and each of the stages of the experiment are examined and appraised, modifications of the original plan may be necessary. In this sense, the process is a cyclical one and should lead to new decisions which will modify the experiment in the light of the evidence gained through the appraisal process.

Orienting Parents to the Change

Earlier in this chapter, a caution was offered in terms of a premature public release of information relative to the proposed nongrading plan being considered. Early involvement of the board of education was deemed essential and the possibility of including selected parents and uniquely qualified representatives of community agencies was also considered. The total plan should also make provision

for orientation of children and parents as well. Since Amer
schools belong to the people, the schools have been fortunate
retaining a close school interest on the part of most parents. Pare...s
are always interested in improving educational opportunities for
their children, but they also will try to make certain that departures
from traditional patterns of action are carefully planned, executed,
and appraised. They have also insisted upon being informed of
changes and innovations that are being used in their schools.

One of the most difficult problems in nongrading a school relates
to parent orientation to the varied abilities of children. The differences in their rate of achievement is not newly discovered; it has
been with us for some time. However, the schools have not made
adequate provision for these differences in their organization and
operation. The graded system, as it is operated in many schools,
appears to deny these differences. In many cases, the schools
assumed a common set of learning experiences at each grade level
accompanied by a common set of objectives. To be sure, they have
also assumed that the objectives are attained in varying degrees by
pupils moving through the program. If administrators and teachers
subscribe to the basic concept of the nongraded school, they must
also recognize these differences, plan for them, and modify the
traditional program for the enrichment and achievement rate. Some
teachers and administrators find it extremely difficult to convey this
idea to parents. In one sense, this entire problem is a product of
years of operation under the graded school concept. In any planned
program of parent orientation, this question must be faced and
adequately dealt with if the necessary parent support for nongrading is to be obtained.

Specific techniques for parent-orientation programs will again be
dependent on local school situations. In some school systems, school-
community relations have been well established, and orientation of
parents can follow the general pattern which has been formed in the
past for other orientation activities. In other communities, agencies
such as the Parent-Teacher Association include provision for adequate parent orientation activities. In still other communities, it may
be necessary to establish the orientation procedures in the absence
of suitable school-community interpretation machinery. A carefully
planned orientation program should, of course, include skillfully
developed materials which can be utilized by the mass media of

communication such as newspapers, radio, television, community forums, and other media available at the local levels.

In preparing materials for parent orientation programs it is important to develop presentations and materials that will reflect the care with which the innovation has been considered. The orientation sessions should include a discussion of the planning process including consideration of some of the problems that stimulated the original investigation. The alternatives considered during the planning process should also be described and specific reasons given for the alternative which was chosen. A review of the range of personnel involved in the planning process should also be made including the board of education, consultants, and members of the community. Parents should also be familiarized with the objectives established for the program and the way in which these objectives are related to the goals of the school system. Finally, the operation of the program must be thoroughly described and illustrated along with the plans which have been made for the thorough appraisal of the experimental program. Future plans for expansion of the program should also be discussed including possible alternatives to be determined as a result of the appraisal process. Whenever it is possible to do so, time should be allowed for questions as the most carefully planned orientation program will not anticipate all questions.

Pupils to be affected by the nongrading experiment should also be oriented to the new program. If a selective introduction is to be made in a school and if it will only include a portion of the pupils in the school, those who are not to be included should also be acquainted with the change; and reasons should be given for the limited introduction. If appropriate, future plans for expansion of the experiment may also be shared with these pupils.

It is probably advisable to plan for parent and pupil orientation at approximately the same time. In this way, pupils will find it easier to discuss the new program with their parents, and inadequate or erroneous interpretation of the program by pupils can be avoided. The general areas to be covered in pupil orientation should be determined by the staff and thoroughly discussed with the children. Obviously, the content of their orientation program will differ from that of the parent program, but each stage of the introductory process should be examined and a selection of information made to be presented to the pupils involved. This will vary with the levels at which the nongrading experiment is to be inaugurated. Again, a question period should be provided to avoid misunderstanding and apprehension on the part of the pupils involved.

Conclusion

The major concern of this chapter has been focused upon the process by which a typical graded school may be ungraded by cooperative staff and community action. It begins with a recognition of problems resident in graded school structure and continues through the stages of investigation, planning, decision making, programming, and culminates in the introduction of the nongraded plan with careful provision for appraisal during the experimental period. The process is designed to do much more than change the form of organization from a graded to a nongraded one, for mere change from one type of organization to another will accomplish little in and of itself. The introduction of a nongraded plan does remove restrictions for students and teachers, but this is really only the beginning. The process described should also alert the teacher to the new possibilities for accomplishment in the nongraded organizational framework. It is designed to develop understanding, to change attitudes, and to deal more effectively with some of the most difficult problems involved in the education of children. It brings with it not only new opportunities but also new responsibilities since the nongraded school offers a system of organization that is completely compatible with basic American educational values.

CHAPTER 5

Research and Evaluation of the Nongraded School

by

ROBERT J. GARVUE

Robert J. Garvue is an associate professor of education at Florida State University. Dr. Garvue had been teaching under a contract with Indiana University and the Government of Pakistan. He has had a long-term interest in research in this field.

EDUCATIONAL INSTITUTIONS have varied histories of modification. During the current period of educational change effected by the earth-shaking event of Sputnik in 1958, one senses a growing belief by the public that this period is among the most profitable in terms of educational output. Faith abounds that children today are learning more and faster. The thrust given to education by the federal government's new and highly funded programs provides more dollars, more means, for potential widespread school improvement. However, the fact is that criteria of determining school effectiveness have not been clarified well at the national or state levels and clarified only in isolated instances at the local level.

In spite of the problems of establishing criteria to measure school effectiveness, institutions which train school administrators are beginning to emphasize the role of educational leaders as agents of change and, in some instances, have structured academic programs accordingly. In addition, teachers are being oriented about the historical naïveté of teachers in politics and about the new role of teachers in effecting change at the policy-making level. Thus, professional educators are taking new political stances in the determination of educational innovations, and in suggesting deletions and modifications in educational practice.

Educational reform issues involve substantive and procedural elements. The substantive elements consist of goals, aims, and ends, while the procedural elements are the means to effect the desired ends. Promising substantive elements include increased critical inquiry and general process ability. Promising procedural elements include flexible scheduling, the wide use of programmed instruction, and the nongraded organization.

With tongue in cheek, a cynical teacher might state that both substantive and procedural educational reforms are brought about in the following ways: One is by administrative mandate that "we are going to improve"; another is to form a committee to investigate and evaluate; and a third is to wait for development of textbooks, films, or programmed materials by the experts or to get *the word* from a book such as this. Another popular method is to adopt voluntarily a model patterned by a school district which has received much favorable publicity. Other strategies could include a combination of these, or a program might be built on research data. Such data, however, will necessarily support broad generalizations and add fuel to conjecture since most of the accumulated research related to school organization is fixed firmly in the setting of the graded school.

Policy Translates Knowledge to Action

Theoretically, policy serves as an instrument to translate knowledge into action. One criterion of the value of knowledge is usefulness, and it is the man of action who devises policies or guidelines to convert words into behavior. Therefore, a school district's policy pertaining to instructional organization—both horizontal and vertical—should be grounded upon knowledge about many variables, including educational philosophy and related goals, staff competencies, learners' differences in ability and motivation, learning theory, plus educational facilities and costs. The extent of such a framework of knowledge is an empirical research problem that must be solved on an individual basis by each of the nation's school districts. Conjecture is that the framework needs to be strengthened. Hopefully, the Elementary and Secondary School Education Act of 1965 and other such legislation will provide the means for needed research in this area.

Educational decision makers frequently are motivated to innovate without substantial justification from research due to factors such as dissatisfaction with the status quo, pressure from varied publics, and the need for schools to become adaptable enough to earn the financial support to thrive. Fortunately, research justification can evolve from so-called basic research, that is, the development and adequate testing of educational theory in areas such as learning, teaching, motivating, and personal development. However, to many practitioners, basic research is thought of as being conducted primarily in laboratories and too far removed from the reality of a public school. Conversely, applied research, which is defined as having to do with the practice of education in actual school settings, offers more promise to practitioners for implementation. Still, there has been far too little research of this type in the schools generally.

Voids in the Research

Usually it has been an assumption of educators that, even though no scheme of school organization can take the place of good teaching, sound organizational patterns can facilitate the opportunity for good teaching. The testing of this assumption is a complex research problem and that data available on the effectiveness of the nongraded organization do not satisfy very exacting standards for significant research. The most glaring research weaknesses are failure to include a large enough number of schools in the study, failure to do longitudinal studies of an adequate number of variables within the framework of a pre-test and post-test design, and failure to evaluate in terms of avowed goals. Valid generalizations and valid research are impossible without such provisions.

Since the nongraded movement is a comparatively recent one, the present programs must be considered as pilot programs. The philosophical stage in the development of nongraded schools is becoming more apparent while the empirical stage—the stage when concepts and assumptions developed during the former period are tested—is hardly underway. A vital research activity will be to observe and collect data accurately concerning hundreds of pilot studies. Data would include information about objectives and goals, behavioral content, administrative policies, culture of the learning situation, pupils and teacher characteristics, varied decision-making aspects, and learning output such as process ability and conceptual and factual knowledge. Analysis of such data could lead to an understanding of the variables present and, eventually, to the construction of sophisticated and controlled studies.

Supporters of the nongraded program, as indicated in Chapters Two and Three, seem bent upon destroying what von Bertalanffy defined as the "equifinality" property of the open systems in education. The term implies that a final state may be reached or a given product produced by systems starting from different initial conditions and proceeding by different means. Nongraded researchers have been determined to prove that the nongraded structure is superior to other organizational forms. At the same time, these advocates of the nongraded school assign instructional goals to the nongraded school which are not always to be found in the statement of goals of the graded school. Most often, nongraded school proponents talk about the goals of increasing a student's responsibility for his own learning, developing skills through interests in broad content areas, and adding to the student's love of learning.

There is an immediate roadblock in the interpretation of nongraded school research data. There is no assurance that results of graded and nongraded programs are defined or differentiated in the research literature. In addition, a purported nongraded form approved by a school board, for example, may not be made operational because of the incapacity of teachers to transfer from a graded form of instruction. This may be more the case at the secondary school level than at the elementary level. Thus, the researcher's dependence upon an administrator's claim that a school is a nongraded one would prove fatal to the investigation.

More definitive abstract and operational statements of the nongraded form and of the graded form needed to be isolated so that appropriate evaluation instruments might be devised. Ideally, then, there would be a logical planning and evaluating sequence from abstract statements of goals, to operational statements of goals, to the development of criterion measures of effectiveness in terms of goal achievement. Operationalism has the difficulty of establishing the identity of an operation since, even when two individuals say the same thing, it actually may not be the same. Identity may not be destroyed by a plurality of designations, but legitimately one could question whether the following are nongraded or reasonably identical: nongraded school, ungraded school, flexible primary unit, ungraded primary, primary progress, continuous progress, and so forth. Too often educators apply labels to programs which are not exact. Thus, those who argue against the development of professional terminology are contributing to the confusion of understanding the critical elements of a program.

Models of School Organization

In order to clarify organizational alternatives, educators have isolated at least three different models of school organization.[1] The models include abstract statements as elements and may not precisely resemble reality in any one of the nation's 31,000 school districts, but they can become a useful tool for investigating the relationship between existing practices and the assumptions supposedly underlying them.

Underlying so-called Model I are the assumptions that the function of the school is to identify, prescribe, and transmit a specific body of subject matter, and within this mode of organization, the student's chances in the race to cover the prescribed material are determined by individual differences. Underlying Model II is the same assumption about the primary function of the school in transmitting subject matter but differences are recognized regarding individual abilities and accomplishments. The vertical lockstep of graded structure is modified to adjust progress according to differences. Underlying Model III is emphasis on processes of learning and a learner-conception of the school function. The nongraded plan replaces the graded lockstep plan, since emphasis is on the individual.

These kind of definitive statements plus operationalized clarifications in the literature would provide other research producers and consumers with more understandable evidence. From the current literature, one could only guess that among the nongraded schools Model II rather than Model III is being followed since the criterion measure consistently is that of subject-matter knowledge as measured through standardized objective tests.

Basic Problems Plague Research

In addition to the problems in controlling variables adequately and in describing comparative models, educational research suffers from the inability of man to solve basic problems of evaluation and measurement in education. The general theory of instruction which dominates the educational scene in the United States is built upon the premise that the primary task of the teacher is to select and organize information for forwarding to the learner. The emphasis in measurement and evaluation is currently upon transmission of information relevant to the cognitive domain of learning, that is, the objectives which deal with the recall or recognition of knowledge and the development of intellectual abilities and skills. Measurement or evaluation in the effective domain—characterized by objectives which describe change in interest, attitudes, and values and the development of appreciations and adequate adjustment vital to nongraded school objectives—is still in the exploratory stage.

In a system based upon informational theory—information defined as concepts, rules, and facts pertaining to cognition, affective and psychomotor events and objects[2]—the extent to which instruction and learning are effective cannot be determined unless there are adequate means of measuring (a) the teacher's (information provider's) objectives and intent at the time he is conveying any parcel of information, (b) the student's (information receiver's) reserve of relevant information prior to receiving the information conveyed at a particular time by the teacher, and (c) the extent to which the student's reserve of pertinent information is increased following receipt of the information conveyed.

The Empirical Stage Is Underway

Since there is a tendency for researchers to prove what they set out to prove, nongraded students fared well in studies reported by Ingram,[3] Skapski,[4] and Zerby[5] in terms of academic achievement.

Since negative findings are as valuable as positive findings, Carbone[6] made a contribution by finding, in his comparison of 122 graded with 122 nongraded pupils with respect to achievement, that graded pupils scored significantly higher (at the .01 level of significance) than nongraded pupils on the *Iowa Tests of Basic Skills*. Carbone included two added dimensions for comparison and found no significant difference on four out of five factors on the California Test Bureau's *Mental Health Analysis*. However, on the instructional practices of teachers, as measured on the *Semantic Differential Scale*, nongraded children tended to describe their teachers as bright, smooth, sweet, relaxed, big, quiet, interesting, soft, and good. Teachers of graded pupils were described as little, loud, boring, hard, dull, rough, sour, stiff, and bad.

In a study conducted in the Bellevue School District, Bellevue, Washington, and reported as "A Second Report of Bellevue's Continuous Growth Program," the purported nongraded program did not effect significantly greater output when compared with the traditional graded form.[7] (See Chapter Seven for a discussion of the Bellevue program.) Intent of the investigation apparently was to indicate a comparison of the difference in mean scores of children in the continuous growth program, as compared with children in traditional classrooms. The mean scores were based on the *Gates Reading Test* and had to do with reading achievement. Seven t-tests were presented. One of the seven t-tests would have been significant at the five per cent level. The remaining six would not appear to be significant in measuring differences in reading achievement between children in the *Bellevue Continuous Growth Program* and children in traditional classrooms.

Buffie[8] compared the mental health and academic achievement of elementary school pupils attending school under graded and nongraded vertical organizations. Eight public elementary schools, four from each of two midwestern school systems, were selected for the study. Each of four schools was matched with a counterpart, insofar as was possible, on the basis of socioeconomic level, school enrollment, average class size (at third-year level only), and experience and training of its teachers (again, only at the third-year level). Buffie found, among other conclusions, that children attending schools under the rationale of the nongraded primary plan do better academically than do their counterparts in the graded primary (particularly children with higher I.Q.'s) and that the nongraded children are better adjusted than their graded counterparts, particularly in the area of social adjustment.

In their analysis of research design, Goodlad and Anderson[9] questioned whether Carbone's and Buffie's samples of graded schools differed from the sample of nongraded schools relative to vertical organization.

Austin[10] researched elementary school nongraded school practices in 1957 and identified four objectives on this form of organization. These were: (1) to provide for individual differences, (2) to provide for continuous, uninterrupted growth, (3) to release young children from strains and tensions, and (4) to eliminate failures and needless repetition. Austin found that social maturity, reading readiness, chronological age, physical maturity, mental age, emotional maturity, and assessments of intelligence were used as factors for making placements of children in the nongraded program.

Blackstock[11] studied schools which had successfully introduced nongraded primary departments and reported, among other things, that there is no evidence that school size or school-district complexity has a bearing on the introduction of this form of organization. A prerequisite to success, according to this investigator, was the full understanding and complete acceptance of the goals and operational requirements by the teachers.

In a study of 50 pupils each in graded and nongraded schools, Hart[12] concluded that "achievement of pupils in arithmetic has been significantly higher in the nongraded program; nongradedness has given pupils self-confidence and has made their learning experience more interesting." A search of the literature revealed other studies which support Hart's findings. Undoubtedly, more studies will add to the understanding of the values of the graded versus the nongraded school.

Research Emphasis

Those educators who are committed to the experimental method as the only means for verifying or refuting claims for educational improvement have learned to anticipate most experiments to be disappointing and frustrating because of recognized limitations in research, and conceptual and technical skills. They recognize, too, that continuous, multiple experimentation is more typical of science than education and that there will be a dearth of clear-cut outcomes when so-called opposing theories are pitted one against the other.

Kaplan[13] has pointed out that there are many kinds of experiments which can be classified according to function. The methodological experiment generally serves to develop techniques of inquiry. Kaplan isolates the pilot or pre-test study as a type of methodological experiment designed to establish the magnitudes of certain variables prior to a major experiment. The heuristic or exploratory experiments are intended to generate new lines of investigation while the fact-finding type is structured to determine magnitudes of particular objects. Simulated experiments are designed to learn what will happen under conditions of a model which is related to a real life situation.

The crucial experiment is an attempt to establish the best alternative or explanation in terms of empirically given data. The crucial experiment may alter the probability data, but it is unlikely that it will conclusively establish one alternative over another. The need for caution in the interpretation and usage of crucial experimental data is implied when competent observers of an identical specific situation often advocate divergent opinions as to a best treatment. On *a priori* grounds, chances are that both observers relate a part of the truth about the situation and a sound strategy seems to be the avoidance of crucial experiments. Reliance should be upon studying interrelationships among many of the experimental variables.

Inadequate Strategies

Because of inherent difficulties, particularly the complexity and variability of social phenomena, a recurrent question is whether experimentation is possible in the behavioral sciences, including education. The complexity of ascertaining and recording all facts of a case is compounded by the perpetual state of change in facts and in time. However, one should be cognizant of the fact that scientific work is, and should be, performed at various levels of abstraction and is performed within a framework of facts that seem to be significant for a particular problem. Admittedly, generalizations from experimental findings are many times impossible since it is likely that circumstances differ from situation to situation. Thus, care should be taken in putting too much emphasis on individual studies.

The validity of various experimental designs is endangered by a number of factors. Those endangering the internal validity—the degree to which experimental designs actually have validity in an experimental situation—might include biases in selection of comparative respondents, differering maturation of respondents over a period of experimental time, changes in instrumentation, and others. External validity, the ability to generalize from experimental findings, could be endangered by the interaction of the experimental variables and selection biases and the effects of earlier treatments upon later treatments in multiple-treatment situations.

The basic processess in accumulating knowledge are to compare, contrast, or differentiate. These processes may be performed within or between groups. For example, educational research literature abounds with reports of research designs of the case-study type in which a classroom of youngsters is studied only once following experimental treatment. If an experimental treatment variable is coded as "E" and the study or measurement process as "M," the design might be designated as follows (time order is indicated by a left-to-right designation):[14]

$$E \xrightarrow{\hspace{8cm}} M$$

Inadequate modification of this simple design might involve the case-study approach again but with a pre-test and post-test arrangement which could be coded as: $M_1 \, E \, M_2$. This design, too, has glaring weaknesses in that vital internal validity is threatened and destroyed by uncontrollable factors such as the maturation of the subjects and the effect of the pre-test upon the subjects' subsequent performance during the second measurement.

When two or more groups are compared, a recurrent design problem is the achievement of equality of groups prior to experimental treatment. There is a growing lack of faith among educational researchers in the matching of groups and a growing increase in faith in the equation of groups by chance through randomization.

Experimental studies in which equation of pretreatment groups is attempted through randomization (coded as R) and are intended to effect positive internal validity can be designated as follows:

R   M   E   M   (1st group, with treatment variable)
R   M   M   (2nd group, without treatment variable)

This is a pre-test and post-test control group design.
  A post-test only control design would be:

R   M   E   M   (1st group, with treatment variable and
                pre-test—post-test)
R   M   M   (2nd group, without treatment variable)
R   E   M   (3rd group, with treatment variable)
R   M   (4th group, without pre-test and without
                treatment variable)

So-called quasi-experimental designs have been conceived to enable a researcher to study actual school settings. The designs are considered to be quasi-experimental primarily due to the researcher's lack of control over the scheduling and grouping of subjects.

The time-series experiments, whereby the experimental treatment variable is introduced periodically, could be appropriate for those who wish to gradually initiate aspects of new programs during a school year in spite of internal and external validity deficiencies. Variations of this basic time-series quasi-experimental design, which includes a non-equivalent control group, could be effected if the researcher were to gain the cooperation of an institution which would not introduce an experimental treatment variable. The design would be designated as:

M   M   M   M   E   M   M   M   M   (experimental group)
M   M   M   M   M   M   M   M   (nonequivalent control
                                    group)

Action Is Needed

There is no grand scheme for determining the effect upon educational output of a nongraded type of school organization. It seems clear that the conceptualization, formulation, and implementation of such a complex research project needs to be a team effort involving public school personnel and university research specialists and technicians. This research task is too enormous for an individual to perform as a doctoral dissertation project, for example, or for a small team with sophisticated capabilities. Public school people can not and should not be expected alone to carry on depth research. The tasks involved in school operation are all consuming and, too, public school educators generally are not trained for research activities.

Multiple and longitudinal experiments need to be conducted, with particular emphasis initially upon methodological experiments or pilot studies to establish the magnitude of certain variables. Those who insist upon conducting crucial experiments should differentiate comparative models clearly. A suggested model of sub-systems and data to be included is that proposed by David Ryans.[15]

Lack of a research justification should neither stifle the initiative of nongraded advocates nor deter innovation of nongraded programs, assuming that activities are based upon such common-sense assumptions that learning is continuous and that instruction must be commensurate with individual ability and the continuous progress of each student. Within the nation's educational systems' network of research checks and balances, critical inquiry will not be monopolized by any segment of the academic or professional circles. The validity of the nongraded movement will not be determined solely by experiments conducted by those with special research competencies but rather by the test of time and by the test of the nation's collective professional competencies. The local school educator's judgment remains, and likely will remain for some time, the best basis for determining the value or lack of value of the nongraded school.

CHAPTER 6

The Future of Nongraded Schools

by

Stuart E. Dean

Beginning in 1957, Dr. Dean was with the United States Office of Education. Prior to this, he had been professor of education and director of Laboratory Schools at Central Connecticut State College. A native of Massachusetts, he has had public school experience as an elementary teacher, principal, general supervisor, and superintendent of schools. Currently, the author is an advisor in teacher education to the schools in Santo Domingo.

A DISCUSSION and review of a movement as basic as nongraded schools must include a look to the future. Does this structural innovation promise that the elusive goal of utopian school organization is at last at hand? Does the underlying rationale suggest a need for a radical change in schools? Does its rapid spread imply that school administrators should join up—or be left behind? Are elements and qualities of a cult emerging? Will nongradedness survive the test of time—or will it falter and fall back in the manner of earlier efforts for improvement? Are we approaching the Armageddon of school administration?

These questions reflect a growing dilemma now being faced by perplexed school administrators, as well as by confused school patrons across the country. Irrespective of source and regardless of validity, these queries symbolize mounting public and professional concentration on this latest proposal, one which offers the twentieth century realization of educational aspirations in place of previous efforts which have fallen short of full educational attainment.

Cycles in School Organization

As is pointed out in the first two chapters, attempts to improve the internal structure of a school toward the realization of more complete educational worth comprise a lengthy list and encompass many years. For more than a century, a score or more such starts have been made. In general, these have been "plans" of school organization, characteristically identified by a label, e.g., The Pueblo Plan, The Platoon School, The Winnetka Plan. These are discussed in detail in Chapter One. Almost without exception each of these was conceived with lofty visionary purpose and sought an improved education for every child in our schools. The repetitive nature of these cycles bears testimony to a continuing belief that our schools have neither quite fulfilled their responsibilities nor realized their potential.

Contemporary involvement with the nongraded movement, therefore, far from signifying a radical change of view, should more properly be viewed as another step in a continuum. It is, in one sense, a recurring symbol of our endless search for the best in school organization, the structure that will enable us to do for children those things which we so earnestly desire and need. Although historically our present stage does represent an almost predictable cyclical development, the accrued factors of social, economic, ethnic, technological, and international change, so pressing throughout the world today, provide this evolutionary development with a sense of urgency that was not present in earlier stages.

The leading question, therefore, as implied throughout this volume and as faced in this chapter, is simply this: Will nongraded schools provide the means by which our schools will meet the changing needs and demands of the times? To which is added the corollary question: Will nongraded schools survive the current era and make a permanent contribution to school administration?

Nongraded Schools: Which Direction?

To rephrase the basic question: Will the nongraded plan of school organization succeed in living up to the claims advanced by its proponents and advocates? If it is successful in providing an educational framework and an administrative structure through which education more nearly meets the needs of learners and more realistically provides for the extreme range of human variability, it will, by weight of its own evidence and demonstration, provide its own answer to this question. In such case, not only will it survive, but it will go on to make important contributions and develop unsurpassed potential.

Unquestionably this answer is too naïve and overly idealistic. Such promise does remain, at present writing, within its potential scope and reach. But to submit this as the sole prediction would be to fail to come to grips with the realities of school practice. As has been emphasized throughout this volume, from the point of view of underlying conceptual philosophy as well as from the experience of everyday practitioners, the plan contains many pitfalls and inherent dangers. Therefore, an authoritative, incisive answer as to the future of nongraded schools eludes most observers at this early stage of development.

On the other hand, it is possible to suggest one or two patterns drawn from history into which nongraded schools might develop in the foreseeable future. In drafting these tentative predictions, full consideration is given to the many interrelated factors as presented and described in this book.

Nongraded Schools: Failure

At worst, nongraded schools will contribute nothing by way of improvement or solution to certain long-standing problems. The movement could follow the course of many previous attempts having only a temporary impact, characterized by a good deal of popular fanfare and professional clamor, but with no appreciable progress and with the status quo prevailing. As with other equally earnest campaigns, it could die aborning and be so lost in the superficialities of mechanics as to dissipate its conceptual potential, thus resulting in little more than a modern-day manifestation of the very situation it sought to change.

There are several reasons why this could happen. For one thing, some may fail to see clearly and fully what the nongraded school truly is, and what it proposes to do. Its viability rests in the creation of an administrative setting for improved teaching, more effective learning, and a strengthened curriculum. But blind faith in nongrading as an organizational technique (in and of itself) is unwarranted and extravagant claims are unwise with reference to its direct and immediate effects on classroom practice. Desirable changes and improvements may come about through the influence of a nongraded philosophy, but it neither guarantees nor predestines such an outcome.

For school personnel to seize upon this plan as the ultimate educational panacea and to assume that it will lead automatically to long-range gains and benefits is to miss the point completely. Unfortunately, the history of similar movements suggests grave dangers of misuse and abuse of the principles and purposes of nongradedness. To seize upon this as an administrative procedure which by adoption or superimposition will solve our major problems and upgrade the quality of our educational services is to remain insensitive to the more compelling issues at stake.

A leading cause for apprehension lies in the nature of the initial approach to the decision-making process. For those who feel attracted to the possibilities of nongradedness or are reached by its rationale, the primary requisite is a careful study of need. The success of existing programs must be thoroughly evaluated. If findings reflect dissatisfactions, a thoughtful approach to a consideration of nongradedness may begin—*but not until!* Far too many determinations of this nature are being made without sufficient evidence. The fact remains there are enough problems involved in operating a nongraded program without foredooming it to failure through irresponsible decision making. There is reason to believe that the movement is suffering some major setbacks from this problem.

Sober concern is also expressed over the so-called "levels" approach. As used here, "levels" implies the concept of educational expectancies for children, expectancies derived from group standards, or prejudged requirements. This meaning of "levels" should not be confused with the way Hillson used the term in Chapter Two. Hillson thought of "levels" in a continuum of content, not as a means for classifying pupils. A truly nongraded school is something more than one which has merely abolished grade designations. To remove these, on the one hand, while at the same time substituting a different set of "requirements," "reading levels," or "check-points," is inimical to an underlying philosophy of individualized progress. Yet this procedure characterizes many of the early programs. It is common practice in many localities to remove the labels of Grades One, Two, and Three while replacing them with 11 or 9 or 17 "reading levels." Such practice is a mere substitution of a varied form of a continuing graded-school philosophy. Widespread adoption of this type of compromise poses a major threat to fulfillment of the nongraded school. Though many nongraded schools have continued to employ common subject-matter sequences while seeking differentiated programs, even this slight step does represent some progress.

Continued reliance on "levels" reveals either an inability or an unwillingness to accept the prime precept of nongradedness. Actually, it is simple in principle, but complex in application. It stems from the axiom of human variability. The child enters school with a bewildering array and range of complex personal qualities at play within himself. From the day of entry, these forces act and counteract at irregular rates and in different directions. Therefore, it is unrealistic to expect many youngsters to arrive at fixed and concurrent levels of academic accomplishment at chronological check points and within prescribed and contained periods of time. Such has been the prevailing doctrine of the graded school. It has been the results of this situation which have triggered the many attempts over the years to release the restrictions and unrealities of operational regimentation. It is to the central purpose of individualizing instruction, in recognition of the dual dimension of variability of learning rate and of latent capacity, that the rationale of the nongraded school is directed.

In addition, there are several other causes for concern for the future of the nongraded school. For one, the manner in which it is introduced can be a source of trouble. As has been pointed out in Chapters Three and Four, the importance of a thoughtful and a constructive approach cannot be overestimated. The virtues of thorough involvement, the wisdom of deliberate preparation, and the necessity for basic understanding have all been painstakingly spelled out. Herein lies a very real source of potential downfall. These prerequisites are so obvious that it is almost unbelievable that any other approach would be attempted. Yet here, again, a growing body of evidence is at hand which clearly reveals that far too many mistakes are being made in these vital preparations.

Finally, grave possibilities of default or defeat must be recognized in the ways in which a nongraded school is administered once it has been established. As previously suggested, the entire concept involves many complex relationships and operational details. Transcending these administrative essentials is the importance of the instructional program. In addition to previously cited sources of breakdown—resolving the basic decision, adequate involvement and preparation, and dependency upon a "levels" approach—other sources of potential difficulty might include the following: difficulty in coping with social and educational change, trouble in reporting pupil progress to parents, problems of vertical articulation within the school system, inadequate curriculum development and modification, frequent pupil transfer and absence, entrenched grouping policies, concern for record keeping, added burden on teachers in changing classroom practices, and complexities of programs of evaluation. Sufficient evidence is at hand to suggest that each of these in itself may present a serious barrier to ultimate success.

It is a matter of record that the two leading causes for collapse of attempts at nongrading schools have been (1) insufficient and inadequate preparation and involvement stages[1] and (2) the perennial problem of report cards, previously a concern for elementary programs.[2] Thus, the possibility remains ever present that the nongraded school movement may not succeed. If ineptly administered, unhappy results may occur. Those who see this plan merely as educational gadgetry are inviting failure. Unless full acceptance of basic purpose and operating procedures becomes the basic commitment, disaster will ensue. Only when the proposal is viewed in broad perspective of nothing more than a way of organizing a school to implement improvement can hopes of success be entertained. At the present stage of development, as intimated in the foregoing section, there are grounds for concern and cause to observe that in many localities where the program is being tried a number of these essential qualities are not yet in evidence.

Nongraded Schools: Success

On the other hand, a strong vote of confidence for the nongraded school may also be cast. In seeking to remedy some of the weaknesses of the graded school by the recognition of individual differences through programs of individualized instruction and continuous progress, nongrading has a persuasive logic supporting it. In seeking to breathe democratic life into educational programs and procedures, it has a powerful philosophy upholding it. In attempting to translate and interpret the deep currents of social change into school action, it has need and urgency directing it.

This book has sought to point out that the favorable climate for this newest development has been brought about by the shortcomings and deficiencies in the graded-school structure, coupled with sharpened recognition, on the American scene, of the importance of individual differences. The obsolescence of the graded school has been hastened and has been highlighted by the many factors of social change and the rapidity with which the impact of social change has had its effects upon our schools in recent years.

The graded school has tended to be an efficient and effective type of *operational* structure but also one which has failed to deal realistically with the *instructional* program. The administrative minutiae of managing a school have frequently overshadowed the primary purposes of a school—teaching and learning—and have relegated them to secondary importance. Frequently, because of rigidity and inflexibility of administrative requirements, the variable needs and natures of the children in our schools have sometimes been overlooked, if not forgotten. Only as these powerful forces of social change and newer social problems have descended upon us, have we begun to question a kind of school organization which has fallen out of step with the times.

Among the social changes which have given rise to this reexamination of the importance of human differences in a democracy is the growth of metropolitan areas. Big-city implosion has created problems in educating shifting populations and the "culturally deprived."

Another example has been the effect on our economy of automation and changing labor markets and the resultant educational changes in manpower development and retraining. Still another is the growing awareness that many children have been severely handicapped through impoverished and deficient social backgrounds as they attempt to conform and comply with the social setting of a typical school. A number of experimental and pilot programs dealing with preschool children and early entrance age possibilities are attempting to fill these gaps. The reopening of the schools in Prince Edward County, Virginia, saw the adoption of the nongraded plan, on the assumption that this would be the best way to meet the needs of children who had been out of school three or four years.

An experiment is underway in a transitional neighborhood junior high school in Passaic, New Jersey, using nongradedness in an effort to compensate for the background deficiencies of the children. A massive attack on these problems in the public schools of the District of Columbia similarly proposes to mongrade the elementary schools in an effort to compensate for deprivations of these children. Thus, the campaign to solve the problems of youngsters who suffer serious social handicaps in adjusting to school is linked increasingly with the nongraded movement in an effort to provide the most effective educational setting.

As an outgrowth of our recent efforts to provide more stimulation in our educational programs for brighter children, with the goal of creating "masses of intellectuals" in answer to forces which threaten our survival as a nation, has also emerged the corollary realization that we likewise have many children in our schools whose intellectual capacities and futures will always be severely limited. A return to this realization is, in effect, a modernized reminder of the basic law of human distribution. Whereas at one time in school organization it was assumed that programs and practices could and should be beamed toward the mythical "average" student and that "norms" represented goals and ideals, the lesson of the times has brought us to a sobering reexamination of these promises. This introspection has, in turn, led us to a revitalized conviction that our schools encompass all the children of all the people. These children represent a range of human capability—and contribution—which, literally, reflects the laws of probability. As this country has reaffirmed its devotion to principles of democracy, and as change of unbelievable magnitude has impinged on accepted practices and values, many of the ways of doing things which have stood the test of time are increasingly coming under searching scrutiny.

The promise of the future for nongraded schools will lie in their potential ability and demonstrated success in two fundamental activities of day-by-day school operation—reorientation of administrative policies and procedures to clear the path for instructional improvement and also a restoration of provision for individual differences in school programs. The achievement of these ends would demonstrate the worth of the nongraded school. If through nongrading our schools we can truly humanize and individualize programs of education for children, we will have made a giant stride. If this were to come to pass, the movement would have succeeded. No one can know at this time whether this will transpire. However, with a reminder that attempts to nongrade schools stem from two basic needs and seek to strike at the heart of two persistent barriers, then strong belief in and hope for the movement's future will persist.

Nongraded Schools: Indifference

Between overwhelming success, at one end, and dismal failure, at the other, lies still another possibility for the future of the nongraded school. To draw again from the history of earlier movements, vestiges and fallout from many of the plans of yesteryear remain with some schools and still seem to be found scattered throughout the nation. At any given point in time, the organizational patterns of the schools of the country run the gamut of types. Some schools reflect traditional practices to which they have clung for many years. Some other schools are constantly innovating and experimenting and are perpetually in transition. Some schools have retained a departmentalized type of organization for many years. Others are moving toward a team-teaching organization. Many schools remain committed to the "self-contained" classroom. Others are moving toward partial degrees of departmentalization. Some persist in a policy of heterogeneous grouping, whereas others are striving for ability grouping. Schools are experimenting with track plans, with programs of individualized instruction, with continuous progress, and with large- and small-group instruction. Other schools are exploring the potentialities of modern technology and are testing possiblities of automated instruction, self-directed learning, and sophisticated teaching aids and teaching materials. Team learning, as well as team teaching, enters into the picture. Still other types of school organization, such as the Dual Progress Plan, the Joplin Plan, the Platoon School, the Winnetka Plan, and others, are to be found in various localities.

Such a spread and variety of practice leads to the simple realization that there never has been, and never likely will be, a universal adoption of one type of organizational structure. Because of a decentralized national pattern of public education and the autonomy of local school districts, no organizational pattern or instructional program has ever achieved national consensus. While it is true that during different periods of history one style of organizational pattern has dominated, and although the pendulum swings from one prevailing pattern to another, at no time can it be reported that a *single* type is to be found in all our schools. Just about every type and style of school organization is to be found in some schools and in some areas at all times.

Such a future possibility is similarly predictable for the nongraded school. It seems highly realistic to expect that this proposal will catch on more permanently in some schools than in others. It is also to be expected that this proposal will have more lasting effect and degrees of continuity in some schools than in others. Therefore, in attempting to project the future of nongraded schools, one may reasonably assume that they will make at least some contribution to the field and will have some measure of lasting effect. However, the degree and persistence of this impact is something which time alone can tell.

Team Teaching

A relationship of considerable promise and one worthy of continued observation and study will be that between nongraded schools and team teaching. Granted that there is considerable confusion surrounding current indiscriminate use of the concept of team teaching and that, admittedly, there are many varieties and applications of its basic principles, essentially it is a type of staff utilization. It is a way of combining the total teaching resources of a number of teachers within a flexible framework, enabling them together to be responsive to the constantly changing needs and directions of a group of pupils. It employs different types of flexible grouping. It is characterized by fluidity in organizational format enabling it to react promptly to the immediate educational needs of small groups of youngsters—to the needs of individuals. It also provides instruction to larger groups by especially qualified or prepared teachers. It enables teachers to teach to strengths while, at the same time, they are not subject to the disadvantages of departmentalization.

Team teaching plans sometimes include additional features and values such as: professional stimulation and growth opportunities for staff members; use of teacher aides; flexible scheduling and time allocations; enriched use of materials and extensive use of facilities and equipment; and the essential spirit of cooperative planning, constant collaboration, close unity, unrestrained communication, and sincere sharing. Many claims are being made for team teaching; some successes are being achieved. It is not, however, so much a specific form of school organizational structure as it is a method of staff deployment and a way of building administrative and instructional flexibility into the school program.

Nongradedness, on the other hand, is a new and different form of what is now being called "vertical organization." As repeatedly pointed out it *is* a method of organization. It is not a new curriculum nor is it a new kind of teaching procedure. But, as pointed out in Chapter Three, nongradedness stimulates different or new teaching procedures for some teachers, especially at the secondary school level. Its function is to provide a means through which the children move up, through, and out of the school from the time they enter. In serving an administrative need, it provides an operational procedure in sharp contrast to the traditional pattern of the graded school. In effect, these two patterns—graded or nongraded—comprise the range of possibility in vertical organization.

Conversely, there are many patterns and ways of horizontal organization of the school. In essence, the horizontal structure provides the means of relating staff to pupils and for organizing the instructional program. Here there are many separate elements involved such as: organization of subject matter, organization of staff, grouping policies, use of materials, organization of pupil personnel services, reporting pupil progress, and other facets of the instructional program.

Thus, we have a constant juxtaposition of vertical and horizontal elements in shaping the internal structure of a school. Vertically, a dichotomy exists: to grade or to nongrade. Horizontally, a number of dimensions and combinations are available. When the horizontal and the vertical are brought together, as they must be in each school, additional combinations become possible.

It is in this blending of horizontal and vertical that the emerging interrelationship of team teaching and nongradedness is of growing significance. It is a development which will bear careful watching in the future. For both are based upon a perceptive understanding of the existence and importance of individual differences. Both seek to free administrative machinery of rigidity. Both are seeking to provide flexible and individualized instructional programs. Each is aspiring to continuous progress for learners. They are intended to create more permissive and more conducive teaching climates and learning atmospheres. In short, both stem from the same rationale and are aimed at the solution of common problems.

While these two organizational elements—nongradedness in the vertical dimension and team teaching in the horizontal—were independently conceived and separately initiated, their coming together could have been anticipated. However, this is not to suggest that programs of either type initially must encompass elements of both at the outset. Nonetheless, experience points to the likelihood the two will become increasingly interrelated in future developments.

Nongraded Schools: Program

In weighing the future of the nongraded school, another central point of major interest will be the nature of its program and curriculum. Will the nongraded school prove to be one which is basically subject oriented, with prime emphasis upon academic distinction and achievement; or will it lead to comprehensive programs for meeting the range of interests and needs of divergent groups of students? Here, as before, nothing more than speculation should be ventured at this time. Admittedly, the program could develop in either direction or assume middle-of-the-road proportions.

As discussed previously in this chapter, one of the persistent problems in attempting the development of the nongraded type of school structure is the strong weight of tradition with its reliance upon some form of "grading." Although grade labels may be erased, the expectancies and the substance of grading remain. Dependence on "levels" lingers as an essential crutch. The creation of an enlightened structure should scarcely be expected to overcome the customs and usages of more than a century. It would be most unrealistic to expect that any struggle to grasp a new philosophic concept should lead to immediate and sweeping changes. Actually, a continuing dependence upon the levels approach is highly understandable in the light of the training, the values, and the experiences of several generations for whom grading has been the only way.

Consideration of this problem sharpens the realization that the greatest potential of nongradedness may lie in the realm of curriculum development and breakthrough. In time, improvement in school programs may become the greatest outgrowth of the movement. Whether or not this will come to pass, again, only time can tell.

This possibility will remain dependent upon several conditions. First, it will rely on whether the underlying concept is sufficiently understood and assimilated to the extent that efforts will be made to interrelate a nongraded theory of school organization with a nongraded theory of teaching and learning, i.e., of individualized, continuous progress. Second, it will remain dependent upon the capability of staffs to reexamine and to readjust curriculum practices in the light of individual differences. Third, grouping policies must be based upon principles of individual differences and continuous progress in harmony with the nongraded concept. Finally, success also will depend upon adjusting operational procedures to the concept of nongradedness. For example, methods of reporting pupil progress will come in for serious scrutiny and deep soul-searching under such a plan, as many localities have discovered. A few examples of actual attempts to get at this problem are given in the Appendix. Parental understanding and acceptances will be of critical importance. Community attitudes and cultural values will have a continuing influence on the kind of program the school will offer. The role and place of standardized tests will need to be reexamined.

Again, both the weight of tradition and the nature of staff training will be major factors in shaping the program of the nongraded school of the future.

Thus far, it appears that the weight of the graded tradition will continue to exert considerable influence on programs in nongraded schools. Despite the fact that the labels of grading have been removed in many schools, the manifestations of grading continue. Unless major breakthroughs occur in this critical front it appears that for the foreseeable future many efforts at nongrading schools will remain subject-matter oriented rather than pupil oriented toward continuous education.

The Culturally Disadvantaged

At the present time, new support for the nongraded movement is being mustered in behalf of programs for the culturally disadvantaged and the socially deprived. Hand in hand with experimental and pilot programs aimed at attacking the problems of the central-city areas and depressed neighborhoods now comes a belief that the nongraded school suggests an effective approach.

When the deficiencies and needs of these children are analyzed, it becomes apparent that some traditional school practices are far too inflexible to be of much assistance. Programs and procedures geared to middle-class social values serve only to exacerbate the basic problems of these children. An educational structure which remains insensitive to the newer problems caused by these conditions is failing to deal with today's realities. Therefore, schools which cling to the administrative rigidities inherent in the graded school are remaining oblivious to social change.

On the other hand, a realistic understanding of transitional neighborhoods, social deprivations, economic limitations, changing racial patterns, inadequate housing, and many other by-products of a changing society can lead only to the conclusion that the organizational pattern of the school must keep pace. We should stop rationalizing that these youngsters fail because of their inability to conform to the requirements of the school. Instead we should accept the responsibility for modifying school programs and practices to meet their needs.

To the extent that the nongraded school adjusts to human variability of capacity and of learning rate then will it succeed in teaching for these children. Again, based upon the underlying rationale of the nongraded movement, individualized instruction, and genuine continuous progress, a strong case can be made for such an approach to these problems and to these situations. In redirecting the teaching, and in reshaping the educational machinery that makes up a school, inevitably the staff will be brought in closer collaborative effort. In turn, this could lead to more practical solutions of the major and serious problems which are confronting schools caught in big city implosion. It is a matter of record already that some success along these lines has been achieved in a few experimental schools which have undertaken to tackle these problems in this manner. It has similarly been demonstrated that traditional school policies and practices simply do not suffice. In the face of newer problems the nongraded school is worthy of at least a trial, as an attempted solution. In theory, at least, there is reason to believe that it may prove to be successful. Certainly, in the grimness and desperation of some present school situations it will be worth attempting. If it should fail, we will have learned something and yet will be no further behind than if we had tried nothing.

Elementary and Secondary Schools

Another future consideration of the nongraded school will be its impact at various age levels. In its first years of growth, it was applicable almost exclusively at the early years of schooling. In a form frequently known as the "nongraded primary unit," it has experienced steady growth. From a start in Milwaukee in 1942 and in Appleton, Wisconsin, in 1947, the rise of nongradedness at the primary level has been continuous. While precise inventory of the number of school districts which have adopted this plan during the past dozen years is not available, there is reason to believe the number is well into the hundreds. A recent United States Office of Education survey of early elementary education reported that 18 per cent of school districts of the country, enrolling more than three hundred pupils, were using some form of primary unit nongradedness.[3] At present writing, it is not unreasonable to believe that there may be several thousand communities now involved in some form of this development in the primary grades.

Growth of the movement of nongradedness in the intermediate school years has not been so rapid. Within the past year or two, indications are that the movement has spurted somewhat in this segment. However, prior to the current period, growth was slow and only a scattering of schools with students in this bracket reported any efforts at nongrading.

Of more recent history has been the development of nongradedness at the secondary school level. The Melbourne (Florida) High School in 1958 and the Middletown (Rhode Island) High School in 1961 were among the first to initiate such programs. Since that time, the movement has continued to spread, although slowly. While it is not possible to report the exact number of programs currently operating in the country there may be several dozen secondary schools experimenting with nongradedness at the present time. Again, indications are that this number of secondary schools will continue to increase.

Thus, from a start with primary grades the nongraded plan of school organization may one day provide all segments of the educational structure. Because of its avowed aim of continuous progress and its provision for individual differences, there are unmistakable signs that the movement will spread, at all levels. Particularly is this likely in those central-city sections where the social and cultural deprivations are so acute. As schools increasingly search for solutions to these problems, the likelihood is that they may turn more and more toward nongraded schools for assistance.

Research and Evaluation

As with all educational innovations, the need for internal research and evaluation is basic. Any plan for instituting a nongraded school should include built-in procedures for appraising its growth and for assessing its effects. Far too frequently, efforts at educational experimentation have overlooked this vital step. Consequently, it has frequently become impossible to arrive at considered judgments of the worthwhileness of the program. Problems involved in evaluation of educational programs are discussed in Chapter Five, along with the status of the current body of studies on nongradedness.

If nongradedness is to stand up and live up to some of its claims and expectations, inevitably, evidence and documentation will be necessary to support its hypotheses. For a movement with the potential magnitude of nongraded schools, high priority should be given to the development of evaluative procedures. Only as purposes are established, can progress then be determined. Therefore, the inclusion of provisions for evaluation, as an essential planning step, serves a double purpose.

Prospects

What, then, is there to say during these formative years of development, for the future of the nongraded schools? First, admittedly, no one can speak with full assurance. At best, only predictions based upon observation, insight, conviction, and judgment can be ventured. Second, to assay a conclusive answer at this stage calls for an impossible degree of clairvoyance. One basic problem for the school today is its responsibility for preparing a youth of today for an obscure tomorrow—a tomorrow which defies both rational understanding and computer analysis. Third, the continued weight of tradition and enchantment with proven school practices of the past, when viewed in the light of historical cycles, strongly suggest that the status quo may continue to prevail for many years to come. On the other hand, we may very well be on the threshold of the first truly significant breakthrough in school organization in many, many years—a prospect hastened by factors of urgency, need, and heretofore unanticipated changes in the social scene and in the world picture.

Nonetheless, the case for the nongraded school may be strongly espoused. Its appeal lies in its dedication to a differentiated education, consonant with human variability, and its determination to free schools of the shackles of unrealistic administrative roadblocks. Against the posture in which schools find themselves these days in the face of changing social conditions and the newer demands brought upon them by the augmented role of education in today's world, the potentialities inherent in the nongraded type of school organization are minimally promising and maximally assuring.

Let there be no doubt that there are many problems in attempting to develop the nongraded school which would conform with the idealism of the philosophic concept. As seen in Chapters Three and Four of this volume, there are many practical problems and moments of potential defeat. Admittedly, in the current sweep of a popular movement there are many misuses, if not abuses, of principles and of purposes. Granted there may be wide gaps between theory and practice. Unquestionably, there will remain many serious barriers to full and effective realization. No one claims that adoption of the nongraded school will solve the many problems which the schools of today face. At very best, it aspires to provide a more favorable setting and a more conducive climate for ultimate solutions of persistent problems.

On the strength of this rationale and in the light of some success to date with the effort, administrators throughout the country, confronted with problems and perplexities, are encouraged to give serious thought to the possibilities which the nongraded school may hold for their situations. If carefully planned and developed and if sensibly applied and administered, there is reason to believe that the nongraded school will enable us to have the kinds of schools and to provide the type of education of which we are capable and which we must have.

PART II

NONGRADED SCHOOLS IN ACTION

CHAPTER 7

Bellevue, Washington, Moves Toward Nongraded Schools

by

Roy Patrick Wahle

Dr. Wahle is deputy superintendent of schools in Bellevue, Washington. This report was prepared with the assistance of Mrs. Gladys Hutchison, teacher consultant.

T WO TEACHERS, each from a different faculty in the Bellevue Public Schools, were overheard in the hallway one day. Said one, "We've accelerated some and we've retained some. I don't like it either way!" Replied the other, "And neither do I!"

From such basic considerations about children, Bellevue's nongraded program was developed. In accord with custom, the faculty of each school selected one project for faculty study during the school year. One elementary school faculty decided to study the problems of maturation. Another planned a study of the problems of gifted learners. The learning and teaching of reading entered into all of these discussions. That was in 1955. By September of 1957, each faculty, somewhat to their mutual surprise, had asked authority to initiate a nongraded primary program. Both faculties saw implicit in such a program the possibility of better mobilizing the schools' efforts to individualize instruction for the children in our rapidly growing school district.

Bellevue's nongraded program was approached from the study of both the slow and the gifted learners. All this happened amid developing realizations that, although traditional and progressive educators had long talked about the doctrine of individual differences, little had really been accomplished. Something must be done concerning the instructional recognition of the individual differences and needs existing among children.

The teachers felt that parents, especially cognizant of the unique problems of their children, were eager to learn about the techniques which might focus personal attention upon each child. If children felt school to be important, experienced greater success there, and gained an increasingly worthy concept of self, few parents would resist the disappearance of older administrative devices, like primary grades, for the proposed nongraded program, the teachers reasoned. And the teachers were right.

The Bellevue Community and Its Schools

The Bellevue Public Schools serve a suburban community separated from Seattle by fresh-water Lake Washington. The school district has 27 schools. Grades kindergarten through sixth are currently averaging 530 pupils each; junior high schools about 685 pupils; and senior high schools about 1,450 pupils. As of September, 1964, there were three senior high schools, five junior high schools, and nineteen elementary schools.

In 1950 there were 72 teachers. Currently, there are 758 teachers. All have bachelor's degrees, 137 have master's degrees, and three have doctorates. The latter are administrators.

The population of the district is youthful. Teachers range in age from 21 to 75 years of age. However, the median age of teachers is 33. Over one half of the teachers in the Bellevue schools have less than eight years of teaching experience.

Pupils come from middle-class homes. The professional, managerial, and skilled classes predominate. Most of the homes are new and contemporary. There has been substantial tract development of homesites with an emphasis upon individualizing neighborhoods. School construction has attempted to complement this trend. The schools, developed with the assistance of different architects, serve similar yet changing educational specifications.

The average Bellevue pupil scores near the top of the nation in standardized tests measuring ability and achievement. Scores generally follow an upward trend as the pupils progress through the grades.

The Nongraded Program—
Its Description and Operation

The nongraded program was not proposed as an inclusive answer to problems of individualizing instruction. However, Bellevue's educators perceived a greater compatibility between the nongraded structure and continuous pupil progress, longitudinal curriculum development, integrated learning, and present day insights into the individual differences of children than that which was observable in the traditional graded program. It was realized that the first experimental attempts with the nongraded school were only a beginning in the long process of revising the school program from kindergarten through the twelfth grade.

As a first step away from gradedness, the teachers decided to develop a nongraded program within groupings initially defined in accordance with the demonstrated ability to read. Nine levels were established in lieu of what had been grades one, two, and three. The use of levels proved to be a first step away from gradedness. Gradually, it has evolved to the point where the level is considered merely a point in the child's development of reading skills. A child is no longer said to be "in Level V," except with reference to reading.

Because nongradedness is identified with no particular pattern of grouping, pupil assignment to classes has varied. This is as it should be. Any arrangement which allows each child the opportunity to progress at his own rate in an atmosphere of increasing success is to be pursued.

The Bellevue schools have proceeded deliberately and slowly. Over half of the elementary schools are now under the nongraded structure. The secondary schools are now initiating studies to inaugurate a nongraded program.

Most of the elementary schools under the plan have at least three sections of each primary-age group. There is a planned overlap of reading levels in each classroom, rather than a strict adherence to separation according to reading ability. However, no one teacher has responsibilities for a complete range of reading abilities.

Plans vary at the intermediate levels. Some follow the primary plan, others have heterogeneous grouping within a single grade level, and still others follow a random plan with intermediate children of every chronological age and reading ability in the same classroom.

In general, primary children of similar chronological ages are placed together, but this is not always true. In some schools, children are grouped across age levels with either two or three ages included in a single class. The grouping in any case depends upon the local situation, the teachers involved, the children, and the neighborhood. Segregating delayed readers, unless they are in a small group in a special room with specially trained teachers, is not recommended in the Bellevue Schools.

First-year pupils in the nongraded program are assigned after kindergarten teachers rank their pupils in accordance with teacher judgment augmented by standardized tests. Principals and the pupils' teachers together group the children for initial placement within the nongraded program. The same procedure is followed at other levels. Principals assign teachers to classes in accordance with their respective talents and interests.

A child may normally continue in the same room with the same teacher throughout the year. With the planned overlap in reading levels, this is possible and expected. However, a child may be moved at any time when another situation meets his needs. Parents, teachers, and pupils are aware of this possibility. Teachers normally rotate from one type of class to another on an annual basis. Some rotate after two years with a class.

Pupil progress is evaluated through individual or group parent conferences, conferences among teachers and other professional workers, and report cards. In the primary years, special reports are issued concerning the acquirement of reading skills at the various levels.

Enrichment of the program is possible at any level. Emphasis is upon a varied and expanded program rather than upon vertical acceleration. A few pupils are able to complete the primary or the intermediate program earlier than others. A few take a little longer than their contemporaries. Accelerated children study subject areas in greater depth by employing advanced study skills, personal research, small individual or group projects, and by exploring creative skills.

Implications For the Building Program

Most of Bellevue's school buildings have been erected within the past ten years. Considerations for the nongraded program have given special emphasis to flexibility in design and construction. There are few load-bearing walls within the interior of elementary or secondary buildings. Greater use of movable walls and the development of multiple-use space has been incorporated. Adjacent outdoor instructional space is provided.

Secondary school specifications are preoccupied with large and small instructional spaces. The development of learning laboratories for mathematics, reading, and social studies are current concerns.

The Learning Environment

Bellevue has attempted to examine various modern instructional and research devices as they have become available. Each is examined in terms of its potential for contributing to the development of the nongraded program. These have included data processing, programmed learning, language laboratories, and television. A district closed-circuit television facility is contemplated. Each building is now equipped for closed-circuit production. These innovations should go a long way toward making it possible to strengthen the nongraded program.

The district is fortunately situated for field-trip activity whether the objective is study of man-made or natural phenomena. Environmentally, every life zone, whether sea life or the land of perpetual snow, is available for study within a day's driving distance from the schools.

Action research is encouraged as a teacher activity in order to enhance a district-wide attitude of questioning and discovery. To date, four research studies and three papers concerning observations of Bellevue's nongraded program have been published locally by the Board of Education under the title, *Six Years of the Continuous Growth Program in the Bellevue Public Schools: 1957–1963.*

Teachers and Change

The challenge in Bellevue is to reveal the complexity of programming instruction for children. The nongraded program may highlight the instruction of our solutions; however, we propose not to retreat from the problems but to face these issues creatively.

A child's true capacity is known to no human being. Children become more ably competitive through building success upon success, rather than failure upon failure. Teachers earnestly desire to enhance each child's self-concept and self-respect. Each child's strengths and successes should be clearly communicated to him, but with a sense that the top limit of his potential has not necessarily been reached. Each child's weaknesses should be communicated to him, but not with a sense of failure on the part of the child. Orienting new teachers to this philosophy is a continuing task. Each year the schools conduct orientation sessions before school opens and during the year.

Teacher Assignments

Mrs. Verna Wiley, district elementary consultant, was a teacher in Bellevue's Continuous Growth Program (nongraded) from its inception in 1957 until 1963. From her experience Mrs. Wiley made the following observations: (1) Extensive and continuing orientation of teachers to the nongraded program is essential. (2) Teacher growth is enhanced through the opportunity to teach all groupings. (3) Teachers who are not easily comfortable in a flexible, experimental situation should not teach in the nongraded program. (4) A very experienced teacher should be placed with a slow moving group; a creative, experienced teacher with an accelerated group; and a teacher new to the program might best be placed with the average group.

Parents and Change

Parents will accept a nongraded program in its many forms—levels, multi-grades, inter-age, temporary, or other groupings—if they are acquainted with the philosophy and organization of the program. Parents need to know the reasons for the specific placement of their children. They must see accomplishments. And the result they most often await is the eager response of their child to the learning situation. With most parents the response of the child is more important than the actual learning itself.

There is no substitute for personal teacher conferences with parents, both individual and group. Other means of parent orientation which we employ are parent-teacher meetings, talks by teachers with their classroom parents, pamphlets, news stories, and parental observations of classrooms.

The building principal, his staff, and his community must be ready for the adoption of the nongraded program before it is initiated in a school. The structure must never go into a school without the philosophy to make it function properly.

Evaluation of the Program—Is It Working?

When the nongraded program was initiated in Bellevue, the initiators hoped that it would be confined to two elementary schools for a period of five years. Public and internal interest would not permit this luxury and it spread rapidly. A period of evaluation ensued. No conclusive evidence was found in the Bellevue Schools favoring either the nongraded or the graded primary program with reference to academic achievement. It was certain, however, that teachers have learned more about children and how they learn as a result of participation in the program. The teachers in the program are not greatly concerned about mounds of material to learn. They are more concerned about the children and the process of learning. So are the parents. And yet, academic achievement in terms of learning products is no less.

Bellevue's research to date may be questioned in accord with right research models. We know that, within our district, all elementary schools operate on a nongraded basis to some degree whether or not they are labeled nongraded. This realization complicates attempts at studying comparative groups within our district.

The Future

The spirit of nongradedness is implicit in Bellevue's philosophy of education. We acknowledge and accept the unique nature of each child. We are dedicated to establishing an atmosphere in the schools and community which will enable each child to find himself intellectually, vocationally, socially, and spiritually. We do not hold any particular organizational system or pattern of grouping as sacred. Our nongraded elementary program has evolved into several forms; some schools are only beginning programs which are recognizably nongraded. We like this gradual approach.

Our secondary schools are deeply moved by a number of realities. The nature of the changing instructional programs in our elementary schools is becoming provocative to them. New techniques —including team teaching, increased emphasis upon individualized laboratory learning in science and languages, newer instructional media, improved instructional materials centers, and better predictive devices concerning pupil performance—are all causing our secondary schools to reexamine their organizational structures, and, more importantly, their instructional attitudes.

CHAPTER 8

Continuous Progress in Appleton, Wisconsin

by

ROYCE E. KURTZ AND
JAMES N. RETSON

Mr. Kurtz is superintendent of schools in Appleton, Wisconsin, and Mr. Retson is elementary curriculum coordinator. Both have played important roles in the development of the nongraded program in Appleton. Mr. Kurtz has been involved in the program's evaluation in recent years, while Mr. Retson has a long history of association with the program. He was a building principal in Appleton before assuming his present position.

THE STORY of "ungrading" in the Appleton (Wisconsin) Public Schools began in the late 1940's. At that time a group of teachers and administrators met to reaffirm what they and other students of child growth and development have known for a long time about how children grow and learn. They also wanted to determine if the instructional practices and curricular policies of the schools were in keeping with their beliefs about child growth and development.

After considerable discussion and study, the following guidelines were established as basic to program planning:

Every child is an individual and will differ in his rate of physical, intellectual, emotional, and social growth.

Each of these four factors of growth have their own characteristics and do not ordinarily occur in concomitant fashion.

Just as *rate* of growth varies, so the tempo changes; and growth spurts and plateaus appear until maturity is reached.

Growth is continuous from infancy to maturity.

Each individual child will differ in the kind of instruction he needs for maximum learning to occur.

Learning is enhanced when each child is placed in a situation where success is, at least, attainable.

Each child faces certain developmental tasks which he needs to work at when the appropriate maturity level is reached.

Having reaffirmed those principles about growth and learning, the committee of Appleton educators then took a penetrating look at existing instructional practices within the schools. They concluded that their practices were, for the most part, not in concert with their beliefs concerning child development. They decided to make some suggestions regarding changes in curriculum practices which should make the schools more child-centered. The imperatives established for the program included:

Within a grade level, children of varying abilities should be given the opportunity to function at their most appropriate instructional level. This would necessitate extensive ability grouping within the self-contained classroom in all subject areas.

A wide variety and large volume of materials should be provided for teachers to use in order to help meet the needs and varying abilities of the children.

Specific records of individual progress should be kept so that succeeding teachers could provide an uninterrupted flow of instruction for each child. This should help insure continuous skill growth and achievement.

The problem approach should be used in social studies and science. A variety of texts and reference materials should be provided to enhance these studies, as opposed to a similar text for each child in the class.

The term "grade" should no longer be used since the term connotes a single fixed standard of achievement for all children at a given chronological age. The standard of achievement should become an individual matter for each pupil, both in the eyes of the child and the teacher. Thinking and planning in terms of three-year blocks of time should replace existing yearly grade levels and grade expectations. It was suggested that the three-year blocks be called "primary" and "intermediate" to differentiate this new approach from the traditional graded organization in the elementary school.

Reporting to parents should be changed from a fixed, standard evaluation (i.e., letter grades, percentages, or numerical marks) to an individualized progress report and/or a parent-teacher conference to supplement written reporting. (Examples of this type of reporting are given in Appendices A through E.)

The administrator and teachers constructed an educational program to place these suggested ideas into practice. They referred to this new approach to elementary school education as the Continuous Progress Plan. The Appleton Public Schools have been using this plan since that time. It has undergone countless changes and refinements since its inception, however.

The Continuous Progress Plan

Following a kindergarten experience, pupils are assigned to the primary school for a three-year program. Children attend classes of conventional size of the typical self-contained type. Teachers may or may not spend more than one year with their classes. Children are grouped according to maturity. Within each room, pupils again are divided into smaller groups for instruction in the basic academic skills—reading, spelling, and arithmetic. There are as many groups in each subject as are needed to give each pupil an opportunity to work at his level of achievement.

Grouping for instruction can begin almost immediately since complete records are kept on individual skill cards. The skill card is a four-page folder on which each child's scholastic progress is charted. (A copy may be found in Appendix A.) Arithmetic skills to be mastered over a six-year period, including both primary and intermediate skills, are listed in sequential fashion. Entries are made whenever a skill is introduced or later mastered. There are similar sections for both reading and spelling. Flexibility is the keynote and children may be reassigned to different groups, even in different classrooms, whenever appropriate.

In all other subjects, children will work together on a given problem. Each child will use material appropriate to his ability and interest. In such areas, the degree or depth of academic investigation will vary tremendously.

First Steps

As a first step in putting the Continuous Progress Plan into action, the administration and teachers secured the permission of the school board for the Continuous Progress approach in the primary grades (one through three) in one elementary school. Staff beliefs were then translated into action in one school.

The parents whose children were to enter this primary school in September of 1951 were invited to an evening meeting to discuss the plan with the committee of educators. Parents took a very active part in the discussion and gave their unanimous support to the new program. Parental cooperation most often has been characteristic of experimental school endeavors when complete explanation has been made available to the parents in this community.

It was decided to depart from some of the more traditional terms for learning levels that had been used, such as first, second, third, or fourth grade. New terminology to designate primary (first, second, and third year) and intermediate (fourth, fifth, and sixth year) was introduced.

The concept of a new organizational pattern soon became ingrained in the thinking and the planning of the teaching staff. The elementary program was organized into three distinct blocks of time for educational purposes. The kindergarten, the three-year primary, and the three-year intermediate blocks constituted the seven years of elementary school instruction.

Report cards became actual descriptive progress reports since a letter or number grade was no longer used to evaluate the child's progress for the parents. Therefore, reporting took the form of a written progress report and two parent-teacher conferences each year. In these face-to-face meetings of teachers and parents, mutual understanding and helpful information exchange were characteristic.

Comparison of Old and New Programs

Appleton educators foresaw that differences would exist between school with a traditional graded structure and one operating under the Continuous Progress Plan. They made the following comparisons as a means of describing the Appleton program:

Graded Structure	*Continuous Progress*
1. It is assumed that all children of the same chronological age will develop to the same extent in a given period of time.	1. It is assumed that each child has his own pattern and rate of growth and that children of the same age will vary greatly in their ability and rate of growth.
2. A child who does not measure up to certain predetermined standards of what should be accomplished in nine months is called a failure.	2. No child is ever considered a failure. If he does not achieve in proportion to his ability, we study the cause and adjust his program to fit his needs and problems.
3. If a child fails, he is required to repeat the grade in which he did not meet the standards.	3. A child never repeats. He may progress more slowly than others in the group, but individual records of progress make it possible to keep his growth continuous.
4. A decision as to grade placement must be made after each nine months.	4. Decisions as to group placement can be made at any time during the three-year period (for social or emotional adjustment, an additional year if needed, etc.).
5. Grade placements are based too largely upon academic achievement.	5. Group placement is flexible, based upon physical, mental, social, and emotional maturity.
6. Fixed standards of achievement within a set time put pressures upon teachers and children which cause emotional tensions and inhibit learning.	6. Elimination of pressures produces a relaxed learning situation conducive to good mental health.

The Lessons of Experience

During the 1951–1952 school year, the pilot experiment was evaluated, found operationally successful, and expanded to more elementary schools in Appleton for the 1952–1953 school year. By the 1957–1958 school year, the plan was used in all elementary schools in the city at the primary and intermediate levels (first through sixth years).

The Continuous Progress Plan appeared successful from the initial stage and has offered a realistic approach to the education of all children. It made provisions for the individual possible for the teacher to accommodate and made provision for raising or lowering the achievement expectation for each child by the teacher.

Parent surveys indicated that there was support for this plan. When measured by standarized tests, children's achievement was commensurate with their ability. The failure rate was reduced from the year 1952 to 1958 as a result of allowing children to hit their stride before a final placement decision was made at the end of each year. Children were given a longer time to allow for the uneven tempos of their growth to become manifest, and this made a better placement decision possible. The implementation of the Continuous Progress Plan was under constant surveillance. And some changes in procedure were felt necessary throughout each year to help insure the optimum growth of as many youngsters as possible—hopefully, all of them.

There have been both periodic problems and minor setbacks but, in general, the nongraded philosophy has prevailed in Appleton since its acceptance in 1951. The Continuous Progress philosophy is a realistic way of thinking about education. It is a plan which, when implemented properly, will tend to erase grade lines; individualize instruction; provide for differences in intellectual, emotional, social, and physical growth of children; and such growth will be continuous, without many of the roadblocks which accompany the traditional lockstep, graded-school program.

The attainment of the desired goals inherent in this plan is contingent, however, upon the willingness and ability of the classroom teacher to interpret and implement the philosophy in day-today work with children. The key to the success of any curriculum plan or change is the ability of the teacher to translate idealistic principles into daily practice.

Perhaps the single greatest difficulty with the Continuous Progress Plan has been creating and perpetuating a thorough understanding among teachers of the underlying philosophy and its implications for implementation.

Since Continuous Progress suggests a philosophy—a way of thinking about education—and not a rigid organizational structure, it has been difficult to carry on enough in-service and orientation programs to reach all of the teachers. The turnover in teachers alone means that many new people who enter the school system have had little or no background in thinking about the nongraded school. Few teacher education institutions give the nongraded concept detailed attention. Often universities lag behind the public schools in introducing teachers to new professional ideas.

Gradation still exists in the physical organization of the Appleton Schools since children are still grouped according to chronological age. This fact makes it very difficult for those who are traditional in their orientation and training to break away from the concept of group teaching and expectations of fixed standards of group achievement. Teachers who have had years of teaching experience in the more traditional school organization have a tendency to slip back into the thinking and practice of their former experience. In these cases, teachers make little provision for individual differences and keep all of the youngsters on the same educational medicine, regardless of their educational ills. This is also true of beginning teachers who come with training in the old traditional approach to teaching. Thus, the principals have a massive re-educational job each year.

Work, Work, and More Work

Parents have not completely reconciled themselves to the terms *primary* and *intermediate* in place of first, second, third, fourth grades, and so on. The latter are terms the public has always known and finds difficult to avoid using. Unless parents happen to be very close to the school situation and have had the interest and opportunity to study it carefully, they will see little difference in what the new program is doing, compared to the traditional school plan.

These problems tend to make the change to complete implementation of the new plan a long and slow process. In order to perpetuate desirable practice in the schools, certain additional steps must be taken. Appleton must maintain strong leadership in the system. Leaders are required who will evaluate, improve, and interpret the philosophy under which the schools are functioning. The system must maintain a practical program of in-service education for new teachers and veterans. The administrators must keep teachers aware of new methods and materials for teaching which may help do an even better job to individualize instruction. In order to have the public's cooperation, the schools must keep the community informed as much as possible about the school's program, using all the communications media.

Mixed Grouping

Constant evaluation must take place concerning any program in order to meet adequately the needs of all boys and girls. A major change which has already helped to bolster the program within the Continuous Progress structure is the establishment of mixed grouping on a limited basis. The mixed grouping is usually known as multi-class grouping, but Appleton educators have chosen the term *mixed* since children are grouped in classes on a heterogeneous basis.

The mixed groups contain children in a self-contained classroom who would ordinarily have been in a first-, second-, and third-year class. Their chronological age spread is three to four years and their abilities and achievement levels show a wide variance. A few such groups in one elementary school at the primary (grades one, two, and three) and intermediate (grades four, five, and six) levels have been established.

The mixed group is the ultimate manifestation of the Continuous Progress Plan and will provide the necessary organizational structure to enhance the Continuous Progress Plan. After five years of experience with mixed groups in Appleton, it is obvious that the mixed-group organization has promise. Teachers in the mixed-group program are discovering and exploring new methods of instruction which better provide for the individual needs of children. By necessity, they are thinking about education in a realistic way. Group instruction is seldom used. The focus is on individual teaching. New teachers, even though unsure at the prospect of teaching such a group, can observe them and, as a result, better understand the values inherent in the Continuous Progress Plan. Parents, especially those who have children in mixed groups, seem to understand more about the Continuous Progress Plan, even though teaching methods are different from what they knew as pupils. According to a local survey, most of the parents who have children in mixed groups agree that this type of organization does have possibilities for the improvement of instruction.

Ironically, the mixed-group type of organization, while epitomizing the Continuous Progress approach to education, offers an entirely new set of problems. These problems stem from the fact that mixed groups do not allow the use of more traditional teaching methods. Thus, it tends to shake their security and may instill some apprehension for a few teachers. Teachers who thoroughly understand children's characteristics of growth and development and are able to implement the Continuous Progress Plan in their teaching have no difficulty with mixed groups. As a matter of fact, they are able to derive the additional advantage of increased personal satisfaction in working with individuals—a feature inherent in this multigrade type of organization.

Not Yet Finished

Even after fourteen years, the nongraded program in Appleton has neither been fully or finally developed. However, it is noteworthy that a lot has been said, done, and learned about the nongraded school. So much so, that it will continue to be developed and flourish. The goal in Appleton is to make good schools *even better*.

CHAPTER 9

Chicago Schools Design A Continuous Development Program

by

EVELYN F. CARLSON AND
JEROME H. GILBERT

Mrs. Evelyn F. Carlson, associate superintendent of schools in Chicago, Illinois, and Dr. Jerome H. Gilbert, former principal of the Tesla Elementary School, describe one emerging program in Chicago, Illinois. Dr. Gilbert is now the principal of the Columbus School, a demonstration school in Berkeley, California, affiliated with the University of California. Mrs. Carlson has been one of the country's leading figures in curriculum and instructional development.

A s WOULD be expected in any large school system in which principals are encouraged to modify the basic city pattern to fit individual school-community differences, variations in organization and programs have emerged in the Chicago schools as principals and teachers have sought to serve youth as individuals. One of these variations has been the nongraded plan. The first Chicago public school to include all of the basic characteristics now ascribed to the nongraded or Continuous Development Plan was organized in 1955.

Over a half-million children are enrolled in the more than five hundred schools of the Chicago public school system. These schools are organized and administered by a central office staff headed by the general superintendent of schools, a deputy associate superintendent, five associate superintendents, and six assistant superintendents. The school system is divided for administrative purposes into twenty-one districts. The field leadership staff is composed of a district superintendent for each district and a principal for each school.

The Beginnings

In 1959, two significant actions brought the schools closer to inauguration of the Continuous Development Plan of instruction. At that time, in one of the Chicago Public Schools' study reports—reports made on a regular basis on various facets of instruction—the city-wide representative staff committee reviewing the elementary school program and its administration and organization recommended the expansion from kindergarten through the third grade of the existing experimental Continuous Development Plan. Also, they called for the initiation of experimentation with the plan in grades four through six.

In 1959, two teachers were appointed to serve as consultants for each of the academic subject areas, one for each subject for both halves of the city. As these consultants worked in curriculum development in the schools, they encouraged faculties to study the Continuous Development Plan. In particular, the language arts consultants held workshops in which the plan was discussed. They spread the word from district to district of developments in the various schools, suggested ways of initiating the program, and discussed what changes were involved in relation to the individual teacher and pupil. The focus was on ways to modify traditional practices to give improved instruction to students through increased personal attention; the goal was to find ways to individualize instruction.

As a revision of the language arts curriculum guide moved ahead, its use for both the Continuous Development Plan and the graded plan of organization was taken into consideration. A chart which provides an overview of the language arts program from kindergarten through grade eight was developed and distributed to all teachers in the elementary schools early in 1963. The chart was useful to the staff of a school operating on either plan of organization.

Between 1959 and 1963 a number of additional Chicago public schools adopted the Continuous Development Plan. In every instance, those concerned were involved in the planning and the implementing of the program. Teachers and principals in a number of districts, under the leadership of the district superintendents, made the plan the object of intensive study for a period of a year. Following this study, many adopted the program for the kindergarten through third grades for all of the schools in the district. In general, schools now operating on this plan have moved into the program at the first-grade level and then added a grade each year.

School Variations and System Development

As might be expected in a program encouraged by the central office but essentially growing from the grass roots, the plan in each school differed in some ways from that used in neighboring schools. While basically this variance was eminently desirable, it presented some difficulties in a large school system and, in some ways, was less effective and efficient than it could have been with more central office coordination. However, the value of the staff involvement was well worth the disadvantages.

A case in point was the development of a report card. In every instance, early in the use of the Continuous Development Plan in a school, the staff realized that changes in the grading system were essential to the success of the plan and turned attention to constructing a new report card. Desirable as this might be in a school system composed of one or two schools, the use of a number of different report cards has definite disadvantages where the school system is composed of more than 500 schools and where the mobility of pupils from school to school within the school system is high.

As the Continuous Development Plan develops, some general guidelines and common materials are needed by all schools and, unless provided centrally, must be developed by each alone. In these instances, a city-wide representative committee can develop the necessary materials for all, thereby conserving the time and energy of teachers and principals that would be spent on special arrangements for their schools, classrooms, and students. Therefore, in 1963, a city-wide Continuous Development Study Committee was organized to establish guidelines for a city-wide nongraded or multi-graded program. This committee consisted of district superintendents and elementary school principals who had experience in this program. Language arts and mathematics consultants were involved as resource persons for the committee.

The first action of the committee was to discuss and reach agreement upon the definition of nongraded organization and upon the elements and functions of both vertical and horizontal patterns of school organization. Nongrading (or multi-grading) was seen as a vertical school organizational pattern which facilitates moving children upward through the curriculum at their individual rates of progress from their point of school entrance to their point of departure.

Before developing a program, complete agreement upon the assumptions basic to the new structure was attained. Briefly, these assumptions are:

1. The administrative structure of the school should be consistent with the function of the school.
2. The administrative structure should take into account what is known about child development and learning theory.
3. An administrative structure that takes into account individual differences within and among children should facilitate the progress of each child through each skill and subject area independent of what he achieves in another area and independent of the achievement of others.
4. An administrative structure that provides a means of establishing continuity of learning and of accounting for varying rates of maturation and achievement permits each child to advance, in any skill area, when he is ready.
5. Administrative structure that provides a method of accounting for the varying rates of maturation and achievement promotes the mental health and develops the self-concept of the child.
6. An administrative structure should help teachers fulfill the functions of the school as previously stated.

Content of the Program

Having established the bases for the Continuous Development Program (the title of Chicago's nongraded or multi-graded program), the committee addressed itself to the question: What instructional areas could be and what areas should be nongraded? Evidence has shown that a sequence in learning mathematics and reading, listening, and writing skills is possible to develop. The committee first agreed to initiate the city-wide program for continuous development in reading and mathematics. Writing skills are to be included some time after the publication of the revised language arts curriculum guide, to be published by the Chicago Board of Education.

The published guidelines of the committee state that all schools using the Continuous Development Program should conform to the vertical nongraded organizational elements involving pupil retention and continuity and sequence in the skill areas of instruction. The *Guidelines for the Primary Program of Continuous Development,* published by the Chicago Board of Education, suggests that diversity and ingenuity might be reflected in the horizontal structure arrangements involving considerations of grouping, curricular approaches, and the use of teacher talents.

The reading and mathematics programs are divided into a series of sequential levels. Children are to proceed through eight reading levels and nine mathematics levels independently. Each pupil begins the regular spelling program when he is ready to start the second-year reading program. The operation of the Continuous Development Program within a school, as well as the criteria for grouping and suggested means for individualization of instruction, are explicated for the teaching staff. In other fields the *Guidelines* state that science, social studies, the fine arts, physical education, and health instruction should be related to the curriculum guides appropriate for the child's year in school. Social studies and science instruction arc to account for the individual abilities, achievement, and interests of each child.

The *Guidelines for the Primary Program of Continuous Development* were devised to implement far-reaching organizational changes and the concommitant implications for learning and teaching. Stress was put on a variety of instructional materials. Suggestions were made for in-service programs for the various faculties. Since schools adopting the Continuous Development Program must have a common understanding of its purposes and operation, and although Chicago has no designated full-time program coordinator, consultants in the Department of Curriculum Development help provide in-service training and act as resource persons for staffs requesting aid. The *Guidelines for the Primary Program of Continuous Development* not only describes the structure of the Continuous Development Program but also serves as a guide for implementation of the program. There is an extensive bibliography on nongraded and multi-graded schools included in the guide. The Department of Curriculum Development, the district superintendents, and the school are responsible for interpreting the program to the community, parent groups, and the press.

The *Guidelines* were only one of the major outcomes of the city-wide Continuous Development Committee's work. The committee also created the design for the new report cards and suggested procedures for their use. The committee is presently at work on pupil record forms appropriate for the Continuous Development Program, a leaflet for use with teachers in initiating the use of the new report cards, and a handbook for parents with reference to the goals of the program and an interpretation of the new report cards.

At this time, more than 300 elementary schools have adopted the Continuous Development Plan.

Tesla School Breaks the Grade Barrier

Tesla School was one of the schools in Chicago that developed a nongraded or multi-graded type of organization before the Continuous Development Program was formulated as a city-wide program. The school is situated in a disadvantaged neighborhood in the Woodlawn section of the city. A significant number of children in a disadvantaged community lack a sense of identity with the demands and goals of the school, manifest underdeveloped cognitive and linguistic abilities, often come to school ill-fed and ill-cared for, and display emotional problems in the forms of withdrawal, aggressiveness, hostility, and anxiety. Many parents evidence a sense of alienation from the school and its goals and a lack of know-how in helping children succeed in school. Almost any combination of these disadvantages leaves children incapable of succeeding within the curriculum and organization of graded schools.

In 1960, the year Tesla School opened, the entire staff for kindergarten through sixth grade decided to investigate the correlation between the school's graded structure and pupil achievements. Test data showed that entering first graders had at least a two-year spread in their ability to learn to read. By the fourth grade, this spread expanded to three and one-half years. The spread of the mathematics achievement scores was two and one-half years at the first grade and grew to over four years at the sixth grade. Mental-age ranges followed a similar variation from first to sixth grade.

This data was collected by the teacher in charge of school testing and vividly displayed on bar graphs for each of the grade levels for which test data was available: first, third, and sixth grades. Three colored vertical bars were clustered for each child: red for mental-age grade expectancy, yellow for reading achievement, and green for mathematics. Not only the differences among children were evident but also the differences in each pupil's reading and mathematics achievements were readily apparent. Most impressive of all, a horizontal black line, indicating the grade level at the time of testing, clearly showed how few children performed near grade level in even one subject, much less in both. The staff realized that "every child being up to grade in all subjects" as a goal in any given grade was unrealistic, and that, in fact, grade levels were largely arbitrary designations.

As a result of this preliminary study, it was decided that a reading program be initiated to meet the learning needs of each child regardless of grade and to provide continuity as children proceeded from first through sixth grade. The principal encouraged the kindergarten through third-grade (primary) teachers to make an intensive study of the learning process, curriculum alternates, and organizational structure as they relate to school success for each child. Several meetings were held with the teachers each week before school started for the children and during the lunch hour. Books and periodicals were purchased and many were borrowed from the library for faculty use. In addition to reviewing the literature, the staff visited schools that considered themselves to be nongraded in organization and program. Within two or three months, the staff agreed upon guidelines for their new program.

The primary grade staff divided into work groups addressing themselves to: (1) testing and placement of pupils; (2) organizing instructional programs of reading, mathematics, social studies, science, and the fine arts; (3) reporting pupil progress; (4) developing criteria for grouping; and (5) searching for ways to develop and use instructional materials to match pupils' rates of learning in the areas of reading and mathematics. The committees met jointly at the end of each week to evaluate each other's progress. Care was taken to see that the plans reflected the realities of child development and agreed with modern theories of learning and mental health. Staff plans were also reviewed by Dr. Robert H. Anderson of Harvard University and by Dr. Kenneth Rehage and Dr. Hartung of the University of Chicago.

By June, 1961, the Tesla School *Multi-graded Developmental Plan Handbook* for teachers, a cumulative record form for reporting pupil progress, a revised Chicago Public Schools report card, and the *Nikola Tesla School Handbook for Parents* had been prepared. With the growth of the city-wide Continuous Development Program, this parent handbook was adopted by District 14.

The Multi-graded Developmental Plan was inaugurated at Tesla in September, 1961, at which time seven classes of grades one and two were multi-graded. Parents were called in for meetings to discuss the new plan. The third-grade pupils entered the program the following year.

The children of the first three years of school after kindergarten comprise the primary unit of the Multi-graded Developmental Plan, later called the Continuous Development Program. While most children move through the primary unit in three years, a few children may complete the work in two years. And some find it profitable to remain in the primary program for four years because they need additional work before moving on. There are no retentions during the first three years pupils are in the primary unit.

Children progress through the areas of reading and mathematics in blocks of work called levels. They move through these mathematics and reading levels independently. For example, a pupil might be reading in level C and be studying mathematics at level B.

Children may proceed through each of these levels at rates equal to their ability to do so. Each pupil begins the regular spelling program when he is ready to start the second-year reading program. As children progress through the primary unit, they learn the science and social studies appropriate in their years in school.

The criteria for selecting pupils for class placement are listed in the order of their priority: (1) chronological age; (2) estimated reading level as determined by tests and teacher judgment; (3) estimated rate of learning as determined by tests and teacher judgment; (4) social maturity; and (5) physical maturity. Children leaving kindergarten are grouped by chronological age, reading level of reading readiness, and by estimated learning rate. By the second year after kindergarten, social maturity and physical size must also be accounted for in class placement. Second- and third-year children generally are in classes with their counterparts of similar age and maturity. Those who deviate widely in reading and mathematics achievement leave their self-contained classrooms for instruction in these areas.

The organization of classes generally takes the following pattern: immature first-year pupils who need continued kindergarten experiences; first-year pupils making average progress; quite mature first-year pupils who are advancing more rapidly than others; first-year pupils and slower learning and less mature second-year pupils; average second-year pupils; advanced second-year pupils and third-year pupils (or second-year pupils and less mature third-year pupils who are advancing slowly); and third-year pupils making average progress. Organization of classes is flexible so that a child is not locked in any one class.

Each class generally has four reading groups and two mathematics groups. Whenever possible, classes are organized with two reading levels with two groups working at the same level. Each group of pupils proceeds at its own pace through the level, one moving faster than the other. This grouping pattern provides flexibility by making it possible, within a class, to change a child to another group when it becomes desirable to do so. This reduces the number of changes of pupils from one classroom to another.

However, from time to time, it does become necessary to transfer the pupil to another room. Every five weeks the principal asks the teachers to submit the names, ages, years in school, reading texts, and estimated rate of learning of all pupils who should be placed in other rooms. Only the teachers who need to be involved are brought together to determine proper pupil placement. Teachers are encouraged to make changes at any time advantageous for the child. Parents are notified of any room changes.

The children of grades four through six at Tesla Elementary School are now working in the intermediate unit of the Continuous Development Program. Although nongrading had been previously limited to reading, the mathematics program will be included next year. As achievement ranges greatly expand by the fourth grade, it becomes necessary to set specific periods for mathematics and reading instruction. Children may leave their classrooms to be with others who are working at their level.

Parents are encouraged to come to school at any time they wish to discuss their children's progress. Parent conferences are scheduled twice each year. The new report cards will be given to parents four times a year.

No program, of itself, will meet the needs of all children. Therefore, the teachers at Tesla School get together for weekly in-service meetings. They have formed three teams (kindergarten and first-year teachers, second- and third-year teachers, and teachers of grades four through six) to work at common tasks and to share ideas. There are no illusions that what has been accomplished is the final answer. Rather, the Tesla School staff believes that our schools are in the process of becoming ever more effective educational organizations and that the Continuous Development Program is a significant step in this process.

CHAPTER 10

The Southern Humboldt Story
from Northern California

by

CLARA SHUMAKER AND
WARREN LINVILLE

*Mrs. Shumaker is a specialist in elementary school
education. She has been a contributor to the development of the program described in this chapter. Dr.
Linville is superintendent of schools in Miranda, California, where a nongraded school has been organized.*

THE SOUTHERN Humboldt Unified School District encompasses a
large geographic area in the beautiful redwood region of northern
California. There are fourteen individual communities and twelve
schools located in this area. The district is bounded on the west by
the Pacific Ocean and on the east by the wilderness area of Trinity
County. It extends from approximately two hundred miles north of
San Francisco to within sixty miles of Eureka.

Nearly two thousand pupils are enrolled in this unified (K-12)
district. Fewer than 20 per cent of the high school graduates go on
to college, and fewer than 20 per cent remain in their home
communities. This is largely due to the declining lumber industry
and the slow economic development of the area.

The schools are of modern frame construction but are equipped in

154

a minimal manner. This is due to the loss of annual tax revenues because nearly 50,000 acres of the real property is under the control of state or federal agencies.

Background of Nongraded Program

During the period of approximately fifteen months prior to the 1958–1959 school year, the director of elementary curriculum for the district studied ways of improving reading instruction. The achievement test scores in reading indicated that primary youngsters were below the national norms. A careful analysis of materials obtained from schools and school districts was completed by interested staff members. Particularly helpful were materials obtained from the National Education Association; the Torrance Unified School District, Torrance, California; the public schools of Wellsville, Ohio; and the Joplin Plan, Joplin, Missouri. Personal visits were made to Torrance, California, and Trinidad, California, in order to observe the type of program in operation in each of these schools.

Pilot to District-Wide Program

Following an initial planning period, it was decided that an ungraded primary program would be most suitable for the schools of the district. Beginning with the 1958–1959 school year, the Myers Flat School was scheduled for a pilot study. The one-room school contained the primary grades, and since the teacher was particularly interested and willing to cooperate, it was felt that this would be the most desirable starting place. The primary youngsters were grouped in reading according to multiple criteria including teacher recommendations, previous records, and informal reading inventories developed by the curriculum director. Achievement scores in reading and spelling were also used for initial grouping.

During the 1959–1960 school year, the program was enlarged to include two primary rooms in the Miranda Elementary School. The following year, 1961, the program was adopted throughout the district. Teachers were given an orientation program by the curriculum director. The orientation has been continued each year and during the preschool program for the 1964–1965 school year a three-day block of time was devoted to a workshop and orientation on the nongraded program.

The Program

When new children enter the school, placing them in proper reading groups is done through the use of an informal reading inventory. The principal or a designated primary teacher is responsible for the testing and placement. Tests which go along with the reading series —in our program, the Scott-Foresman series—are given to the children after finishing each reading level. If a child passes the test satisfactorily, he begins the next level of reading. If he does not pass the test satisfactorily, he is given another book on the same reading level in another reading series. After this book has been completed, the child is usually ready for the next reading level.

Frequently, there are children who are able to progress faster than the average children. These children are taken out to form another group. In some cases of acceleration, a child becomes a "group" himself. However, as a general rule, primary children do not enjoy working alone. Instead, they want to be a part of a group. Enrichment is provided for these children through supplementary readers and library books. For these more able learners, the material is presented somewhat faster according to the progress of the child. Also, Level VII of the program is an enrichment level for the able children to read after finishing all third-year material and before entering the fourth year in school.

No level or step is omitted or skipped in the program by any student. The skills and material on each level are important to all children. However, the time required for developing these skills depends on the children involved. Hence, the slowing down and acceleration practices are effective and practical procedures.

Since 1958–1959, changes have been made in grouping which have proven more practical and effective. When enrollment allows, the children are divided into groups of high and low abilities for each of the levels with a teacher assigned each group. Within each group, there may be as many as four or five reading levels. This type of organization and grouping permits the children to do more effective work in reading, arithmetic, language arts, and especially in science and social studies. The two latter subjects can be geared to the children's abilities, and enrichment can be bounded by the limits of the children's ability.

The Key

In the evaluation of such a program, it is obvious that success still depends on the teacher. Factors on which the teacher's success depends are:

1. Understanding the child.
2. Careful attention to sequence of material.
3. Proper use of correlated independent work.
4. Supplying sufficient reading material for use when children are ready to use it.

There seems to be great satisfaction in the district among teachers and parents in the improved way in which the slower developing children and the faster developing children are taught and progress. Underlying all nongrading, for both primary and intermediate grades, are the purposes of the nongraded program. These include:

1. To provide continuous growth of children in all areas.
2. To provide for individual differences.
3. To relate sequential development of subject matter more realistically to child-growth patterns.

Thinking and planning to ungrade grades four, five, and six started with discussions by the board of trustees and the staff. A pilot program was instituted in the 1965–1966 school year. The ultimate goal of the board of trustees is the operation of a total district nongraded program (K-12) by 1968–1969.

Sequence of Reading Levels

The reading-level sequence is the cornerstone of the nongraded plan in the elementary schools. As the program extends to other content areas and grade levels, similar sequences of content will need to be established. Below is the reading sequence for the elementary schools.

			Sept. 1964– June 1968	Sept. 1964– June 1967	Sept. 1964– June 1966
One school year	LEVEL I	*Reading Readiness*			
	LEVEL II	*Pre-Primer* (4 levels)			
	LEVEL III	*Primer* (1 level)			
	LEVEL IV	*First Reader* (2 levels)	Slow Developing Child ↓	Average Developing Child ↓	Very Rapid Developing Child
One school year	LEVEL V	*Second Reader* (2 levels)			
	LEVEL VI	*Third Reader* (4 levels)			
One school year	LEVEL VII	Enrichment units for fast pupils who completed Level VI in less than three years			↓
	ENTRANCE TO FOURTH GRADE				

FIGURE ONE

CHAPTER 11

Continuous Plan of Pupil Progress in Cabool, Missouri

by

NEAL NEFF AND
D. A. FERGUSON

Long before many educators were knowledgeable about the nongraded concept, Neal Neff and D. A. Ferguson were operating such a program in Cabool, Missouri. Mr. Neff is the principal and Mr. Ferguson is the superintendent in a small but progressive school system.

CABOOL, MISSOURI, is a small town in the south central part of the state. Its population prior to 1948 was about 1,500 people. The only industry of note at that time was a large creamery. The school system consisted of a secondary school of about 300 students, and an elementary school of about 350 students. The latter was supervised by a principal. There was a very active Parent-Teacher Association which was genuinely interested in the pupils and the schools.

In 1948, the superintendent and the teachers began an evaluation of the school program and its traditional organization. Convinced of the need for the school's adaptation to the peculiar needs of the community in which it was situated, a joint committee of parents and teachers began a study on the method of evaluating the work of the individual student in the school. Keeping constantly in mind that the school existed for the individual child and should be geared to his needs, a report card was drawn up which was not competitive but diagnostic in nature. Meetings were held with the local clubs and the Parent-Teacher Association to discuss the treatment of the child as an individual and how he learns. Trial reporting sheets were drawn up and used for a year. They were then revised and printed in permanent form to be used for a three-year period.

The faculty and administrators decided to move slowly in changing the school organization, but they were committed to make important changes. From the beginning, the group was in accord that ungrading the school was desirable. Teachers were convinced that a change was needed badly and that, as the adjustments moved forward, each move must be evaluated carefully as to its pedagogical soundness. The motive was not to create something new *per se*, but to decide what was best for boys and girls and then effect it. The faculty was qualified to do this. All of the staff were degree people who had specialized in primary, intermediate, and upper-grade professional work.

As the town grew, the school was able to hire a guidance person, a librarian, and a reading specialist, all of whom were essential to a staff engaged in change in these areas. Also, the school was able to secure capable teachers for teaching the mentally retarded. Teachers were chosen with a philosophy cognizant of the values inherent in individualized instruction. As the school grew, over a period of ten years, it reached an enrollment of 700 students and a corps of 28 teachers. The faculty, in a large measure, was handpicked for working in a school with a sensitivity for the unique needs of children. A single salary schedule and agreeable working conditions induced long tenure and produced a stability seldom attained in communities of similar size.

Students As Individuals

The native intelligence of the children indicated normal distribution and compared favorably with the intelligence of children in many other American communities. The fact that the school was located in the south central part of the state meant that many of the families were substandard economically and culturally. Some children had little access to magazines, newspapers, or books. Other children had little background experience because they had traveled only short distances from their homes.

For the above reasons, it seemed advisable to devise an administrative framework which would encourage a pace of learning conducive to more individual attention from the teacher. If teacher and pupil were released from grade barriers, more time could be spent on perfecting reading skills all through the elementary years, more favorable study habits could be produced, and the teaching could be done in large areas of interest which would encourage habits of independent study. More and more, the teacher could set up problems with the students concerning "why" rather than "how." Inquiry supplanted memorization of large bulks of facts.

With the elimination of grade lines, the school's administrative machinery enabled a child to go as far in one year as he could and then begin there in August when he came back after the vacation months. The education of a child through school came to be thought of as continuous during his progress through the elementary years, and the program which resulted was referred to as the Continuous Plan of Pupil Progress. This concept was not analogous to the segmentation produced by grades. So the school came to think of children as first- , second- , or third-year students, not as first- , second- , or third-grade pupils.

The administration and faculty of the school came to the decision very early that the framework of the school should be adaptive so that it could accommodate itself to the individuality of the children as their needs varied. The school was to exist for the child, not the child for the school. If this were true, such a school would have to be unique in the truest sense of the word because there were no other children just like the ones at hand, nor any other community like the one in which they lived. Likewise, there was no other faculty with the same strengths and weaknesses.

Flexibility, Testing, and Grouping

With free communication between the teaching staff and the administrative staff, the latter became permissive and tried not to be dictatorial. The teacher was considered as the specialist in his room. Flexibility was the order of the day. A child was to be assigned to a teacher, not promoted from grade to grade. He was to be allowed to move from group to group within a classroom or from room to room within the building during the school year.

A regular testing program was put into operation under the direction of a guidance teacher. New students were tested immediately upon enrollment in order to ascertain placement for instruction. Achievement tests were given each spring to obtain the statistical data to be used in assigning students to teachers the following term. Intelligence tests were administered to the third- , fifth- , and seventh-year pupils each year. As an aid in grouping for instruction, the students were listed from the highest to the lowest achiever in reading. On this sheet were also listed the chronological ages, mental ages, and intelligence quotients. This information, along with the teachers' opinions concerning a child's emotional and mental maturation, furnished the data for pupil assignment at the close of the school or the beginning of the fall term. This procedure was referred to as selective grouping.

In the assignment of students to teachers, it was attempted to keep the teacher load down to 30, but ultimately, the numbers sometimes reached 35 for each teacher, due to the activity of the local factories and the annexation of local rural schools to the Cabool Town District. At times it seemed wise to attempt homogeneous grouping. Most of the time the children were assigned to a teacher in such a range or distribution as to ease the numbers of groups to be found within a classroom.

Various methods of grouping were utilized, dependent upon the teacher available and the student problems involved. Since there were two teachers for each age group, it was possible at times to assign the top one-fourth and the lower one-fourth to one teacher on the basis of reading achievement. The other teacher received the middle half in such an arrangement. At other times, it seemed advisable to divide the student lists into halves, one teacher taking the advanced half and the other teacher taking the lower half. Part of the time the students' names were arranged in order of achievement scores in reading, from high to low, and divided by quintiles, each teacher taking alternate groups.

When the Continuous Plan of Pupil Progress was being organized, it was thought possible to allow a child to accelerate through the elementary years. Since a school must operate within the bounds of limitations placed upon it by the community, it seldom was feasible to practice acceleration to any great extent. Such practice was controversial, as it is in many communities. There are always so many existing indeterminates to weigh and consider. However, enrichment of the program of studies appears to be an acceptable and helpful practice.

During a fourteen-year period the Cabool Elementary School staff was required to exercise much creativeness. With the creation of a flexible administrative framework to accommodate a child-centered school, inventiveness was taxed at all times to produce records and forms to fit the uniqueness of the situation. No printers of official forms produced any of the official records necessary to mark a child's progress as it fluctuated throughout his eight years. New cumulative folders were designed by the staff and accompanied the child until they were surrendered to the guidance department of the secondary school. Even the reporting cards were customized, one for the primary department, one for the intermediate department, and still another for the upper department. (An example of the kind of report parents receive is given in Appendix B.)

Differentiated teaching within the regular classrooms cared for the slow, average, and fast learners. A constant search was made to locate materials to instruct the above-average pupils on their various levels of achievement. A central library, or curriculum center, was constantly taxed. A county bookmobile proved to be of great value in supplementing the schools' resources.

Public Education About the School

Keeping the community informed about changes in the school is an important task of the administration, whether in a graded school or a nongraded school. The lines of communication must be kept open through the various media which the particular community may offer. In Cabool, parent education classes were held each fall, for one night each week, and lasted for a period of five to seven weeks, depending upon the interest manifested.

The topics each year were varied and included pupil evaluation, the significance of the intelligence quotient, testing, how children learn, and the teaching of reading, language arts, mathematics, and science. Other subjects which seemed pertinent to needs of the current year were discussed. The Citizens' Advisory Commission, a group of local citizens of which the superintendent of schools was ex-officio member, met six times a year. This commission served in an advisory capacity to the superintendent and the board of education and proved to be valuable in the dissemination of information throughout a district that covered many square miles by 1963. The P.T.A. functioned diligently and faithfully over the years. Of course, the local newspaper and radio stations were readily available and frequently used to tell the school story.

Evaluation from Cabool

The administrator of a nongraded school will not necessarily claim that more academic achievement is attributable to the nongraded structure, but there are some things which he may credit to his new organization. Experience at Cabool suggests the following:

1. The flexible organization of the school enables it to foster the individual interests and needs of the child.
2. Effective grouping of children and a differentiated curriculum provide for more effective teaching of the bright, the normal, and the dull-normal child.
3. It is true that teachers encounter fewer learning plateaus among students in a nongraded school, because they do not become burned out by the presentation of indigestible masses of academic effluvia which some individual has imposed from above.
4. Truancy and classroom discipline problems are reduced. This is true because the teaching is adjusted to the abilities of the children and they are not taught at a frustration level.

It is difficult to predict the future of the nongraded school in Cabool. Those who began with the first programs of twelve or fourteen years ago would never have believed that the movement would ever reach the proportions it has assumed today across the country with approximately one out of four elementary schools in the nation employing some type of nongradedness. No doubt the trend will continue toward more individualization of instruction, and administrative services will be created to care for such a program.

The writers envision a combination of team teaching and non-gradedness. The large assembly of children under direction of the head teacher will conduct the large background areas of study. The smaller breakdowns of children into groups for study can be made on the basis of ability. The two types of organization are most compatible and make possible a more truly continuous educational program for each child.

CHAPTER 12

The Monteith Plan

by

MARSHALL C. JAMESON

Formerly principal of the Monteith School, where he was instrumental in the development of an exciting elementary school program, Dr. Marshall Jameson was coordinator of elementary schools for the Waterford Township Schools in Pontiac, Michigan, until his recent retirement.

U SUALLY A story has a beginning, a long middle which is the heart of the story, and a brief closing, and spends most of its time leading up to the climax, the "how-it-all-came-out" part. As far as the Monteith story goes, it must be said at the outset that only the beginning of this story has been completed. How the story comes out, what the endeavors of the staff of this Grosse Pointe, Michigan, elementary school will eventually result in, may not be known for some time. If a strong and successful beginning can be prophetic, then the result will be something of merit for public education.

Up to the time of this writing, the author knows of no truly, completely nongraded elementary school in this country. There may be such schools, however. But the important thing is that many, many schools are aggressively moving toward such a school— moving toward putting into operation in the school program the concept of continuous growth and moving away from the deadening

166

structure of grades. Thus, after more than a century, we are actually beginning to put into practice some of what we have long known about child growth and development—known but ignored. Thousands of elementary school children are now having some educational millstones removed from around their necks and are being allowed to learn as rapidly as they can without being hurried and as slowly as they need to without being shamed, mistreated, or failed.

Organizing a nongraded school has been the aim of the Monteith staff and parents since September of 1957. While a long way from their goal—a goal which is revised as more is ascertained about how children learn and about their limitlessness of learning—real progress has been made. The Monteith School is not a completely nongraded school. This is so with most schools which so claim or which, like ours, have been named a nongraded school by others.

Developing the Plan

Having spent seven years on the development of a nongraded plan, one might wonder if it will ever be completed. Perhaps the central part of this story and its ending will come rather quickly, and it will have created a new method in story writing.

The writer returned to the Monteith School in the fall of 1956 from a sabbatical during which he met and worked with Dr. Robert H. Anderson of Harvard University, a pioneer in thinking about the nongraded school. The author became the leader in first organizing a staff study of the possibilities of The Primary Plan, a three-year nongraded block, and then directing, as principal of the building, the initiation and progress of what was called The Monteith Plan, after first getting permission from the superintendent of schools and the board of education.

A very exciting and interesting story could be written about those beginning years. How much all of us learned! We were our own university with each other as instructors. If nothing at all to change the school's program had come out of our seven years of working together in this endeavor, what we learned would have been well worth the hard work, the long hours, and the serious study we showered on the project. However, a lot did happen to the school's program.

The Setting of the Story

Grosse Pointe is a prosperous Detroit suburban community. Many wealthy families reside here, most gravitating towards beautiful Lake St. Clair. Residing in Grosse Pointe, also, are many business and professional people along with thousands of average, middle-class wage earners. Many parents are college graduates, most homes have two car garages, the children go to summer camp, and the parents usually come to Parent-Teacher Association meetings. The community strongly supports its schools and the parents work closely with the schools and their faculties. They want good educational facilities for their children and are willing to pay for such facilities. In such a setting, progress toward nongrading an elementary school began.

Monteith was for many years the largest of ten elementary schools in the school system, its largest enrollment reaching 900. Currently, there are about 750 children enrolled, kindergarten through grade six. "Grade six?" the reader may ask, "in a *nongraded* school?" Yes, we call our groupings grades and probably will for another twenty-five years, so ingrained is the idea in our system. However, it is not the label that is important, but what the thing really is. The organization for the past fifteen years has been the so-called "self-contained" classroom in which one teacher teaches everything—or almost everything. Someone else teaches vocal music, instrumental music, physical education, speech, and French. But the homeroom teacher does most of the teaching.

The 30 teachers include 12 male teachers. The staff boasts both veteran and young teachers. Both kinds, together with a variety of in-betweens, give a staff a wholesome balance. And let it be said here that the old wives' tale about older teachers resenting change is only that, a tale. Not so here, nor, I suspect, in most schools. All the teachers are college graduates and over 60 per cent have their master's degrees. It is a dissatisfied staff, dissatisfied with many aspects of elementary education which can be improved, evaluated, questioned, and—most important—changed.

With an average I.Q. of 115, Monteith pupils, like most Grosse Pointe pupils, score well above the average on all achievement tests.

While the author has yet to meet a teacher, principal, or superintendent from a school which does *not* also score above the national
medium, Grosse Pointe children do achieve well. Youngsters come
to school with enriched backgrounds, interest in learning, and a
good attitude toward education, though often pressured mightily to
succeed. But like schools anywhere, these children suffer the same
handicaps from a graded structure as children anywhere.

Children in this school are grouped according to their place along
a continuum based on reading proficiency. They are not grouped by
intelligence test results, for we claim not to group on the basis of
ability, believing that we really are incapable as teachers of knowing
what ability is, let alone being able to measure how much of it a
child may or may not have at a given point.

Kindergarten children are grouped late in May for the fall classes.
We use a standardized reading readiness test plus teacher judgment.
Children who are ready to read and who show no evidence of a
need for further readiness or delaying activities are grouped together. Those children who actually need, for a while in the fall, a
continuation of their kindergarten program are grouped together. So
it is with all classes throughout the sixth grade. Each June, after
administering an achievement test and employing teacher judgment,
the teachers do the regrouping together and classes are set for the
next year. In a larger school, where there are three or four groups,
this kind of grouping can be more precise. However, even in a
school with only one section of each grade, such grouping is
advantageous, we believe.

In our grouping plan, in a fifth grade of four groups, for example,
the most advanced group would contain only children who read on
an advanced level, all above grade six. Their reading instruction
would be on a level far above grade five, and they would have
poked through and ignored the graded ceiling of grade five, with
learning having no set limit. Conversely, in the least advanced
group, being no more fifth graders than they are moon children, the
students would receive instruction at the level where they are and
need to be, and this will be anywhere from grade two to grade four.
There are those who will argue in opposition to this manner of
grouping, but we will not argue back. For us, this method has had
meaning and we have seen its value. This kind of grouping is merely
the way in which the Monteith teachers felt they could best put into

practice some of the promises of the nongraded structure. Another school in its nongrading efforts may group by intelligence, another by achievement, and yet another by age or sex. And some may not group at all. We recognize that there is no single way and no required way of grouping in order to enjoy some of the values of the nongraded philosophy.

In this, our plan, all children remain in the elementary school seven years including kindergarten. Some children may need to stay another year or two and are entitled to stay longer, as long as there is education there for them and they are learning. A Nebraska farm father always warned his sons when they came in the from the field never to force the horses away from the water tank as long as they were thirsty and there was still water in the tank. Can't we do as well for children in the elementary school? We do not believe in hurrying children through the elementary school. Thus, no child is ever double promoted. If he learns well and rapidly, we place more learning before him; some children may be working in advanced areas in all subjects. Here is where the elementary and junior high schools need to harmonize their programs, philosophies, promotion procedures, and so on.

A major flaw in the Monteith Plan was this: We were unable, as we developed our plan, to make the curriculum changes which go hand in hand with a nongraded philosophy. Changes were made but mostly by the individual teachers with administrative support and encouragement. However, a single building by itself finds it most difficult to make important changes in curriculum design. It is still a part of a greater whole. If such a curriculum change is not an all-school cooperative venture, then a single school is handicapped and often criticized.

Three Questions

At this juncture, it might be well to answer three questions which are usually asked by those interested in learning of a school's experience in the nongraded area.

1. *What different physical facilities are needed?* There is no more need for any particular kind of equipment, material, or facilities

for a nongraded school than for any other kind of school. Neither is there a need for any special kind of teacher or for more teachers than any other building has.

2. *How does one mobilize a faculty for change?* The question was partially answered earlier. As the dissatisfaction of teachers was discussed further, upon returning from the sabbatical, the writer talked about the program with the whole staff and invited anyone who wished to become a member of a Monteith study group. Nothing was forced upon anyone, for even the parents had a choice of having, or not having, children in the Primary Plan.

3. *How are parents oriented to this change?* We began our program by going to the parents of the kindergarten classes. We decided it would be best to develop kindergarten children as our first group of nongraded children. So, after Christmas of that study-year, after the staff had agreed to give the idea a trial, the principal and teachers began a series of meetings with the parents from individual kindergarten classes. At the time, we had six kindergarten classes. During the winter the plan was discussed with them in small groups and several times at all-parent meetings. At such meetings we had experts address us. About March first, at a general meeting, almost in evangelistic fashion, the question was given to the parents, "Do you want your child to be a part of a nongraded group in the fall?" Fifty per cent of the parents said "yes" during the next week. Thus, in the fall of 1957, we began the plan with two groups of first graders in the Primary Plan and two groups of regularly graded first graders. Parents whose children landed in the regular grade had not voted against the plan. They just had not learned what it was all about. Once they learned of the plan, they rushed to get their names on a waiting list. (Topics to be considered in conferences with parents are given in Appendices C, D, and E.)

Monteith First—Who Was To Be Next?

Grosse Pointe has ten elementary schools. A natural comment might be: "Since you say the nongraded scheme is working so well at Monteith, we presume all the other schools have since gone to the nongraded organization." But no others have. Undoubtedly, other schools are getting at some of the problems we believe we get at better with our kind of grouping. But no other Grosse Pointe school has moved into it as we have. This might suggest that the Monteith Plan holds so little promise that no other school can justifiably go into it. We do not believe this is so. Since each building in this system is somewhat independent, each principal and his staff are free to develop a program, experiment, test, and organize differently. Schools other than Monteith have found other interests and have developed them. No school can claim all advances, embrace all ideas, move on all fronts, or attempt all trends. Therefore, we feel it is very natural that only Monteith has chosen to work so pointedly in this one direction. After all, our story has not reached its conclusion. If that conclusion is an impressive one, then perhaps other schools will move in this direction.

Evaluation

The question, "How have you evaluated the Monteith Plan?" is often asked. We have not evaluated the plan in any formal manner, that is, using tests, comparing children in the plan with others not in the plan, and so on. Often, school people emulate the lightning bug, lighting up always where they have been and losing sight of where they want to go. We try something and hardly has it taken in a few breaths of life before we begin to evaluate it. Some things do not have to be evaluated. They are obviously good without ever having had a formal, exhaustive, publishable study of evaluation.

Since in our nongrading efforts we organized slowly, moving one grade at a time into the plan, we have only recently gone through all the grades with the plan as we have so far conceived it. When the nongraded structure has finally been created, only then are we ready to begin to think about evaluation. But only after another five years from the time when nongrading is complete should the school be ready to evaluate the program.

If we seem defensive or evasive regarding proof about what has happened at Monteith under the plan to this stage, we do not wish to be. We do believe there have been some positive results, many of which defy measurement. For how can we measure:

a child's release from the fears and damning effects of failure?

the emotional betterment of children as they live in a milieu of success instead of failure?

the satisfactions which occur to teachers who no longer have to lead children into academic trouble caused by the timing and prepackaging of education?

the positive attitudes of children toward learning which we sincerely believe our efforts have brought about?

the enhancement of the learning climate of a school in which it is claimed that every child is reading successfully, at the level where he is reading? And why should children not be kept in a successful reading level, regardless of the grade they may be in?

Under the Monteith Evolving Plan, we feel we have:

released children to learn at their own rate and pace;

taken the limits off of learning;

eliminated those terrible deterrents to learning, the report cards;

recognized and put into practice some principles known from research such as recognizing that failure is harmful to children, retention seldom accomplishes its purpose, and children learn in spurts, which should be accommodated in terms of each child;

stopped setting the same goals and standards for all children.

How can we ever measure these? We do not know how. We cannot even prove by any tests we know of that we love children. But we do. Our concern for their total welfare cannot be measured by any standard test or researched in any way. But we do have a concern.

CHAPTER 13

The Peter Boscow Primary School, Hillsboro, Oregon

by

RICHARD H. HART AND
ALTON O. SMEDSTAD

Mr. Hart is the principal of the Peter Boscow School and has served as a visiting instructor at the Pacific University. Mr. Smedstad is the superintendent of schools in Hillsboro, Oregon.

IN THE ATTEMPT to provide an authentic developmental program of instruction for every child, the Hillsboro elementary schools have progressed through various phases of improvement. Concern over the inadequacy or lack of a genuine developmental program in reading instruction, some fourteen years ago, launched Hillsboro on a continuous trial-and-error plan of improvement that has resulted in the nongraded organization.

Fourteen years ago, an investigation revealed the practice, prevalent among most intermediate and upper-grade teachers, of assigning all pupils, without regard to achievement or ability, to grade-level texts for reading instruction. Also, the investigation revealed the resultant frustrations of the retarded readers and the sheer boredom of the abler ones. Unfortunately, this is not an unusual situation. Even in this enlightened day, grouping to provide for the wide range of pupil abilities is not a consistent practice among intermediate teachers.

Change through administrative edict was required as an immediate attempt to improve the situation in Hillsboro. Each teacher at
each grade level was now expected to have at least three groups for
reading instruction. As a device for initial grouping within each
classroom, teachers were introduced to the mysteries of the informal
reading inventory. Time and in-service training made it possible for
the teachers eventually to become relatively effective in utilizing
these procedures.

This step toward a more adequate program of reading instruction
inspired the provision of adequate reading materials, not only at
grade level, but above and below grade level. It was now possible
for a teacher to instruct all pupils in a basal reading series, regardless of the level of instruction. The reading materials were not only
appropriate to the needs of a given group but were also new to the
group. No pupil was asked to study a text that he had read on any
previous occasion.

Obstinate Problems

Experience helped the teachers recognize the inadequacy of the
three-group procedure in meeting the needs of all pupils. It was
apparent that in most cases teachers would need more than three
groups. But it was also obvious that it is difficult to prepare for and
manage more than three groups. This led to the practice of teachers
on a grade level shifting pupils during the first few weeks of school
in order to form more realistic groups within each classroom.

From this point, the staff evolved what is designated as the One-
to-Five Plan of grouping children for classrooms based on reading
achievement. In regard to reading achievement, pupils were evaluated as (1) most able, (2) above average, (3) average, (4) below
average, or (5) slow learners. At that time there were three teachers
at each grade level in the Peter Boscow School. In the attempt to
reduce the range of reading achievement in each classroom, teacher
A was assigned the 1's and the 3's; teacher B was assigned the 2's
and the 4's; and teacher C was assigned the 3's and the 5's.

The principal and teachers apparently were transfixed on the
horns of a pedagogical dilemma. They felt the need for further
grouping to meet more adequately the needs of all pupils. Yet they

were cognizant of the fact that as a teacher increases the number of instructional groups, he decreases in his effectiveness as a teacher as the result of increased preparations and the reduced amount of teaching time available to each group. How could this dilemma be resolved? Is it possible to organize an elementary school so that every pupil, without exception, is working at his own best rate and at his own level?

A Nongraded Language Arts Program

The search for an improved method of organizing an elementary school logically led to a more careful analysis of the data available concerning pupil achievement. The results of the reading battery of the California Achievement Test as administered to all intermediate-grade pupils revealed a wide range of achievement. An informal reading inventory administered to all intermediate pupils confirmed these results. Although the performance of a relatively small group of pupils was right at grade level, many pupils were able to perform at a level significantly greater or at a level significantly lower than the grade-level expectation. This phenomenon, with minor variations, was common to all grade levels at Peter Boscow School.

These data disclosed the need for seven or eight levels of reading instruction in every classroom. For example, in a typical fifth-grade classroom, the range of reading achievement varied from an easy third-grade level to seventh-grade level and beyond. However, in the combined intermediate-grade classroom there was indicated a need for thirteen levels of reading instruction. It was obvious that there was a duplication of teaching effort, teachers teaching similar groups at the same level of instruction. This fact called for a new approach to language arts instruction.

It was proposed that for the purpose of language arts instruction (reading, English, spelling, and use of library), the intermediate grades be ungraded. This would provide a needed flexibility in grouping pupils and in the organization of the curriculum. Pupils would be grouped according to their language arts achievement without regard for the usual grade placement. It would now be possible for pupils to make continuous growth regardless of ability or lack of ability. The teachers felt this would enable them to be more thorough and comprehensive in their teaching and they would be more able to meet the needs of all pupils. Thus, they would be more effective as teachers.

A developmental program was to be initiated with every pupil studying on his own appropriate level and progressing at his own rate. There was to be no undue pressure on any pupil to perform at a level beyond his capacity. But at the same time, no pupil was to be bored or allowed to rest on his laurels. All pupils should find the work challenging and stimulating. The able learner and the slow learner would be in a position to make progress beyond normal expectation.

Community Approval and Implementation

The community of Hillsboro has a population of 10,000 and lies about 17 miles west of Portland, Oregon. While children of all socioeconomic levels attend school, the majority of the pupils are from middle-class homes. Pupils also reflect both suburban and rural backgrounds.

Eight hundred pupils are enrolled in the Peter Boscow School, in kindergarten through the sixth year. The 29 teachers have taught for an average of eleven and a half years. Three teachers have no degree, the majority hold the bachelor's degree, and a minority are at the fifth-year and master's degree level of formal education.

At a dinner meeting with the board of education, the professional staff with the principal as spokesman presented the proposed plan to the board. First, the problem of adequately providing for the needs of children of varying abilities was presented. Charts showing the wide range in ability were displayed. And, finally, the proposed solution to the problem was discussed with the aid of more charts. The board of education received the plan with enthusiasm and gave approval. The plan was then presented to the Peter Boscow School Parent-Teacher Association. The principal again explained the educational problems and the new proposal. Questions were raised, but no objections were registered by the parents. They liked the rationale of the new plan.

When the proposed plan had been refined to the point that it was acceptable to the staff, it was put into operation. All fourth-, fifth-, and sixth-grade classrooms were ungraded at once for the purposes of language arts instruction. A great amount of thought had been given the problem of grouping pupils, as the teachers and administrators were convinced that this was basic to any success that might be forthcoming. The staff also shared the conviction that the groups and the program of studies must be flexible. Therefore, provisions were made for the adjustment of pupils from one group to another whenever the teacher believed this to be desirable. Provisions also were made to provide for continuity in the curriculum for all groups at all levels.

Although each teacher had an achievement-grouped class, the teachers found it necessary to do some grouping within the class for instruction in specific skills. A teacher might find that he could instruct his entire class as one group for instruction in grammar, while he would need another group for teaching phonetic and structural analysis skills.

Evaluation

As time passed, the teachers were convinced that the nongraded language arts program was a success. The majority of parents were also of the opinion that the new program was more beneficial to children.

The administration was also pleased with the results but, in addition, felt the need for a more objective evaluation of the results. At the end of one year a carefully controlled study (considering the problems inherent in using classrooms as control and experimental groups) comparing nongraded classrooms with graded classrooms revealed a significant difference in reading achievement in favor of the nongraded classrooms at all levels. The mean differences in reading achievement were all significant at the 1 per cent level of confidence.[1]

The Nongraded Primary

The success of the nongraded language arts program in grades four through six and its immediate and enthusiastic acceptance by children and parents were the prime initiators of the Peter Boscow Nongraded Primary School. During a discussion of the problems of readiness in first grade at a parents' meeting the following September (1957), an inquiry from a parent as to the feasibility of adapting the nongraded intermediate program to the primary grades initiated the staff study that led to the present nongraded primary school in Hillsboro.

The nongraded primary school organization in Hillsboro is not a new method of teaching or a departure from effective procedures long used by competent primary teachers. It is a means of making more functional a philosophy of education that recognizes modern advances in the field of child psychology and human development. It is an administrative procedure that makes possible a more flexible organization for grouping pupils. It is designed to encourage and promote a philosophy of continuous pupil growth. Briefly, it will enable teachers to more adequately meet the challenge of varying abilities in all aspects of the curriculum.

After the primary staff and the administration had studied nongrading in other school systems (Milwaukee, Wisconsin; Cardston, Alberta; Park Forest, Illinois; and Provo, Utah), a nongraded program was carefully designed for Hillsboro and by Hillsboro teachers. The Hillsboro nongraded program is not a copy of any other program but was developed by the teachers and principal to meet the needs of pupils in a specific school situation.

Again, when the professional staff was of the opinion that the proposed plan for a nongraded primary had met the most exacting standards set by the superintendent, it was presented to the board of education. The board accepted the proposal. At another meeting, the proposal was presented to the parents of the school who also accepted the proposed plan. The following September (1958), the nongraded primary school plan was begun.

Grouping

Children in the Hillsboro nongraded primary are grouped in terms of achievement. Reading achievement is the primary criterion for placement in a group, although other factors (maturity, emotional stability, arithmetic achievement, etc.) receive consideration.

Classes are organized into comfortable working groups without regard for traditional grade placement. No pupil is placed in a group where he would be more than one year older or one year younger than the other members of his class.

Even though the classes are achievement grouped, each teacher usually finds that he has at least two working groups of pupils. Whenever a teacher discovers that a pupil no longer fits comfortably in a particular group, due to the fact that he has made more progress or less progress than the other members of the group, an adjustment is made. The pupil is then placed in a group of similar ability and achievement. If there is not such a group in the pupil's present classroom, the pupil is transferred to another classroom. A nongraded plan makes flexibility in grouping possible.

Continuous Growth

The language arts and arithmetic curricula of the Peter Boscow Nongraded Primary School have been organized into eight levels of achievement, plus a readiness level as the foundation of the program. It is more realistic to think in terms of eight or nine levels of achievement, rather than the traditional three grades. This not only reduces stumbling blocks to stepping stones but facilitates the implementation of a concept of continuous growth. It also provides a more precise indication of pupil progress and achievement at any given time. This principle lies at the heart of the nongraded primary.

Today, if it is known that a certain pupil is in the second grade, this is no indication that the child has reached a specific level of achievement. The nongraded primary has new meaning for both parent and pupil, as opposed to the meaningless appellations: first grade, second grade, and so forth.

Pupil Progress

A child who is gifted intellectually and is also socially and emotionally precocious may complete the nongraded primary program in two years. Less than one per cent of the pupils do this. A child who completes the work normally expected of an average pupil at the end of three years in the primary school is placed at an enrichment level. At this level, the pupil receives both an enrichment and accelerated program of instruction prior to moving into the fourth grade.

In the Hillsboro nongraded primary school there is no retention as it is thought of in the traditional, graded school. No student is asked to repeat a course sequence. A slow-learning pupil may spend four years in the nongraded primary, but his progress is continuous, step by step, up through the primary school.

Parents are advised of their child's progress in parent-teacher conferences which are held in November and March. In addition, a written report is sent home whenever a child completes a level of achievement. At the end of three years the teacher and the parent will both have more understanding as to whether or not the child should spend a fourth year in the primary school. This eliminates the shock that some parents experience at the mere mention of retention. The majority of pupils spend three years in the primary school, as is the custom in the graded elementary school.

Matters About Which More Might Be Said

The Hillsboro nongraded primary school was implemented without any changes in physical facilities. Instructional materials already available were utilized. No special funds were budgeted for the nongraded program, either. Technology has played no role in the nongraded instructional program in Hillsboro.

However, nongraded organization facilitates desirable curriculum change. It provides the flexibility necessary to cast off obsolete methods of working with students and encourages experimentation with more promising and appropriate curricula. In the authors' opinion, most graded schools should be prepared for such change before nongrading is seriously considered. Otherwise, the possibilities for improvement may not be fully realized.

Evaluation

A matched-pair study of reading achievement, comparing nongraded primary classrooms with graded classrooms in Hillsboro, was conducted by the school psychologist.[2] Pupils were matched on the basis of chronological age (within one month) and intelligence quotient (within three points). Intelligence quotient measurements were obtained from the Science Research Associates Primary Mental Abilities Test which is administered in September to all six-year-olds as part of a district-wide testing program. Reading achievement was measured utilizing the Reading Battery of the California Achievement Test.

At the beginning of the fourth grade, after the pupils (matched pairs) had spent three years in the Peter Boscow School nongraded primary (experimental group), the mean reading grade placement score for the nongraded pupils was 5.92 and for the graded pupils was 4.81. This difference of one year and one year and one month in favor of the nongraded program is statistically significant at the one half of one per cent level of confidence.

A matched-study comparison of arithmetic achievement was conducted, comparing arithmetic achievement of pupils in graded primary classrooms.[3] Arithmetic achievement was measured utilizing the Arithmetic Battery total score obtained from the California Achievement Test, 1957 edition.

Children tested were drawn from the same community (Hillsboro) and were matched on four points: sex; I.Q. as measured by the California Test of Mental Maturity, 1957-S-Form; chronological age; and socioeconomic status. The control group had spent three years in a graded program, and the experimental group had spent three years in the Peter Boscow Nongraded Primary School. The groups were comparable in every way. Instructional methods and materials utilized for both groups were similar; teaching time and emphasis given arithmetic instruction were also similar; and class loads were comparable for both groups.

The results of the comparison revealed a mean difference of five months in arithmetic achievement at the end of three years in favor of the pupils who had been in the nongraded primary. This difference is significant statistically at the two hundredths level of confidence.

Conclusion

There is nothing inherent in the graded organization that is essential to a child's progress in school. A graded system tends to foster unrealistic standards and to be inflexible in meeting the needs of all pupils. A nongraded system can be flexible, fostering standards that challenge and interest the able learner without frustrating the slow learner. The teachers in a nongraded school find that they can be more effective and comprehensive in their teaching. Children appear to be happier and more secure without fear of retention and with competition controlled so that all pupils have a reasonable opportunity to succeed.

It is also important to emphasize the fact that the professional staff at Peter Boscow School believe they only have begun to take advantage of the opportunities created by a nongraded plan. This system holds abundant promise for the future.

CHAPTER 14

The Torrance, California, Approach

by

JOHN H. HULL

As superintendent of schools, Dr. John H. Hull has guided the development of the nongraded program in Torrance, California. Dr. Hull has served as a college professor and has written extensively for educational journals.

M ANY EDUCATORS become frustrated by the traditional grade concept that produces the same method of mass education for all students. Several times in Torrance we had learned the lesson that changing names does not change thinking. New programs result from new ways of teaching and learning and not from adding new names to old practices. It was determined several years ago that if we were going to change professional thinking in Torrance, we were going to have to face the teacher with a problem that required a new approach. Our solution was to place children from three different grade levels in a single teacher's classroom.

Problem Approach

This resulted in a host of problems. What was the teacher to do about them? The teacher must make differentiations in the curriculum by allowing for varying abilities and interests and tailor the program of each child to his individual rate of learning. This is what should have been going on in all classes—but it was not. The new class organization in Torrance resulted in the development of techniques for teaching over a broad span, instead of teaching to one specific level. Once the multi-grade teacher grasped the idea and made it work, the so-called straight grade-level teacher next door made the change too. She was not going to be outdone!

Differentiated instruction resulted throughout the school system. Standard test scores in multi-grade rooms went way above the district-wide norms because we received the benefit of doing something about increasing the achievement of all students. Instead of teaching to the middle group, teachers were challenging the gifted, improving the retarded, and still not ignoring any other student.

The multi-grade organization retains the advantages of the graded organization in keeping track of children administratively but does not stifle teachers' progress in moving outside of restricted content areas. Educationally, a child works as fast as his ability and interest warrant. He is not held down by the grade in which he is harnessed. He may be below grade level in some subjects and above grade levels in others. There is both variation between and within students.

Although graded labels are maintained, the philosophy of continuous education permeates the entire program. Students are simply taken as far as they can go in each academic area. However, there is also another major distinction that should be clearly recognized. Contrary to most all other grouping patterns, the Torrance multi-grade pattern is based upon having greater differences in every aspect of child growth and development, including age, ability, achievement, and social maturity. Such a grouping plan is based upon the point of view that children learn more from those who are different than from those who are similar to themselves. Maturity, be it social or academic, is gained by living and working with those who are more mature, or by having responsibility for those who are less mature. Negated completely is the common pattern of collecting or grouping children of similar characteristics.

The Little Red Schoolhouse had "something" and we're trying to recapture that "something." In effect, an attempt is being made to combine the best of two educational worlds in the Torrance program.

Questions and Answers on the Multi-Grade School

1. *How many years does a child spend in a multi-grade class?* If a child started in the first year, that child would have the opportunity of staying with the same teacher for three years. A child could have two teachers in a period of six years (1-2-3 and then into 4-5-6). However, since this program is voluntary, a parent may take a child out at any time and ask that be be put in a graded organization.

2. *What testing devices were used in the original program?* Several tests were used in the original study of the multi-grade program. They included all of the California Achievement tests, the California Test of Mental Ability, the Vineland Social Maturity Scale, and the California Test of Personality. All tests were given in the fall and again in the spring.

3. *Is the rate of growth of a third-grade student as fast as that of a first-grade student in this program?* Yes, if one believes in individual instruction, then all students grow at their own rate. The results of the study showed that older children gain from helping younger children and younger children learn from older students. The studies also proved that the wider the range of experiences and interests, the greater the stimulation to learning.

4. *How do you cover content, especially social studies?* All subjects in this program, as well as all classes in this district, are taught on the individual basis. Social studies for multi-grades are broken down as follows: (a) Grades 1-2-3: Natural Environment, How People Live and Work Together, Transportation, How People Communicate and Cooperate, and How Differences in Communities Influence People's Lives; (b) Grades 4-5-6: How the United States Came into Being, How the United States Developed, How People Live in California Past and Present, How Our Region Relates to the Nation, Seeing California as Part of the United States and World, How the United States and Canada are Interrelated, How People Live in Another Culture, How the Nation Looks to the Future, and What Is the Effect of Scientific Discovery on the Life in the World Today? Teachers use a multiple text. Since the same

teacher will guide children throughout the entire three-year period, there is no need to divide the subject matter into years.

5. *How was the original program evaluated?* Most of the data of the study were secured from standardized tests. The gains that the multi-grade pupils made in all areas were compared with gains made by regular grade pupils for the same grade levels. The district also made a comparative study involving all six grade levels with six other graded schools in the system selected on a random basis. Results were in favor of students in the multi-graded rooms.

6. *What is the I.Q. range of the multi-grade class?* The I.Q. range is the same as in any other class within the district. Those I.Q.'s below 70 are placed in the educationally mentally retarded program.

7. *Would a small school make a difference?* Probably not. It would seem to be a more natural setup in a small school. The schools in Torrance where the multi-grade classes are located have student enrollments of over 800.

8. *Will mobility of population hamper this program?* No, experience has shown youngsters who transfer out of the program do as well if not better than those in a graded program.

9. *Is there any extra clerical help in this program?* No more clerical help is given these teachers than that offered to teachers in graded schools.

10. *Are there any limitations in any area of instruction?* None whatsoever in the multi-grade classes; the sky is the limit.

Additional Observations

The basic organization of the multi-grade classes consists of groups containing approximately equal numbers of first, second, and third graders and an intermediate multi-grade group containing approximately equal numbers of fourth, fifth, and sixth graders.

By increasing the general spread of differences, the learning situation in the classroom is enriched. No thought is given to expecting all students in the multi-grade room to do the same learning activity on the same level of investigation. Learning experiences are individually designed and personally executed.

Even if the children in the multi-grade classes still think of themselves as being at a particular grade level, the grouping within the classroom in the areas of reading, arithmetic, and social studies cuts across grade-level lines and is different in each of these areas of study because of the difference in the achievement levels of the individual pupils in the classroom.

Since the multi-grade pupils clearly demonstrated greater personal and social growth, some feel that this represents the major area in which the multi-grade structure is superior to a regular grade program.

Information Pertaining to Multi-Grades

The idea of the multi-grade was developed by Dr. Walter Rehwoldt, with the cooperation of Dr. Welte LeFever of the University of Southern California, and Dr. J. H. Hull, superintendent of the Torrance Unified School District. Dr. Rehwoldt presented the original idea of comparing multi-grade classes with the regular grade classes to the administration of the Torrance Unified School District in 1954. After some modifications, the superintendent recommended approval of the program. The program was duly authorized by the board of education and put into effect at the Walteria Elementary School in September, 1955, with seven multi-grade classes in operation at the school.

The first step in the development of the program was to secure an administrator and teachers who were willing to participate. After this was done, a series of general meetings by grade level was planned in order to present the idea to parents. Following only two general meetings, these was sufficient positive response by parents to establish the program.

A careful statistical analysis of the growth of children in both the regular grade and multi-grade classes in the district was made for the school year of 1955–1956. In general, virtually all comparisons in the areas of social development, personal adjustment, and maturity favored the multi-grade pupils. In the majority of cases, the achievement progress on the part of the multi-grade pupils in the academic areas of reading, arithmetic, and language also favored the multi-grade pupils. These comparisons were made on the basis of the matched-pair technique (matching was by sex, age, grade, I.Q., and fall achievement score).

Evidence indicates that children learn more effectively in the multi-grade system. But we have no evidence that retention is any greater in the multi-grade system than the retention of children in other classrooms over an extended period of time. More studies are needed over an extended period of time to assess the long-range gains in student achievement.

In Torrance, we do not think that a multi-grade is the only answer to improving the quality of instruction. But we are convinced that the teacher who will move into the multi-graded organization with the objective of trying to do something about each child's problems will find himself a better teacher. Good teaching, after all, is helping each individual learn, appreciate, develop, and think to the best of his ability.

Because of the general acceptance of the multi-grade program, the board of education made it possible for the program to expand, providing the children were placed in the classes by parents' request and the teachers volunteered for the classes. Following this decision, three additional schools in Torrance started multi-grade classes in September, 1958–1959. By the 1960–1961 school year, there were 78 multi-grade classes in Torrance's 30 elementary schools.

The benefit from this program has been the wide practice throughout the district of individualizing teaching, of differentiating instruction, and of recognizing the variable rates of learning which exist in all classrooms. As a device for stimulating the improvement of instruction, multi-grades in Torrance have been a tremendous success.

Thirteen Basic Hypotheses
Concerning Multi-Grade Grouping Study

1. Older children learn a great deal in such a group by helping younger children. Older children develop willingness and ability to assume responsibility for helping others.
2. Younger children profit from the stimulation of working with older children and learn much from them.

3. A multi-grade group reduces the artificiality of the graded pattern of school. Grade standards are minimized. It becomes more natural for teachers to work with children where they are and take them as far as they can go in the multi-grade group regardless of their grade.
4. Greater emphasis is placed on individual and on small-group instruction than in total-group instruction.
5. Such grouping results in greater cooperation among teachers. Teachers solve problems as they seek answers to individual problems.
6. There is a greater acceptance of individual differences on the part of the pupils when they are in multi-grade groups. These differences are more obvious, hence pupils are more inclined to accept those who are different from them.
7. Morale is greater in such a group since the basis for contention, rivalry, and competition with the rest of the class is largely removed.
8. Circumscription of the grade is removed so that the teacher does not feel he has to cover a given amount of material, but can devote his attention to the individual progress of the children.
9. Discipline is better in such a group as older pupils act as a quieting influence.
10. These groups are more natural since pupils often choose younger or older students with whom to work and play outside of school.
11. A wider range of ages brings a wider range of experiences and capacities to the group, thus enriching the opportunity of each individual for learning and for being valued rather than envied or patronized.
12. Greater social growth takes place where pupils are of wider age range.

CHAPTER 15

The Cedar Falls, Iowa, Story

by

VERNA SPONSLER AND
MARVIN ZIEMAN

*Miss Verna Sponsler is an elementary school principal
and Mr. Marvin Zieman is the assistant superintendent
in charge of instruction in Cedar Falls, Iowa. Both
have played important roles in the development of the
nongraded program in their community.*

CEDAR FALLS is the home of the State College of Iowa and, thereby,
one of the cultural centers of Iowa. The community supports several factories and many places of business. Thus, Cedar Falls has a
range of high, average, and low socioeconomic levels. The intelligence testing program and the Iowa Test of Basic Skills Battery
have revealed that there are more students in the high range of
academic ability than in the low.

The Primary School

The primary program is for children in the first three years of
school. Children are simply referred to as being in the Primary
School instead of in a particular grade. As instruction is given, a
complete record of each child's progress is kept. The following is an
example of the kinds of data collected. In each academic area the

191

faculty have identified desirable instructional outcomes. These are arranged in sequence without reference to grade level.

CEDAR FALLS COMMUNITY SCHOOLS
CEDAR FALLS, IOWA
Standards for Primary School Levels: Reading

Level 2, Reading-Charts
Short, Transitional Period

Is aware of point-by-point correspondence between oral and printed word. (Child dictates sentence as teacher writes it.)

Is aware that sentences are composed of words separated by spaces.

Understands short sentences as units of thought.

Understands that the period completes the unit of thought.

Understands that one or more sentences may be used to tell a story.

Level 3, Reading
Pre-primer

Has grown in ability to understand and use oral language.

Is able to give sustained attention for longer periods of time.

Listens attentively to what others are saying.

Scrutinizes words from left to right.

Recognizes words in either book type or manuscript and in capitalized or uncapitalized form.

Is able to remember word forms by associating meaning with printed word.

Is able to remember word forms by careful observation of visual details.

Is able to use meaning clues in identifying words.

Has well developed auditory perception of rhyming words.

Has well developed auditory perception of initial consonant sounds.

Uses phonetic analysis to attack unfamiliar words.

A level is used to designate a pupil's position on the educational continuum in each content area. There are twelve areas in the program. Standards are set for each of the twelve areas. Growth in reading ability is considered in the gradations of each area in the primary school. Instructional outcomes have been developed with more precision in reading and mathematics than in the other areas.

Although grouping is essentially based on reading skills, competency in other subject areas is not neglected. Because of the importance of reading to successful achievement in other subjects, we believe that a good reading program will strengthen the work in other academic areas in the Primary School. Also, we have set up a gradation of standards to measure a pupil's progress in primary mathematics, social studies, language, science, and physical, social, and emotional health.

Pupil Assignment

During the latter part of May all kindergarten children are given a readiness test. The kindergarten teachers then meet with their principal to study the test results, discuss the anecdotal records, and review the materials kept in separate conference folders for each child. The teacher's judgment of each child as to his academic, social, physical, and emotional development has a definite place in this discussion and in the decision as to group placement for the coming year. The teachers then classify the children into workable groups for September. Readiness for reading serves as an important basis for grouping. The number of groups depends upon the number of rooms to be used for the primary classes. Children are grouped chiefly at their performance or achievement levels rather than in terms of any assessment of their potential ability.

After classes have started in the fall, a teacher may find that a child is moving more rapidly or more slowly than others in the group in which he has been placed. If the teacher believes that the youngster will continue to do so, he is moved immediately to another group, preferably in the teacher's own classroom. If the teacher does not have a group that will meet the child's needs, he will discuss the child's general academic progress and his social and emotional development with the principal and with a teacher who has a group that will more nearly meet the child's needs. If, after a careful consideration, the teacher feels that a move would be beneficial, the child will be transferred into a classroom that will challenge him to do his best. The parents are called and the reasons for the change are explained.

This flexibility in placement of children is worthwhile for new enrollees in the schools. A child entering one of the Primary Schools from another community is assigned to a group on a temporary basis and may be changed if the group does not meet his needs. Each new parent moving into this community is given an explanation of the Primary School and how it operates, as well as an explanatory handbook. If the parent has questions concerning the plan, he is urged to discuss the Primary School program with the principal or with the child's teacher.

A pupil leaving our system is given a transfer card which tells the receiving school where the child should be placed in a graded school.

Introduction of the Primary School

The actual operation of the Primary School began at the end of the 1958–1959 school year. Principals and kindergarten and first-grade teachers studied the readiness and achievement assessments of the kindergartners in their building and grouped them so that children with common abilities, insofar as was possible, started together. The pupils then were assigned to the teachers who were to teach the first six levels. Each teacher, wherever possible, was to have only three groups.

Those children not quite ready for formal learning were placed in the junior primary so they could attend school all day and develop readiness at a quicker rate than by attending kindergarten only one-half day. Very immature children were left in the kindergarten.

When school began the next fall, principals and teachers, after the first week or two, took another look at the grouping arrangements. Changes were made which were necessitated as a result of growth by some children over the summer months.

During the year a few children were moved from one group to another to allow for more opportunity for academic growth. The same procedure was employed in placing the second group of children into the Primary School at the end of the 1959–1960 school year. The teacher's committee met with parents of these children so that everyone understood the function of the Primary School.

The 1958–1959 kindergarten children entered the Primary School in the fall of 1959. Beginning with the fall of 1960, the plan moved into its second year. By the 1961–1962 school year the Cedar Falls Primary School was in full operation.

Evaluation

The faculty utilize a number of means in checking on the effectiveness of the Primary School program. The program's predetermined standards furnish a direct check on pupil progress. Testing, at regular intervals, supplies a means of evaluating the scholastic-achievement dimension of the program and gives information on how well each student is doing. The primary teachers check with each other and work closely together. This furnishes a constant check on how well individuals and groups are doing. The principal, guidance counselors, and special consultants from outside the system evaluate the program from time to time.

A Primary School evaluating committee has completed the first assignment of evaluating the establishment and operation of a Primary School in the Cedar Falls Community School District. The major objectives of the evaluation were to find if there was evidence:

1. Supporting the belief that children do better in a program that adjusts itself to the child's rate of development.
2. That the teacher operating with more freedom to make adjustments is able to be more effective in his teaching and also feels positive about his pupils' accomplishment.
3. That the individual child benefits from going through a Primary School program.
4. That parents are satisfied with their child's progress and experiences in the Primary School.
5. That the administrators are better able to evaluate the work of the teachers and pupils in a Primary School than in a traditionally organized school.

The first phase of the study was conducted by Dr. Edward Buffie of Indiana University. He evaluated the test results of 234 elementary school children who were given instruction under the two plans, 117 children in their third year in Primary School and 117 children in a regular third grade. The general purpose of his investigation was to compare the mental health and academic achievement of elementary school pupils attending school under two different plans of organization—the graded and nongraded primary school.

One significant finding in this study was that children of high-average and above-average ability achieved more success in the nongraded school than in the graded school. This finding was reinforced after interviewing all the primary teachers in Cedar Falls. They, in general, believed that this Primary School plan did more for the average and above-average student than was previously the case in the graded school. Also, the teachers judged that at least as much was accomplished by the below-average child in the nongraded school as in the graded school.

A parent questionnaire, serving a second phase of the evaluation study, was answered by some 260 parents out of a random sampling of 300. The results offered substantial evidence that parents believed in the Primary School concept and that they also thought it was doing more for the children than the graded school. They strongly favored its continuance.

A wealth of information was obtained from a questionnaire given to each teacher and from interviews with all primary teachers which made up the third phase of the study. In general, this information dealt with evidence regarding the first four objectives of the study. The following brief set of summary statements reveals the attitudes and professional opinions of the Primary School staff:

1. Parents have a sound understanding of the objectives of the Primary School, but more parent education would be helpful.
2. The Primary School is doing more for the average and above-average pupil than was done in a traditionally organized school.
3. Modification of some of the standards used in pupil evaluation are advisable. The reading and mathematics standards are very acceptable.
4. Although teachers in all of the buildings indicated the grouping was satisfactory, some improvement could be made.
5. While some children still use grade designations to refer to their place in school, they are moving toward recognition of the Primary School as a nongraded unit.
6. Primary teachers feel that a closer working relationship has been established in their group of students.
7. Teachers feel that the Primary School helps them to become more aware of the individual student's needs and that it provides the freedom needed in order to satisfy those needs.

8. Parents have more confidence in the professional staff and in the school because of parental understanding of the Primary School organization and because of the knowledge the faculty demonstrate they have of each child.

Elementary school principals during the past three years have had brought home to them the necessity of knowing the individual child and his family. Principals have shown their response to the shift in organization mainly by:

1. Submitting more referrals to the guidance department,
2. Requesting more supplementary materials,
3. Holding more in-service meetings,
4. Relating interesting situations in principals' meetings,
5. Maintaining a closer relationship with primary teachers.

It is important that this program be carefully studied and reevaluated from time to time for necessary revision and improvement. Therefore, a committee has been assigned to be on the alert for needs or trouble spots which may arise.

Future Plans

We have an elementary study committee made up of eight teachers and the director of instruction to study curriculum changes that need to be made in the organization of the upper elementary grades.

Achievement grouping has been done in some subject areas in grades four, five, and six. That is, the teachers of each grade level have grouped children needing help in developing reading skills in the same class. In this way teachers can concentrate on the weak areas and give more help to individual pupils. The children are regrouped for other subjects according to their performance. In a few cases we have crossed grade lines in our grouping for better instruction in the upper elementary grades.

Improvement of the Program

At the present time, it is quite evident that nearly all concerned—parents, teachers, children, and administrators—are satisfied with the progress of the Primary School. There is still work ahead for committees, individual teachers, and administrators as the need for future changes becomes evident. We believe that it is desirable to fit the nongraded organization to meet the needs of each individual school community. The plan described has proven a satisfactory one for the Cedar Falls schools.

CHAPTER 16

Breaking Grade Level Barriers at the Webster School, Pontiac, Michigan

by

EDITH ROACH SNYDER

*Dr. Snyder has been involved in the nongraded move-
ment for a number of years. In addition to being
principal of the Webster School, she has written
widely in the field of individualized instruction and
has been active in the Association for Supervision and
Curriculum Development. She has been a professor
for summer sessions and workshops in the field of
elementary education.*

WHEN TEACHERS and administrators evince genuine concern and
anxiety for the welfare of today's children, when they objectively
identify the actual needs of children, and when they recognize the
factors which prevent fulfillment of these needs, then change begins
to take place in the schools. Desirable learnings occur when the
educational environment is conducive to creative and constructive
activity. Teachers must feel free to evaluate the existing curriculum,
to express their ideas, and to participate in planning for improved
educational experiences of children. Progress begins with the re-
designing of a school program which gives priority to meaningful

learning and the methods which foster it. Education becomes meaningful when the school program recognizes the needs of the learner
and the demands of the society in which he lives.

The Webster School staff's concept of curriculum broadened as
research, individual study, and discussions centered on different
aspects of the educational process. While the content of learning
received major emphasis, the plus factors—security, desirable attitudes toward self and society, optimum climate for learning, and
provision for experiences with democratic values—were not ignored.
The Webster staff was confident that a desirable school program
recognized all educative procedures which contributed to the development of a good citizen. It was the belief of this group that if some
or all of these factors could be incorporated in a school program, the
child would learn more and learn it better. It was on this basis that
the staff set to work to implement such a philosophy in a nongraded
program.

The School Community

Webster School is one of 28 elementary schools in the industrial city
of Pontiac, Michigan. The school is located in a typical American
community. Families live in middle-class homes and are merchants,
professional people, businessmen, office workers, or factory employ-
ees. The school has approximately 800 students. There are a few
ethnic groups; Indian, Spanish, Chinese, Negro, and American
Indian. The majority of children come to school adequately clothed
and well fed.

Webster School is an old school, built shortly after the first World
War; however, the floor plan is modern and it has large rooms. The
school community is slowly changing from a restricted residential
area to an area spotted with commercial establishments. Many of
the large one-family homes have been converted to two- and three-
family apartments. The school serves a large geographic area. Some
children come by bus but most are within walking distance.

The present school organization is the self-contained classroom.
The average pupil-teacher ratio is approximately 30 children per
teacher. The staff is composed of both experienced and new
teachers. There are a minimal number of annual staff changes.

Approximately half the staff hold master's degrees or are working on the degree, and all teachers have bachelor's degrees.

Staff Interest

Noteworthy is the teaching staff's constant effort to improve teaching performance. This effort has characterized the performance of the first planning group that worked with the school principal on the development of a practical nongraded teaching block geared to the developmental needs of children. The sympathetic, inquiring climate in which the original teaching group developed its plans had its beginning at Webster School. The encouragement teachers give children to try new learnings is paralleled by the encouragement which the principal gives teachers to try new approaches to learning.

The idea of the block program or nongraded school was first presented to parents whose children were completing kindergarten. A statement of philosophy was followed by recommendations for implementation. Parents were then invited to participate in a general discussion and suggest ways in which the plan might be improved. The decision to accept the three-year block plan, which meant that children would spend three years in one room with one teacher, was made by the parents. Their decision was an unanimous one. Parents' satisfaction with the initial three-year block was attested to when they evaluated it with teachers and principal and then requested that their children continue in a second block for grades four through six. This block plan provided children and teachers with a common learning-teaching environment for a longer period of time.

A Program For Children

Organizational changes in the program were made to provide a structure where children and teachers could work for longer periods of time than in usual practice. Teachers were certain that much time was lost in changing children to other teachers and rooms at the end of a semester or two. It takes time to learn what students can do and how they work best. Also, students profit from prolonged association with one teacher and develop real rapport with their teacher over several years. A two-year block was considered good, but perhaps a three-year block would be better. Knowing a child takes time, and at Webster School the teachers felt the knowledge gained over a longer period of time would be reflected in constructive teaching.

Visitors at Webster frequently ask, "What do you mean by a nongraded school?" Also, "Does the block plan mean ability grouping?" The children at the end of the kindergarten year remain in their kindergarten group and move easily into the primary block. The group to which each child is assigned is by chance and not based on any regimented plan. Both the original planning staff and the present-day staff say, "Give us a cross section of children; we will adjust the instruction to them."

The children remain in the same room with the same teacher for a three-year period. This block of time allows the individual child to develop within an educational framework familiar to him and in which he feels secure. It provides the teacher with increased opportunities to observe, understand, and plan for both the individual and the group. The expanded block of time also encourages teachers to subscribe to, and actually practice, a teaching approach that allows children to develop and learn at their own pace. The time block makes possible more parent-teacher contacts which contribute to better understanding of, and sympathy for, individual children. The child's room teacher is his guide and his counselor for three years. Many resources are fed into each group to enrich the curriculum. Each child learns as much as he can every day. The motto "No child may go out the door at the close of the day without having at least one successful experience" is a practical and satisfactory one.

At the end of the three-year block, the children move into a second block for another three years but with a different teacher in a different room. Occasionally, it happens that an extremely immature or accelerated child will profit by being transferred to a younger or older group. When parents, teachers, and principal agree that evidence indicates that a change in placement will benefit the child, the change is made. This could also be true on the upper-grade level. This does not necessarily happen at the end of the year or at the end of the block. It happens whenever there is need for such an adjustment.

Environmental factors have generously contributed to the success of the program. In addition to curricular experiences being adjusted to meet the needs of children, physical equipment is inviting and child-like. A room becomes a child's second home. The rooms are colorful and well-equipped. In addition to a piano, record player, tape recorder, and filmstrip projector, each room is set up informally with rocking chairs, davenports, reading centers, interest centers, lamps and other equipment built to fit into a relaxed setting.

Fundamentals of the Webster School Program

1. PLACE:
   Pontiac, Michigan (25 miles north of Detroit).
2. TIME:
   Conception of program, 1945.
   Development through total school in eight years.
   Organization with improvements in practice today, 1967.
3. KINDERGARTEN GROUPING:
   Alphabetical on enrollment (some factors affect group placement: transportation, working parents, etc.).
4. PRIMARY BLOCK:
   Children enter from kindergarten.
   Remain in same group through elementary school (few exceptions).
   Remain in same room, with same teacher, and same children for three years.
   Maximum growth expected of each child through planned learning experiences.
   Rapport and understanding established and developed through parent-teacher-child conferences.
5. UPPER-GRADE BLOCK:
   Group moves intact to new room and new teacher for a three-year period.
   Primary block teacher bridges the gap to upper-grade block through conferences with the new teacher.
   New teacher begins instruction where learner is.
   New teacher continues expansion of planned learning experiences for the individual and the group.
   Program places increased emphasis on creativity, exploration, experimentation, and develops the role of the individual in the group.
   Recognizes and uses educationally valuable community resources.

6. EVALUATION OF BLOCK PROGRAM—NONGRADED SCHOOL:

Provides each teacher with a cross section of children (achievement, intelligence, socioeconomic, culture—no plan for grouping).

Provides opportunity for long-term planning.

Establishes good relationship between child, parent, and teacher.

Provides a more intelligent and related use of human resources, specialists, community agencies, etc.

Promotes continuity in learning.

Provides a program honoring readiness.

Gives greater depth to understanding the child.

Provides the flexibility needed to accommodate individual differences.

Individualizes instruction and applies this principle to all areas of learning.

Gives children security and stability and successful experiences which contribute to improved learning.

Develops a permanent kinship between school, home, and community.

Evaluation

The improvement and extension of the educational experiences of children should be the only valid reasons for changing school programs. There is much evidence—subsequent records, achievement testing, leadership roles, scholarship awards, and citizenship traits—which indicate that the boys and girls who live and learn under this program are living and learning well.

A child who had entered junior high school and had received a report card for the first time was asked by her elementary school teacher, "Sharon, does it make any difference in how hard you work because you are receiving a report card?" She replied, quite indignantly, "Of course not, I always do my best." Somehow, this statement sums up the attitude toward learning shown by children who have experienced the climate of the nongraded school.

In addition to some of the things listed above, which the Webster School staff use as criteria for evaluating a good educational program, there is also a benefit to children as parents and teachers work together to understand and to help the child. To know the parents is to better know the child.

In the block program parents often become valuable resource people. They frequently help with parties, outdoor education, field trips, mending library books, kindergarten registration, etc. They want to be a part of their children's school, but, somehow, school people in the past have not had the inclination to incorporate parents in the planning and the operation of the school.

Probably the greatest device in helping children to learn is the parent-teacher-child conference due to the cooperative effort it brings about. The parent-teacher-child conference encourages self-evaluation by teachers, parents, and the children themselves. All three participants in this type of conference can afford to be objective because each stands to gain through better understanding.

Conclusion

Attitudes toward learning are enthusiastic at the Webster School. Exploration and experimentation are the order of each day. Children work as hard as they can work in a program characterized by academic growth and concerned with values. It is a program enriched by people and things.

Creativity dominates this climate. It takes a certain kind of relationship in a classroom, a generous amount of motivation, a stockpile of working ingredients, and an excitement about different ways of doing and learning. The quality of learning depends upon the child's quality of living in his twenty-four-hour day. If he has the opportunity to create at school, it follows that he will create at home and in his community. It is not just the way he attacks his reading or his arithmetic, but it is a way of life. He has freedom to create on his level of accomplishment, not necessarily at the fourth-grade level or any specific grade level.

Students are involved in task setting. It is for a teacher to live with a child for three years, to be able to understand him and his parents better each year. And each year the teacher uses that increased understanding to help the child realize his learning potential. The block plan creates a haven of good mental health for teacher and pupils. To be in a position where a teacher need not threaten a child because he is eight years old and not doing third-grade work provides a security for both child and teacher. The uniqueness of the individual child is recognized and properly respected in the nongraded program.

A child lives with children his own age, but as an individual he may work on levels which differ from those of other members of the group. He may explore with a different approach. He may learn different things about the same interest area of the group. He finds satisfaction in doing all he can do and doing it as well as he can. His classmates enjoy his findings because he shares his experiences with them. There is continuity to his learning because his teacher knows where he has been and helps plan where he is going.

CHAPTER 17

The Nova Nongraded High School, Fort Lauderdale, Florida

by

Arthur B. Wolfe

After traveling extensively throughout the United States visiting significant school programs, Arthur B. Wolfe participated in the development of the Nova School program. Mr. Wolfe is assistant superintendent of the Broward County schools in which Nova High School is operated.

Constant change, sometimes breath-taking, is the keynote of contemporary life. Education cannot afford to stand still while the rest of the society's institutions move forward in self-improvement.

Old methods of teaching are being challenged by the Broward County Public School System, which serves a populous section of Florida's lower east coast including such fast-growing municipalities as Fort Lauderdale, Hollywood, and Pompano Beach. In an area where school enrollment has increased by more than 367 per cent in the past decade, coping with population changes has become a way of life to Broward educators. They have recognized that more is required than merely building new schools and hiring additional teachers to meet increasing educational needs. Emphasis must be put on quality as well as quantity in the instructional system. The schools must shape the policies and practices to accommodate the full development of every youngster.

Fortunately, the attitude toward learning is favorable in Broward County. Parents are deeply concerned with the development of a better educational program for their children. Business and industrial leaders are fully aware that a superior school system is the backbone of a growing community and an absolute necessity for stable economic expansion. The dynamic and far-sighted leadership of educators, the willingness of the public to accept new ideas, and the need for vastly improved public school programs have resulted in a new and exciting experiment to improve instruction.

The Nova Plan

Known as the Nova Plan, a bold departure from traditional programs is being implemented at the South Florida Education Center —a vast 545-acre educational complex which eventually will include tax-supported schools encompassing kindergarten through junior college, plus a private four-year university with a graduate school. This instructional program, when finally formulated within the next few years, will present a continuous integrated progression of learning opportunities unparalleled in the history of education. While the various elements of the Nova Plan are to be found in various good schools throughout the United States, no school has combined these elements as part of a single program, as has Nova High School.

The Nova School has not been subject to many of the routine policies and traditions under which other schools operate in the county. This separation was planned so that new procedures could be developed and new courses of action employed to upgrade the total school program at all levels.

The concept of the South Florida Education Center was born in March, 1960, when Dean Dessenberger, then chairman of the Broward County Board of Public Instruction, decided that a weed-covered, surplus government airfield could become a living monument to education. Tireless efforts by the school board members and Broward's professional educators resulted in acquisition of the land and the construction of a new plan for public school education.

After a period of intensive research and planning, educators presented the Nova Plan to a large number of parent, business, and civic groups within the various communities throughout the country. The responses were enthusiastic.

Nova High School, which opened in September, 1963, was the initial unit of this center. It was unlike any other school in the country. Nova did not have an experimental course of studies, but its concept of teaching was innovative. Physical features, equipment, teaching aids, and instructional methods employed at Nova have been tested and proved individually in other school systems. Nova's uniqueness rests in the fact that, for probably the first time anywhere, all of these proven devices and techniques are being brought together with superior teachers and modern buildings for maximum efficiency. Focus is being put by the staff on new instructional techniques.

Nova's primary purpose is to utilize scientific methods of learning in a scientific age with an educational program truly tailored to individual needs. Nova is trying to bring into practice the theory of "taking each student as far as he can go."

The organization to help motivate each student to develop his maximum capabilities lies in utilizing the nongraded method of progression in the Nova High School. As a student masters one of a series of achievement levels in a course, he may continue to the next on any day of the school year. Since each level must be mastered in turn, no one can fail and no one is required to repeat an entire year's work in any subject. Students progress through the school's program at their own rate. They depart from the basic program of studies as interest and ability dictate.

However, eliminating grades *per se* is only a part of the overall picture. Operating on a trimester system, Nova has lengthened the school day and year. The daily schedule includes five regular class periods, each 70 minutes long, plus an optional period when students may do research or participate in non-credit co-curricular activities. The school year totals 200 days—40 days longer than the national average, 40 days longer than required by Florida law, and 25 days longer than any other public school system in the country. Such a schedule places increased demands upon both teachers and students. Both are meeting the challenge.

Teachers at Nova were selected on the basis of their willingness to try new ideas, academic qualifications, and previous experience—in that order. Their byword has been flexibility. The average teacher is almost 30 years old and has approximately five years of teaching experience, although the 60-teacher staff includes 15 beginning teachers and a handful of bona fide veterans. More than two thirds hold master's degrees or doctorates and those with bachelor's degrees have indicated they want to continue graduate studies.

Nova's opening marked the beginning of both a new school and a new world for nearly 1,500 students in year levels seven through ten. These boys and girls came from 80 elementary and junior high schools representing all of the geographical areas of the county. Admission was on a voluntary basis.

Nova includes a cross section of students, not just those who have above average intelligence. However, the interests and abilities of the total group have proven to be well above the average. It was immediately evident that this totally new approach to education held considerable promise for the students. Teachers, too, have been enthusiastic about the Nova Plan.

Perhaps the most intriguing feature of the program for students was the means whereby each student progressed at his own rate, commensurate with his abilities and interests. Among parents, this promise of continuous progress probably was the greatest single factor contributing to the widespread interest in this school. Schools often have been accused of fostering instructional programs aimed at a mediocrity of learning through group teaching. Such instruction can overwhelm the poor student, fail to challenge the talented student, and frequently offer nothing of lasting value to the average learner. At Nova each student, regardless of talent and intellect, is challenged and motivated to do his very best.

The focal point in the instructional program is the study unit, a chameleon-like creation which must assume the characteristics of a text, study contract, curriculum guide, lesson plan, and resource reference. Any given unit must clearly outline the nature of areas to be studied, exhibit understandable continuity, issue a challenge to the student's interest regardless of how infinitesimal interest might be, and still compensate for variances in individual ability and understanding. Within each study unit, a variety of work is accomplished by various students.

These requirements are not impossible to achieve, although the first impression may leave room for doubt. Teachers often feel that unless something can be of rousing success on the initial try, it should not be undertaken. However, the courageous teacher may very well make an excellent beginning with a relatively simple design. Only through use and refinement of materials can come the satisfaction and confidence necessary to organize a good program for continuous progress.

A "Hard-Core" Curriculum

Nova emphasizes a "hard-core" curriculum. All students are required to take English, mathematics, science, a foreign language, social science, technical science, and physical education each school year.

Students initially were grouped on the basis of grades and test results from schools which they previously attended. Further testing and evaluation during the school year resulted in some adjustments and students now are grouped according to achievement. Learning situations are organized to meet specific needs. Methods range from large-group instruction, with teaching teams and guest lecturers, to regular classroom instruction, small-group discussions, and individual research.

Talented students who progress rapidly may be graduated early with faculty permission. However, no one will be graduated in less than two and one third years above the ninth-year level. Nova's purpose is not to graduate students early but to give them more education over a longer period of time and in greater depth.

Physical Facilities

The curriculum at Nova is complemented by a physical plant which in itself is a departure from tradition. The environment was adapted to a pre-planned instructional program; the program was not restricted to conform to physical facilities. Classrooms have been constructed with movable partitions so that students may study in large or small rooms, as the day's activities dictate. Work space also has been built for small discussion groups and for individual research. In addition, ample room is available for teachers to confer, plan instructional programs, and coordinate materials.

The traditional library has been replaced by resource centers located in the language arts, mathematics, and science buildings, where reference books share space with tape recorders, microfilm readers, and teaching machines. While these instructional aids were expensive, they did not boost Nova's overall costs. Neither did such items as air-conditioning, carpeted floors, and special acoustical materials—all of which combine to make an atmosphere more conducive to learning.

These innovations were financed by omission of facilities which long have been considered standard equipment in conventional schools. Nova has no large assembly-type auditorium, no huge spectator-sized gymnasium, and no expensive kitchen and cafeteria. Students either bring their lunch or purchase food at snack bars, supervised by a dietitian, and eat in a protected outside dining area. The success of a nongraded program by no means is dependent upon such changes in physical facilities, but certainly these modifications play an important role in making school responsibilities easier for both students and teachers. The Nova Plan could be instituted in an ancient building since the intrinsic value of the Nova Plan is its instructional program.

Multimedia Teaching Devices

This philosophy of providing the best possible education has made Nova a prime showcase for automation. Overhead projectors and tape recorders are installed in all teacher centers. Students who miss an important lecture need not rely on second-hand accounts. They merely go to the resource center and listen to a playback on tape. In addition, closed-circuit television not only permits telecasts throughout the school but enables video tapes to be made of discussions and lectures for use at later dates. The TV system also allows the school to take advantage of programs telecast over South Florida's educational channels. Here, again, the expense of such a program has been offset by savings in construction costs.

Teachers Need A New Approach

Nova's radical departure from traditional education techniques obviously demanded a new approach by teachers, especially those acclimated to conventional classrooms. Instructors learned to "think Nova" during an intensive orientation period: a three-day introductory session during the late spring of 1963, a six-week stint for a portion of the faculty during the summer, and an additional three weeks for all personnel immediately preceding the September opening.

Despite the advantages of a nongraded system, it was clearly recognized that this was perhaps the most difficult program to implement of all those possible to consider. The enthusiasm of students was somewhat greater than that of the faculty, whose zeal was tempered by the enormity of the task.

Teachers soon discovered they were being placed in an entirely new role as instructional consultants. The autocratic position as a lockstep teacher shifted to that of a consultant, counselor, and resource person. For example, the teacher must evaluate the student's progress through entirely different methods than mere question-answer and test-paper feedback, so popular in lockstep teaching. Although these methods were utilized to some extent, they are not the only criteria for assessing student accomplishments. Teachers must make evaluations in terms of a student's total performance—the amount and quality of work he completes in class assignments, oral contributions, and depth studies.

Faculty thinking also had to be revised on such matters as sharing classroom responsibilities, increasing planning to utilize a wide range of curriculum materials, and allowing for a greater degree of individual instruction. It is rather difficult for a teacher to relinquish even a little of his traditional autocracy in the classroom. After all, the Nova Plan was requiring teachers to teach in a way they had not been taught. Changing from teaching by telling to teaching by consultation was not a minor professional variation.

However, the way has been smoothed, to a great extent, by providing as much time as possible for important planning sessions.

The selection, organization, and presentation of materials require careful and time-consuming effort. There must be a continuity of materials so that students can recognize and understand relationships of concepts in all subject areas. To this end, teacher aides and clerical personnel are being utilized to relieve instructors of paper work and permit them to devote more time to instruction and instructional planning.

Parents Are Enthusiastic

Parents overwhelmingly favor the Nova Plan despite the fact that they, too, have increased responsibilities. Their participation in the school program focuses in two major areas. First, parents are requested to emphasize continually to their children the importance of education, to encourage them to develop their special interests and talents, and to help them recognize that attending school is a privilege, not a chore. Second, parents are asked to give time to the school—to help organize and sponsor social activities, assist with auxiliary services, such as in resource centers and in the health clinic, and volunteer as clerical assistants.

Nova students must provide their own transportation or pay bus fare to and from school, pay a fee to defray expenses for additional instructional materials and automated teaching devices, and purchase special textbooks not available from state sources. When school administrators explained the Nova concept to parent groups while the school was still in planning stages, the magic phrase, "to upgrade our educational program," was the only selling point needed. Even before advance registration ended in 1963, students had to be turned away. The 1964–1965 complement of 400 new students was filled early in 1964, leaving a waiting list of more than 500 applicants. Before Nova first opened, parents of students accepted for enrollment attended an orientation session for a detailed briefing on school policies and an outline of parent-student responsibilities. A second progress report meeting was conducted for parents several months later.

From the beginning, Nova was planned as a nongraded school and opened on that basis with year levels seven through ten and with eleventh and twelfth years to be added successively. A kindergarten and elementary school opened in September, 1965, and three additional elementary schools, plus a school corresponding to the junior high level, are planned for the future to complete South Florida Education Center. All of these schools will be organized on a nongraded basis.

Since the Nova Plan will be coordinated from kindergarten through the university level, students soon will have unlimited opportunities for continuous progress. It will not be extraordinary for an elementary pupil talented in a particular field to be studying that subject on a junior high or possibly senior high level if justified by his rate of progress. The same holds true for exceptional junior and senior high school students who will have access to the junior college and, with special arrangements, to the private university as well.

Nova's nongraded program still is too new to be evaluated under the rigor of research procedures. Preliminary observations and subjective evaluations by the Nova staff, county supervisory personnel, and visiting educators rate the program with a unanimous "A." Plans already are underway for the gradual introduction of nongraded programs in other schools throughout the county. "Whatever proves successful will be incorporated in the rest of our school system, even if some modifications are necessary to fit these programs into existing school plant," said Dr. Myron L. Ashmore, superintendent of Broward County schools.

Perhaps the best proof of the effectiveness of the nongraded program is demonstrated in the Nova students themselves. They have volunteered to participate in this new program, traveling distances up to 15 miles twice each day, and have accepted the longer school year. Student morale is high and progress on an overall basis has been better than originally anticipated. The pattern of continuous progress probably has been the greatest single motivating factor for students. Slow learners find encouragement in mastery, not despair in failure; rapid learners discover the joy of meeting and conquering new challenges, not boredom in senseless repetition.

Everything, of course, is not viewed through rose-colored glasses. First-year problems, formidable in any new school, are multiplied in Nova. Innovations in equipment as well as instructional techniques are piled one on top of the other. Teachers and students alike are learning a whole new way of education.

Nova administrators are quick to concede that it takes time to adjust and then predict that it will take from three to five years before the nongraded program is refined to a maximum degree of value. Human resources do not change as quickly as technical innovations can be introduced.

Nevertheless, the Nova staff still believes that the total knowledge gained by its students through this method will far exceed that gained by utilizing traditional techniques. Teachers are eagerly awaiting results of a full-scale evaluation to be completed within the next two years to see whether they are correct in all they believe about the nongraded program at Nova High School.

CHAPTER 18

The Middletown Project: A Nongraded Secondary School

by

JOSEPH H. GAUDET

Joseph H. Gaudet has guided the development of the Middletown Project, one of the first nongraded secondary school programs. Superintendent Gaudet was the principal investigator in the study supported by the Fund for the Advancement of Education which designed the new program for the Middletown (Rhode Island) High School.

EARLY IN 1957 the Middletown School Committee appointed an advisory committee to examine the need for a high school and to report its findings with recommendations within six months. This was done and the report recommended that the town at once set about building a six-year high school. The school committee accepted the report and adopted the recommendations made by the advisory committee.

By May, 1958, authorization had been given by the voters of the town to assure the construction of the high school. For the superintendent and his staff, this required careful preparation of a plan describing the school's proposed functions in order to specify the form of the new school. In July and August, 1958, ten meetings were held with the school committee, the staff, invited guests, and consultants. The latter were superintendents and high school principals from various New England cities and towns. These meetings were planned as orientation meetings in order to enable the school committee to decide how the new school should be organized for instruction.

In January, 1959, an all-day session was held in one of the school auditoriums. A panel of nine school administrators discussed modern thinking about the functions of a comprehensive high school and the latest trends in school planning and building construction. The general public, the school committee, and several town and state officials were present at this meeting. The architects chosen to develop this school were in attendance also. This assembly helped crystallize the thinking of the community about the program of studies for the new high school.

From Function to Form

From January to December, 1959, numerous meetings were held with different groups of citizens, the staff, and consultants in a very real attempt to spell out in detail the educational specifications of this school. The erection of a high school in a community which had never had one of its own became a highly involved enterprise. Educators were successful in cooperatively developing what seemed to be absolutely necessary, a *Statement of Philosophy and Purposes* which was representative of what Middletown citizens wanted their high school to do and to be.

In summary, this *Statement of Philosophy and Purposes* dictated that:

1. Each child is entitled to an education and that education should be unique to his own abilities and capacities.
2. In order to achieve maximum educational benefits for each child, existing modes and patterns should be disregarded if it becomes apparent that other ways will lead more surely to our main objectives.
3. The classroom teacher is fundamentally the key to the good education of a child and, therefore, curriculum and technique must reflect the best judgments of the teacher.

Next, it was time to draw up a blueprint of what to teach and how to teach it. A grant from the Fund for the Advancement of Education made it possible for the professional staff to work intensively on the new program with remuneration. The Middletown Project came into existence. And with the co-sponsorship and assistance from Rhode Island College, the faculty began an eighteen-month study of how to implement the officially adopted *Statement of Philosophy and Purposes*. With a staff inexperienced with high school teaching beyond grade ten, this was a more formidable task than at first envisioned. High ideals necessitated detailed and original planning. Old practices had to give way to new ones.

The following describes the Middletown Project. In effect, this was a charge to the staff participants, and it served as a checklist for their planning and evaluation of operational procedures.

The Middletown Project

1. The Middletown Project is representative of a basic philosophy of educational purposes, freely drawn and essentially self-serving to the needs and interests of the youth of Middletown. It must exemplify and be responsive to the role and functions of a secondary educational institution during the latter half of the twentieth century.

2. The Middletown Project seeks in operational detail to:
   a) Provide a program of education tailored to meet the needs of the individual student.
   b) Deploy, capitalize upon, and otherwise commit the best capabilities of each staff member to the good of the greatest number of students—an application of the concept of team teaching.
   c) Provide the opportunity for, and encourage the development of, talent and capabilities possessed by various students and discernible in their behavior.
   d) Make available staff services and physical facilities for the further advancement of learning beyond the days and hours of what we know as the normal school day, including adult education and summer school programs.
   e) Arrange and regulate the learning schedules for the various disciplines as will best suit a proper and fruitful pursuit of

knowledge and understanding. This would mean that the school day would not be subjected to a rigid system of six 45- or 55-minute periods; the step length of learning periods would be set according to the needs of the specific subject matter being studied.

f) Provide an adequate program of guidance and counseling, along with a system of pupil program reporting that will be significant and meaningful to the individual student.

In setting forth these objectives, it was acknowledged that their implementation and attainment would be dependent upon certain factors which may or may not be significantly mitigating. Among these are:

a) availability of staff,
b) physical plan limitations,
c) the ability of the taxpayer to finance the program in full,
d) varying demands which may be made by law or society which would take precedence.

The Pattern Emerges

The pattern of educational programming for each child attending Middletown's six-year high school is based on the thesis that a child progresses academically as fast and as far as his God-given talents will permit. This, in turn, is based on an assurance that whatever a child is doing academically is what he can do best of all and, hopefully, includes all that he can do in the matter of specific choices of disciplines.

Symbolically, as shown in Figure One, all of the children are placed in the center of a circle at the beginning of their tenure in this six-year program. Each child proceeds at his own academic rate toward the outer perimeter as fast as he can. The normal limits of the perimeter represents six years of academic pursuit for the child with normal mental ability. Then it follows that, as time goes on, children will be at many different positions in the academic cycle. It also follows that all children will not necessarily be together in conventional groups, nor at the same traditional grade levels.

Scheduling in this situation became very complex. The complexities in scheduling were due, in part, to the limitations of space, staff,

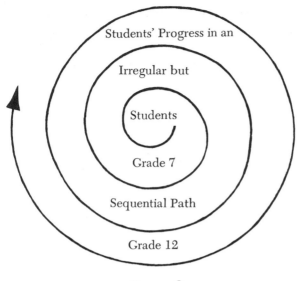

FIGURE ONE

and human inabilities to change teaching practices. However, developments in data processing, schedule planning, and new administrative techniques lead to the belief that schools can expect some help in the solution of both scheduling and in-service education problems. Research and experimentation currently going on in these areas should give a valuable thrust to schools' efforts at nongrading.

The Curriculum

The curriculum of Middletown High School was designed to measure progress by achievement and to schedule groups accordingly. The curriculum for each discipline—in the humanities, the social sciences, the physical sciences, the commercial courses, and the manual arts—has been constructed to cover learnings in each area for 60 months of study. Each discipline is laid out in discrete, measurable units of learning or by organizing concepts. Thus, the English curriculum, over a six-year period, consists of 212 units, the social sciences curriculum has 441 units, and so on. Classes are set up for 25 pupils, all of whom are working within a related cluster of concepts. Students master each successive concept at varying rates.

(Appendix F gives a student's program of studies and Appendix G shows the school's time schedule, using periods of varying lengths.)

The curriculum calls for regrouping classes, at intervals, more frequently than in the traditional school, where it is done by the semester or year. It presents a difficulty because of human inability to construct pupil, teacher, room, and subject schedules in short periods of time. Thus, the Middletown Project is difficult to manage because of the technical problems of scheduling and rescheduling. This technical difficulty should be solved in the near future with the use of data processing and new administrative techniques in scheduling.

The professional staff also had to be concerned with the managerial aspects of opening a high school in addition to studying the curriculum. The following are some of these concerns:

1. *How long should teaching periods be for each subject?* It was decided that they need not be uniform in length and thus there are 35-, 50-, and 70-minute periods.
2. *What subjects shall be taught?* Some are required by law—English, American history, and physical education. The other subjects at Middletown are similar to those one would find in any good comprehensive high school.
3. *How shall we teach?* With us, thus far, this is generally along traditional lines, i.e., one teacher for each subject for every class, although some beginnings have been made in what is broadly called team teaching and inter- and intra-departmental sharing of the teaching of subject matter. Some integration between subjects was effected: English and social studies and mathematics and science are handled in a special way.
4. *How shall a pupil's program be determined?* This is being done by counselors who have a 50 per cent teaching load and a 50 per cent guidance and counseling assignment. There are six counselors and one full-time guidance director.
5. *What about a child's permanent record for the purpose of providing transcripts to other schools upon transfer?* The point system, whereby credit is given for successful achievement in the various disciplines, along with his mark, denoting quality of performance, can be converted into a standardized, traditional type of transcript which, in effect, relates achievement in terms of one, two, three, or four years of English, foreign languages, mathematics, etc.

6. *What about the marking and reporting system?* Pupils are issued a report four times per year. The report is constructed to show the pupil his progress in terms of achievement in whatever subjects he is taking by using a bar graph to denote his progress. He will find that he is progressing at a normal speed, less than normal speed, or faster than normal speed. He will also be given a mark, A, B, C, or D, to denote the quality of his work.

7. *How are in-coming pupils to Middletown High School placed?* Their transfer records are evaluated and after appropriate testing, as needed, a pupil is placed with a class which is doing the same work—as much the same as possible—as his class in the previous school.

The Middletown Project in Operation

The problem of implementing everything desired by the staff turned out to be both the severest and the most stimulating kind of challenge. The step-by-step conceptualized curricula, in some cases, were not satisfactory in practice. Concepts sometimes were in the wrong order, badly spaced, pedagogically meaningless, or out of balance. This was due, in large measure, to inexperience in judging the relative merits of concepts and the time needed to teach them, as well as to insufficient development of understanding about the conceptual technique itself. It was plainly evident that revisions and deeper analysis were in order. This is continuing and is part of a regular staff study.

The ability of teachers to handle what is, surely, a more sophisticated and discriminatory way of teaching bears scrutiny. The school suffered from a lack of teaching experience on the part of many new and young staff members. A firm command of good methodology is absolutely essential at Middletown High School. Unfortunately, one cannot assume that a teacher has the ability to teach because he has graduated as a teacher. The administration intends to do something about this: (1) to conduct regular staff meetings on methodology, and (2) to observe teachers in action more frequently than in the past with personal conferences to follow these visitations.

This lack of understanding of the philosophy and implementation procedures of the Middletown Project on the part of some teachers was due to the fact that some members of the faculty—perhaps twenty—joined the faculty at the last minute. Some teachers were bewildered; others felt more sure of themselves but were more heartily committed to the traditional way of teaching.

It may seem that there was an excessive amount of confusion and defeat. This was not the case, but it must be remembered that the goals and objectives had been well agreed upon and the ills and pains of this creaking mechanism were all the more obvious to those who had so painstakingly structured the program. Furthermore, it is generally agreed that the program can be perfected and by no means should it be scrapped.

Three Years Prompts Some Observations

The students understand quite well that academic achievement is a personal matter and that progress is recognized, evaluated, and credited to them personally. Individual motivation is a much more critical factor than might be the case in a traditional system. The pupil who possesses it to a high degree advances rapidly, while the less ambitious or lackadaisical very often makes less academic progress than he should, considering his intellectual ability and capacity.

The Middletown Project functions best with the normal, well-motivated students. Students whose academic performance is below the normal level become a burden on the operational capacities of the Middletown Project. There is increasing evidence that students can make remarkably fast academic progress if given the opportunity to learn at their own pace. This is the key tenet of the Middletown Project. As we approach a full six-year cycle in the Middletown Project, an increasing number of students are successfully completing the normal high school academic requirements in one or more disciplines by the eleventh year. The slower student, the student whose intellectual ability is such that he moves more slowly, does not drop out but joins his peers at a slower rate.

The Middletown Project requires teachers to use a variety of classroom methodolgies. The group-lecture method plays only a small part in the way a teacher conducts a class. It is the rule, rather than the exception, to find groups of students at different levels of achievement in any one class. The teachers are unusually aware of the academic achievement of the individual student. They must conduct him from one curricular concept to the next as slowly or as rapidly as he achieves mastery of the subject. While this is difficult for the teacher to do, it is rewarding and becomes dramatic evidence of the teacher's power to motivate and assist students.

The role of the counselor becomes extremely important in the nongraded school. Students look to their counselor for guidance, encouragement, and advice. Those whose progress is slow must be guided into areas of study where success can be attained. The fast-moving student must be provided with schedules and programs to meet his needs. Care must be taken to guide the normal achiever to his own best interests.

The burden on the administration becomes one of thoughtful adjustment of staff, space, and schedules in response to the never ending demands of change. Use of the limitations imposed by a fixed number of teachers, a fixed number of classroom spaces, and a fixed number of clock hours per day becomes the measure to which the administration can fulfill the promise and objectives of the Middletown Project. In the three years during which we have operated, it is fair to say that everyone—especially the principal, the guidance director, and the various heads of departments—are trying to fulfill the promise made to each child at Middletown High School in the *Statement of Philosophy and Purposes* adopted by the School Committee in June, 1960.

For the past three years no high school staff has worked harder to fulfill an ideal and a philosophy. It has been difficult and frustrating at times; but, however noble the aspirations, the faculty could not have made any progress without the faith and support of the people in the community and without the confidence of the school committee. The problems of the second year were neither as big nor as numerous as those of the first year. These problems will be solved by the trust placed in the staff and faith in the principles set up seven years ago.

CHAPTER 19

A Continuous Progress Plan at Brigham Young University, Provo, Utah

by

Edwin A. Read

Dr. Read, formerly the director of the Brigham Young University Laboratory School, is now the director of the William Stewart Laboratory School at the University of Utah.

T HE STORY of the Continuous Progress School at Brigham Young University began in 1959. At the time, a new director was appointed at B.Y.U. Laboratory School. The laboratory school, which included all grade levels and was part of a large university, which many of its graduates entered, was an ideal setting for development and experimentation in education.

One of the attractions of Brigham Young University was the dean of the College of Education, Dr. Asahel D. Woodruff, a widely recognized educational psychologist and an advanced thinker in the field of curriculum. With Dean Woodruff working on improved curriculum designs and on more effective instructional procedures and Dr. Read, the new director, seeking to describe a more efficient educational system than the graded school, it was natural that these two men should get their heads together. In the establishment and success of the Continuous Progress School at Brigham Young University, other factors were no less important than those mentioned above. The university president, the dean of the college of education, and many faculty members of the college held the opinion that the laboratory school should be an experimental and research department, taking leadership in searching for ways of improving public school education. The laboratory school faculty, a select group, was also interested in experimentation and pilot demonstration projects. These common interests made it possible for the college dean and the laboratory school director to work successfully with a representative committee in the formulation and description of an educational system which was labeled the Continuous Progress Plan.

Since the laboratory school is a department of the Brigham Young University, and, as such, has no legal connection with the Provo public schools, students are admitted by application. There are many more applications than there are vacancies in the school. An honest effort is made to maintain a heterogeneous school population in order that any experimental program under way would involve students who are fairly typical of those in the public schools. However, two factors tend to make the students at Brigham Young University Laboratory School similar: first, either they or their parents are anxious to have them enrolled in the school; and second, they tend to have similar cultural backgrounds. Similarity in cultural background also made the introduction of the Continuous Progress Plan relatively easy at the laboratory school.

Developing a Plan

As indicated earlier, a committee representing the laboratory school and three other departments within the college of education worked out the details of the Continuous Progress Plan. Laboratory school personnel were kept fully informed of the committee's work. And by the time the system's description was completed, there was relatively little in it that was new to the faculty.

The proposal for the implementation of the plan was to introduce it through a small portion of the elementary and secondary programs. The subjects selected on the elementary level were reading, spelling, and arithmetic; on the secondary level, English and mathematics. Selecting these basic subjects had the advantage of involving all students in the experimental program while still not committing the entire educational program to the new concept. On the secondary level, it had the advantage of requiring the participation of only a few teachers, thus making involvement somewhat optional.

Once approved by the faculty, the experimental program had to be taken to the community, or in this case, to the parents of the children enrolled in the laboratory school. This was done through the Parent-Teacher Association, whose advisory committee had already been introduced to the plan and had expressed support. Two presentations were made to the Parent-Teacher Association. Visual devices were used extensively in order to help parents understand the plan. The attitude of the vast majority of parents toward the nongraded idea was enthusiastic.

The Continuous Progress Plan is an appealing idea to most parents and teachers. It calls for the establishment of a sequential curriculum of carefully selected and important concepts, symbols, skills, and habits free of artificial progress barriers such as grade levels and promotion dates. It proposes an educational system which will make it possible for students to progress through this curriculum at their most efficient rates of learning. As a means of accomplishing this, it suggests individualized approaches to instruction in each of the various subject fields. With the aid of curriculum materials especially designed for independent use, it encourages students to compete with their own records and to achieve up to the level of their own established academic standards, while also permitting them to engage in self-initiated, undeclared competition with classmates of their own choosing. A large share of the responsibility for progress is placed upon the shoulders of the individual student. This not only develops a sense of responsibility but also stimulates and encourages initiative.

Contents of the Plan

The curriculum of the Continuous Progress Plan might be thought of as a core of essential, common learnings carefully selected, articulated, and freed of artificial barriers which tend to restrict and force a lockstep on the progress of students. Surrounding this central core of learnings is an unlimited field of related learnings which are open to students who have the interest and inclination to pursue them.

The curriculum of the Continuous Progress Plan is divided into four major divisions, each of which is further subdivided into steps, or levels, for the convenience of progress and curriculum designations. The four major divisions are: the entrance division, divided into four curriculum levels; the cultural division, divided into four levels; the pre-specialization division of five levels; and the specialization division, with a varied number of levels depending upon the nature of the post-high school program in which the student is engaged. The curricula of the entrance and cultural divisions correspond roughly with that found in the elementary school, while the curriculum of the pre-specialization division corresponds with that of the present secondary school. The specialization division corresponds with today's post-high school programs, both vocational and collegiate.

While the entire curriculum is open and available to all, most children in the primary school will be engaged in the curriculum of the entrance division. This curriculum is the door or entrance of the formal educational program and, as such, is designed to perform very special and limited functions. It places major emphasis on the essential tools of learning, including the language arts—reading, writing, spelling, learning how to study, and using numbers—and how to use them in the acquisition of knowledge.

The major purpose of this aspect of the curriculum is to provide the students with the tools and methods of inquiry. No longer is a child frustrated by the task of having to acquire knowledge before he possesses the prerequisite tools of learning. During these early years he is helped to discover the thrill which comes from acquiring new ideas through the use of the skills of investigation he possesses. This increases the appetite for new skills which are, in turn, used in a constant search for a greater understanding of the world around him.

While involved in the curriculum of the entrance division, children are organized into modified self-contained classes on the basis of age. Individualized approaches to teaching and learning are employed throughout this program in order that each child may progress at his most efficient rate of learning.

Movement, Flexibility, and Progress

The content subjects are used as the vehicles for teaching basic skill subjects. Special interest projects are undertaken by these younger children either in the classroom or in the project rooms of the instructional materials center as they begin to practice their newly acquired tools of learning.

Once a child shows that he is adequately prepared for a more formal study of the content fields, he is introduced to the curriculum of the cultural division. Under the guidance of the teacher, and with the aid of specially designed study kits or guides, children in the cultural division of the curriculum use all their acquired skills of inquiry in a study of the social sciences, physical sciences, and other related fields of learning. They work on projects individually or in groups, meeting with the teacher periodically for the purpose of clarifying concepts and receiving directions. The ideal of enrichment based upon individual interests and needs is now totally possible since students can progress at their own best paces. They can now digress from the common core of the curriculum into related studies of particular interest and value to them.

While it is recognized that learning skills will be strengthened and improved through their use in the search for knowledge, formal instruction in basic tools such as reading and spelling is continued as part of the curriculum of the cultural division. For the rapid learner, this results in an ever-widening phase of skills and in more efficiency in the use of the skills he possesses. For the slow learner, it results in steady growth rather than the frustration which comes from being pushed ahead in work beyond his depth. Like the more able student, the slow learner enjoys some success and growth each day as he progresses through the curriculum at his best pace. It is believed that this concession to his rate of learning will result in acceleration for him through all the following years of school in contrast with the faltering progress he would make in the present school system where he frequently faces the impossible task of keeping up with more able learners.

Most students who enter the secondary school will be ready for the pre-specialization division of the curriculum. Some learners, the more able scholars, will have advanced some distance in the study of this new aspect of the school curriculum since they had been introduced to it while still in the upper elementary school, while others, the slower learners will still be involved in the curriculum of the cultural division. The students in the secondary school are not organized into classes for instruction. The class organization has relevance only to student government, activities, and social functions. Instead of going to a first-period class, the student begins his day by going directly to his own individual study station or carrel, which serves as his home base. It is from this station that he plans his study activities which will include independent study, research in the instructional materials center, project work in laboratories and shops, individual and group meetings with teachers, discussion sessions with other students, physical activities, and other activities as prescribed by the nature of his program.

Independent Study and Small Groups

The amount of time spent in individual study will vary from student to student, depending upon his initiative, his capacities for learning, and his particular temperament. Many students will spend approximately fifty per cent of their time in independent study. Much of this individual study will be done at their individual study stations or carrels where they keep their books, progress charts, and other study equipment. It seems entirely possible that in the future many of these study stations will be equipped with television screens, ear phones, and facilities for simply dialing video-taped lectures and demonstrations. The individual study station is equipped with a signal or inter-communication device whereby the student can notify an assistant teacher of his need for help. This assistant either proceeds to the student's carrel or converses with him over the inter-communication system.

These study stations, or carrels, are located centrally and adjacent to the instructional materials center. Nearby, are teaching studios, discussion or seminar rooms, testing rooms, project rooms, and laboratories. The average student spends approximately forty per cent of his time working in small groups in these facilities.

Small clusters of students are called into the teaching studio by the professional teacher for common-need or expressed common-interest instruction. These groups range in size from one to fifteen students. They are composed of students who have either expressed or demonstrated a need for the same instruction. In these small group or cluster sittings, students exchange ideas, make reports, and receive instructions from the teacher. Such meetings last only as long as is necessary to achieve the objectives of the lesson. Many clusters or individuals receive all the help needed within a five- to twenty-five-minute class period and then return to their study stations in order that the teacher might meet with other students. Some groups of students proceed directly from the teaching studio to discussion rooms where they continue their discussion under the direction of a student leader or an assistant teacher. It is by means of this system of study and instruction that each student is able to progress at his most efficient rate of learning. He is guided in his studies not only by his teachers and assistant teachers but also by a study kit, or guide, which directs him from one learning experience to another as he seeks to acquire important skills, habits, concepts, and their related symbols.

Evaluation

As each unit of study is completed, the student prepares himself for an evaluation of his learning. Even before the test is taken, the student knows what standard he must achieve. His individual standards in each subject have been established in conferences with teachers, counselors, and other members of the instructional team. There is a quantity standard, in terms of the amount of progress a particular student should be able to accomplish during a given unit of time, and a quality standard, in terms of depth of learning. For example, some of the more able students will have standards of one and one-half to two times the amount of work normally accomplished by most students. Slow learners will not be expected to cover as much of the curriculum in a given unit of time as the average student. However, they will be expected to demonstrate satisfactory levels of learning in terms of their own established quantity and quality standards. Thus, the progress of all students is measured in terms of their individually established standards. Students who are falling behind their established time schedule are quickly identified through a daily record system and are called in to meet with teachers or counselors. If a student fails to meet his established quality standard in a given test, he is required to undertake further study in order that he might raise his level of performance before being allowed to progress to the next unit of study.

Facilities

Certain unique instructional facilities will already be evident to the reader. They include, at the very heart of the school, an instructional materials center which houses all types of learning resources and provides space for listening, viewing, conferring, and developing skills. Spaces are also provided for teacher and student production of materials and programs.

The emphasis on inquiry and the search for knowledge calls for laboratory-type facilities which house the necessary equipment and materials for individual and group research and investigation. Other unique facilities include carrels, teaching studios, and testing rooms. Discussion and seminar rooms are not unique to this type of school since they are found in a number of the better schools throughout the country.

Not all of these facilities can be found in the B.Y.U. Laboratory School. Individual study stations, or carrels, are provided for students while they are studying those subjects included in the experimental program—high school mathematics, high school English, and foreign languages. Certain carrels are equipped with ear phones and telephone dials so that students might listen to lectures and other recorded materials stored in tape decks, which are remotely controlled. Teaching studios are also used effectively as spaces where students and teachers meet to discuss and clarify concepts which have been acquired by study and other means of investigation. A testing room is located near the carrel area and adjacent to one of the teaching studios. A secretary supervises this room, providing students with appropriate tests from a locked file which contains carefully constructed unit tests for each of the courses in the experimental program.

Stronger Beliefs

No controlled research has yet been conducted with the Continuous Progress Plan in order to compare it with similar groups of students in a more conventional graded high school. However, a careful study of student progress has caused the laboratory school faculty to believe more fervently in the Continuous Progress Plan than it did when the idea was adopted four years ago. Students in the laboratory school continue to achieve well above the national norms on standardized tests. The more able students now find it possible to complete one and one-half to two years of work in an experimental subject each year. As a result, many of these students have been able to graduate early from high school and begin a study of advanced placement courses for college credit. The less-able student finds himself able to succeed in courses which would normally be too difficult for him to achieve above a D or failing grade. Working at his own rate, he can achieve satisfactory levels of attainment even though it may take him more than a year to complete a course.

Some of the most promising results are found in the elementary division of the laboratory school where children of all abilities are enjoying success in terms of their own capacities for learning. While associating with children of their own age, these pupils continue to progress at their most efficient rates of learning as they move into aspects of the curriculum for which they have readiness. In one primary classroom will be found children who are just learning to read, mixed with others advanced to the third- or fourth-grade reading level. Similarly, in spelling, children can be seen working at their own rates and at the levels for which they have readiness. It is not uncommon to find second-year children, with a particular flair for the language arts, spelling on a difficult fourth- or fifth-grade level.

After four years of experimentation perhaps the best measure of the program can be found in the continued support which the program receives from parents. Each year about 600 applications are received for the approximately eight vacancies which occur in the entire laboratory school.

While the program has not expanded greatly during its few years of existence, it has improved significantly as curriculum materials have been developed. These curriculum materials are produced by teachers who are given released time for the development of instructional resources. These curriculum materials include study guides, tapes, filmstrips, programmed materials, and records. After several revisions, most of these materials are proving to be highly satisfactory as tools for individual study. With these aids and the opportunities for progress provided through this new system of education, students are learning to be scholars who recognize their responsibility for progress and who possess the skills and study habits necessary for the pursuit and acquisition of knowledge.

APPENDICES

SELECTED BIBLIOGRAPHY

NOTES

INDEX

APPENDIX A

PROGRESS REPORT

Elementary Department, Appleton Public Schools,
Appleton, Wisconsin

PROGRESS DURING THE YEAR
SPRING REPORT

	IN LINE WITH ABILITY	SHOULD DO BETTER

READING
STRENGTHS
WEAKNESSES
WORK IS · LEVEL FOR AGE

SPELLING
STRENGTHS
WEAKNESSES
WORK IS · LEVEL FOR AGE

LANGUAGE
STRENGTHS
WEAKNESSES
WORK IS · LEVEL FOR AGE

ARITHMETIC
STRENGTHS
WEAKNESSES
WORK IS · LEVEL FOR AGE

SOCIAL STUDIES

SCIENCE

MUSIC

ART

PHYSICAL EDUCATION & HEALTH

COMMENTS (Fall Report)

Times Tardy

COMMENTS (Spring Report)

Times Tardy

ACADEMIC ACHIEVEMENT
FALL REPORT

	IN LINE WITH ABILITY	SHOULD DO BETTER

READING
STRENGTHS
WEAKNESSES
WORK IS · LEVEL FOR AGE

SPELLING
STRENGTHS
WEAKNESSES
WORK IS · LEVEL FOR AGE

LANGUAGE
STRENGTHS
WEAKNESSES
WORK IS · LEVEL FOR AGE

ARITHMETIC
STRENGTHS
WEAKNESSES
WORK IS · LEVEL FOR AGE

SOCIAL STUDIES

SCIENCE

MUSIC

ART

PHYSICAL EDUCATION & HEALTH

APPENDIX B

REPORT OF PUPIL PROGRESS

Intermediate Department, Cabool Schools R-4, Cabool, Missouri

APPRECIATION AND PARTICIPATION IN:

I. MUSIC & ART

PERIODS 1 2 3 4

1. ENJOYS HEARING MUSIC
2. TAKES PART IN GROUP SINGING
3. SHOWS AN INTEREST IN RHYTHMS AND MUSIC
4. SHOWS INTEREST IN FUNDAMENTALS
5. SHOWS INTEREST IN ART ACTIVITIES
6. EXPRESSES HIMSELF WELL IN ART
7. IS CAREFUL IN USE OF MATERIALS

ATTENDANCE RECORD

PERIODS 1 2 3 4

DAYS PRESENT
DAYS ABSENT
TIMES TARDY
HEIGHT
WEIGHT

LIBRARY READING (Number Read)

PERIODS 1 2 3 4

"A" GROUP—FICTION
"B" GROUP—SOCIAL SCIENCE
"C" GROUP—SCIENCE

· HOME REPORT

PERIODS 1 2 3 4

1. DOES YOUR CHILD GET 10 TO 12 HOURS SLEEP EACH NIGHT?
2. DOES HE EAT BREAKFAST?
3. DOES HE DRINK COFFEE OR TEA?
4. ARE THERE ANY PHYSICAL DEFECTS THAT WOULD RETARD HIS PROGRESS?
5. DOES HE SEEM TO ENJOY SCHOOL?
6. DOES HE WORRY OVER SCHOOL?
7. WHAT SUBJECTS SEEM MOST DIFFICULT
8. DOES HE HAVE HOME DUTIES?
9. HOW OFTEN DOES HE GO TO MOVIES OR SCHOOL NIGHTS?
10. HOW LATE IS YOUR CHILD ALLOWED TO WATCH TELEVISION?
11. ARE THE TELEVISION PROGRAMS CAREFULLY SELECTED?

* All facts asked for in this report will be helpful to the school. It is hoped parents will fill this out as completely as possible.

PROGRESS IN BASIC SKILLS

EXPLANATION OF MARKS:
S—STRENGTH IN THE TRAIT—SUPERIOR TO GENERAL CAPACITY.
N—NORMAL DEVELOPMENT AND GROWTH.
W—WEAKNESS IN THE TRAIT.
I—MARKED IMPROVEMENT.

I. READING

PERIODS 1 2 3 4

1. SHOWS INTEREST IN READING
2. UNDERSTANDS WHAT HE READS SILENTLY
3. READS WELL ORALLY WITH EXPRESSION
4. WORKS OUT NEW WORDS ALONE
5. LOOKS UP WORD MEANINGS INDEPENDENTLY
6. READS VOLUNTARILY MANY KINDS OF MATERIAL DURING FREE TIME

II LANGUAGE ARTS

1. EXPRESSES IDEAS CLEARLY
2. USES CORRECT ENGLISH IN WRITTEN WORK
3. USES CORRECT ENGLISH IN CONVERSATION
4. SPELLS CORRECTLY WORDS FOR HIS LEVEL
5. SPELLS WORDS IN WRITTEN WORK CORRECTLY
6. WRITES NEATLY AND PLAINLY

III ARITHMETIC

1. KNOWS AND UNDERSTANDS THE NUMBER FACTS FOR HIS LEVEL
2. CAN USE FUNDAMENTAL SKILLS FOR HIS LEVEL
3. CAN SOLVE THOUGHT PROBLEMS FOR HIS LEVEL

SOCIAL STUDIES & SCIENCE

1. KNOWS THE HISTORICAL AND GEOGRAPHICAL FACTS FOR HIS LEVEL
2. HAS AN APPRECIATION FOR SOCIAL PROBLEMS
3. TAKES PART IN PLANNING AND WORKING OUT PROJECTS AND UNITS
4. MAKES WORTHWHILE CONTRIBUTIONS TO CLASS DISCUSSIONS
5. KNOWS SCIENCE & HEALTH FACTS FOR HIS LEVEL

CITIZENSHIP AND PERSONALITY DEVELOPMENT

THE TEACHER HAS CHECKED ONLY THOSE ITEMS WHICH SEEM TO GIVE THE BEST INFORMATION ABOUT THE PUPIL.

I. WORK HABITS

PERIODS 1 2 3 4

1. FOLLOWS DIRECTIONS
2. MAKES GOOD USE OF TIME
3. IS NEAT AND ORDERLY
4. BEGINS WORK PROMPTLY
5. COMPLETES WORK BEGUN

II SOCIAL BEHAVIOR

1. RESPECTS SCHOOL PROPERTY AND PROPERTY OF OTHERS
2. GETS ALONG WELL WITH OTHERS
3. IS DEPENDABLE
4. HAS GOOD LUNCH ROOM MANNERS

III EMOTIONAL DEVELOPMENT

1. ACCEPTS CRITICISM AND TRIES TO PROFIT BY IT
2. HAS SELF CONFIDENCE
3. IS HAPPY AND WELL ADJUSTED

IV. PHYSICAL AND HEALTH HABITS

1. HAS GOOD POSTURE
2. TAKES PART IN OUTDOOR PLAY ACTIVITIES
3. SHOWS GOOD SPORTSMANSHIP
4. REFLECTS GOOD SLEEP AND REST HABITS

APPENDIX C

First Year: Primary Plan Conference Form
Monteith School, Grosse Pointe, Michigan

Pupil .... Teacher ....

Year in Plan .... Date ....

1. Attitudes:
2. Behavior:
3. Attention to Directions:
4. Carry-through on Responsibilities:
5. Interest Span:
6. Health Habits:
7. Independence in Work:
8. Relations With Fellow Pupils:

LEVELS OF DEVELOPMENT

Level Child Is In At This Time	1	2	3	4	5	6	7	8	9

Reading Progress:
Teacher Comments:

APPENDIX D

Second Year: Primary Plan Conference Form
Monteith School, Grosse Pointe, Michigan

Pupil .... Teacher ....

Year in Plan .... Date ....

1. Attitudes:	5. Health Habits:
2. Behavior:	6. Quality of Work:
3. Attention to Directions:	7. Carry-through on Responsibility:
4. Interest Span:	8. Relations With Other Pupils:

LEVELS OF DEVELOPMENT

Reading Level Child Is In At This Time	1	2	3	4	5	6	7	8	9

Reading Progress:

Arithmetic:	Writing:
Language:	Spelling:

Teacher Comments:

242

APPENDIX E

Third and Fourth Years: Primary Conference Form
Monteith School, Grosse Pointe, Michigan

Pupil .... Teacher ....
Year in Plan .... Date ....
Days Absent .... Times Tardy ....

Behavior	Ability in Organizing
Health Habits	Listening Habits
Study Habits	Responsibility
Quality of Work	Others:

LEVELS OF DEVELOPMENT

Reading Level Child Is In At This Time	1	2	3	4	5	6	7	8	9	10

Reading:	
Arithmetic:	Science:
Language:	Physical Education:
Writing:	Music:
Spelling:	Art:
Social Studies:	

(Teacher Comment will be found on the back)

APPENDIX F

Student Schedule, Nongraded High School
Middletown, Rhode Island

1964 – 1965

KANE MICHAEL   67

	STUDENT NO.	HOME ROOM	COUNSELOR	PREVIOUS CREDITS
	44662	104	0	– – –

MIDDLETOWN HIGH SCHOOL
MIDDLETOWN, RHODE ISLAND

STUDENT SCHEDULE

SUBJECT AND YEAR	COURSE NO.	TEACHER NO.	PERIODS	ROOM	
STUDY HALL	10		A134		
MECH DRAW 1	859	069	A25	254	MR L BAILEY
ALGEBRA 1 T	332	835	B	244	MISS F STILLMAN
STUDY HALL	10		C1		
PHYSED	907		C24	BGYM	
WOOD 1	851	869	C35	311	MR R SULLIVAN
BIOLOGY	435	036	D	203	MR P ALMEIDA
ENGLISH 9	127	333	E	252	MRS A GROSS
EARLY WLD HIS	228	444	F	240	MR K KERR

APPENDIX G

Time Schedule, Nongraded High School
Middletown, Rhode Island

	Monday	Tuesday	Wednesday	Thursday	Friday
8:05* / 8:15 / 8:20	H.R.	H.R.	H.R.	H.R.	H.R.
	A–1	A–2	A–3	F–4	F–5
9:05 / 9:10 / 9:25	B–1	B–2	B–3	E–4	E–5
9:50 / 10:15	C–1	C–2	C–3	D–4	D–5
10:40 / 11:05			D–3		
11:15 / 11:25	D–1	D–2	E–3	C–4	C–5
12:35 / 12:40 / 12:50	E–1	E–2	F–3	B–4	B–5
1:25 / 1:40	F–1	F–2	G–3	A–4	A–5
2:30	X–1	X–2	X–3	X–4	X–5
3:30					

* Home Room late bell at 8:05

Selected Bibliography

Compiled by JAN SMITH *and* MARILYN BEEBE
UNIVERSITY SCHOOL, INDIANA UNIVERSITY

Anderson, Richard C. "The Case for Non-graded Homogeneous Grouping," *Elementary School Journal* 62:193–197, January, 1962.
The author discusses, in progress report fashion, changes in school organization of the New Brunswick, N.J., schools. In this, the first of two articles, nongraded homogeneous grouping is explained as the design used. Also included is a frank appraisal of the number and quality of research reports available to determine the effectiveness of nongraded homogeneous grouping.

Anderson, Robert H. "Ungraded Primary Classes: An Administrative Contribution to Mental Health," *Understanding the Child* 24:66–72, June, 1955.
Anderson feels that the ungraded program gives better opportunity for good mental adjustment among pupils, especially for both extremes of a class. He presents his reasons with some practical examples from the Milwaukee, Wis., and Park Forest, Ill., programs.

————. *Teaching in a World of Change.* New York: Harcourt, Brace and World, 1966.
Team teaching and nongraded schools are discussed as two of the major innovations and changes characteristic of our times.

———— and John I. Goodlad. "Self Appraisal in Non-graded Schools: A Survey of Findings and Perceptions," *Elementary School Journal* 62:261–269, February, 1962.
A summary report received from 89 communities which have nongraded schools is the mainstay of this article. Included in the report are subjective assessments of strengths and weaknesses of the programs in the following areas: pupil achievement, pupil adjustment, pupil progress, classroom atmosphere, impact on teachers and curriculum development, and parent attitudes.

Asbell, Bernard. "High School for Sky High Learning," *Education Digest* 29:26–28, March, 1964.
Here is a stimulating report of a nongraded plan at Melbourne High near Cape Kennedy. Specific examples are cited of procedures used in such classes as English and the sciences.

Austin, Kent C. "The Ungraded Primary School," *Childhood Education* 33:260–263, February, 1957.

This article has outstanding sections on new teacher orientation and public relations for the ungraded program. All of the examples are taken from the Park Forest program.

———. "The Ungraded Primary Unit in Public Elementary Schools of the United States," *Dissertation Abstracts* 19:73–74, January, 1958.

Austin traces the development of the nongraded school and reports on his recent survey of nongraded schools.

Backroth, Sister M. Bernaedo, C.P.P.S. "An Evaluation of Ungraded Primary as an Organizational Device for Improving Learning in St. Louis Archdiocesan Schools," *Dissertation Abstracts* 19:2819–2820, May, 1959.

This study represents one of the early attempts at evaluating the non-graded organization of elementary schools.

Bair, Medill, and Richard G. Woodward. *Team Teaching in Action.* Boston, Mass.: Houghton Mifflin, 1964.

Team teaching and its relationship to nongrading is explored and investigated. In many respects, team teaching and nongradedness go hand in hand. The book for the most part deals with the development of team teaching.

Ballew, Sheri. "Melbourne High School," *National Association of Secondary School Principals* 47:67–68, May, 1963.

Here is still more about the nongraded Melbourne High School.

Beggs, David W. (ed.) *Team Teaching: Bold New Venture.* Bloomington: Indiana University Press, 1964.

In this volume, the possibilities of utilizing team teaching at all levels is explored and some considerations for inaugurating and evaluating team teaching programs are provided.

——— and Edward G. Buffie (eds.). *Independent Study: Bold New Venture.* Bloomington: Indiana University Press, 1965.

In addition to theory, practical suggestions for developing independent study programs in both elementary and secondary schools are discussed.

Blake, Roy F. "Small Group Research and Cooperative Teaching Problems," *National Elementary Principal* 43:31–36, February, 1964.

Here is a lucid article which summarizes research on small groups and implications for team cooperation and leadership problems. Possible structural and operational solutions are given.

Brinkman, Albert R. "Now It's the Ungraded School," *Education Digest* 27:5–7, October, 1961.

A pep talk on the virtues of an "ungraded" or "primary" school is emphasized throughout.

Brown, B. Frank. "A New Design for Individual Learning," *Journal of Secondary Education* 37:368–375, October, 1962.

Mr. Brown exposites ways in which the present educational system must readjust the content blocks and organization of students and faculties to meet the challenge in this new educational era. The author is principal of the nongraded high school at Melbourne, Fla.

———. *The Nongraded High School*. Englewood Cliffs, N.J.: Prentice-Hall, 1963.
The complete story of one of the nation's first nongraded high schools —Melbourne High School—is described in detail.

———. *The Appropriate Placement School: A Sophisticated Nongraded Curriculum*. West Nyack, N.Y.: Parker Publishing Co., 1965.
The multiphased curriculum is discussed in detail as this relates to the nongraded curriculum in primary, intermediate, junior and senior high schools.

———. "The Non-graded High School," *Phi Delta Kappan* 44:206–209, February, 1963.
This article deals primarily with nongraded innovations in the secondary schools with a brief discussion of the implications for colleges. The grouping procedure plus curriculum phases are described briefly. A summation of the changes in physical environment and teacher-student attitudes after three years of ungradedness is included.

———. "The Non-Graded School," *National Association of Secondary School Principals* 47:64–72, May, 1963.
The author discusses the components he sees necessary for a promising and productive nongraded secondary school. Most important among these is the element of independent study. Included in the article are reports from Melbourne, Fla., Middletown, R. I., and Steauket, N. Y.

———. "An Ungraded Secondary School," *National Association of Secondary School Principals* 45:349–352, April, 1961.
An assessment of high school programs of the past and present is made. Suggestions of new approaches are also given.

———. "The Ungraded High School," *Overview* 2:61, May, 1961.
A positive statement of the advantages of ungradedness at the secondary level, which are explored in detail. One drawback is noted.

Buffie, Edward George. "A Comparison of Mental Health and Academic Achievement: The Nongraded School vs. the Graded School." Unpublished Ed. D. dissertation, School of Education, Indiana University, Bloomington, 1962.
Another of the early attempts to evaluate nongraded and graded schools. This study favors the nongraded form of elementary school organization.

Carbone, Robert F. "Comparison of Graded and Non-Graded Elementary Schools," *Elementary School Journal* 62:82–88, November, 1961.
The basis for this article is the author's doctoral research. Carbone tested three hypotheses: Is there a difference in achievement, mental health, or teacher instruction methods between the graded and nongraded approach? He discovered a significant difference in favor of graded schools in terms of achievement and mental health.

————. "Non-Graded School: Myth or Miracle?" *Montana Education* 39:17–18, November, 1962.

The author bases this article upon the results of his research. A very basic question is raised regarding the nongraded school.

Dean, Stuart E. *Elementary School Administration and Organization.* Bulletin No. 11. Washington, D. C.: U. S. Department of Health, Education, and Welfare, 1960.

A survey regarding the growth and future of nongraded schools is reported.

Doll, Edgar A. "The Four I.Q.'s," *Exceptional Children* 24:56–58, October, 1957.

Criteria for grouping practices could be based upon the "Four I.Q.'s" —the intelligence quotient, the inner quest, the ideal qualities, and the innate quirks. Each is explored in depth.

Dufay, Frank R. *Ungrading the Elementary School.* Englewood Cliffs, N.J.: Prentice-Hall, 1966.

Using the Parkway Elementary School on Long Island as his major focal point, the author describes an ungraded elementary school as well as the processes for bringing about such change.

Duval, Frank H., Elizabeth Theiss, Sylvia Stryker, and Edith McKinnon. "Three Heads Are Better Than One," *Grade Teacher* 81:61 ff., May, 1964.

An excellent overview of practical problems such as ungraded terminology, organization of student groups, and teacher responsibilities at the intermediate level is provided. Some of the activities are illustrated with pictures.

Eisman, Edward. "What's Brewing in Bassett?" *Audiovisual Instruction* 8:136–137, March, 1963.

A preview of the continuous education program that will be introduced at Bassett High in California is described. The program will be implemented through extensive testing and sustained by the assistance of many technological devices.

Eldred, Donald M., and Maurie Hillson. "The Non-Graded School and Mental Health," *Elementary School Journal* 63:218–222, January, 1963.

Emlaw, Rita. "Organizing Schools for the Future," *Educational Leadership* 14:288–292, February, 1957.

Here is a very interesting article describing significant movements which have begun in the schools today and will play an important role in the schools of the future.

Fallon, Berlie J. *Educational Innovation in the United States.* Bloomington, Ind.: Phi Delta Kappa, 1966.

The editor provides abstracts of over 600 best school practices initiated between 1957 and 1964.

Filbin, Robert L. "Continuous Progress for All: Implications for the High School," *American School Board Journal* 143:11–14, October, 1961.

Mr. Filbin attempts to present the need for an ungraded approach on the secondary level. He gives some excellent examples of experiments which help his ideas to be more convincing.

Forbes, Mary M. "So How Is A.V. Different in a Non-graded Program?" *Audiovisual Instruction* 8:578–579, October, 1963.

A short but enthusiastic affirmation that A.V. material may be used to advantage more freely under a nongraded system.

Gaudet, Joseph H. "Middletown High School," *National Association of Secondary School Principals* 47:70–72, May, 1963.

Described is one of the nation's first nongraded high schools.

Gilbert, Jerome H. "Multigraded Development Plan Focuses on Pupil Achievement: Telsa School Breaks through Traditional Graded Structure," *Chicago School Journal* 43:209–214, February, 1962.

The Telsa School is described in some detail. It was one of the first Chicago schools to move in the direction of nongradedness (referred to as continuous education).

————. "Telsa School Broke the Lock Steps," *Elementary School Journal* 64:306–309, March, 1964.

A discussion of steps taken in the Woodlawn community school of Chicago to lessen early school failures is provided. The author discusses the socioeconomic factors behind failure, philosophic reasons for moving into a program of continuous education, and specific methods utilized to implement the program.

Goodlad, John I. "Classroom Organization," in *Encyclopedia of Educational Research*, ed. by Walter Scott Monroe, pp. 221–226. New York: Macmillan, 1960.

The author provides a historical overview of both vertical and horizontal school organization practices. He traces trends in graded vs. nongraded approaches through the recent decades. He raises pertinent questions concerning class size, large group in structure, child security, and use of electronic media.

————. "Inadequacy of Graded Organization—What Then?" *Childhood Education* 39:274–277, February, 1963.

Mr. Goodlad points out several principles of child development which have been ignored by present school organization and suggests solutions for them. He illustrates graphically the overlapping approach of ungraded placement.

————. "More about the Ungraded Unit Plan," *National Education Association Journal* 44:295–297, May, 1955. (This publication will hereafter be referred to as the *N.E.A. Journal*.)

A general appraisal of how the ungraded program works in actual practice is made. A compact discussion of the emphases and outcomes of 16 programs is also given.

————. "News and Comment," *Elementary School Journal* 59:1–17, October, 1958.

Described is a comprehensive report on action to improve schools in the communities of Englewood, Fla., Flint, Mich., Fort Wayne, Ind., and University City, Mo.

———. "Promising Practices in Non-graded Schools," *Education Digest* 27:8–10, October, 1961.
Here is an optimistic view of nongraded elementary schools as a much needed and rapidly emerging concept. Two variations of the concept are discussed. The first view identified is one that seeks to encourage learners of varying abilities to move at differentiated rates of progress, while the second is described as one that emerges out of a complex philosophical background which bears the slogan "teach the whole child."

———. "Ungrading the Elementary Grades," *N.E.A. Journal* 44:170–171, March, 1955.
An artful presentation of the rightful place of organization as it relates to good instruction is made.

———. "What about Non-grading Our Schools?" *Instructor* 70:6, May, 1961.
A summary of basic factors that point to the need for a nongraded organization are treated in limited detail.

——— and Robert H. Anderson. "Educational Practices in Non-graded Schools: A Survey of Perceptions," *Elementary School Journal* 63:33–40, October, 1962.
Many different concepts of nongradedness are explored in depth.

——— and Robert H. Anderson. *The Nongraded Elementary School.* New York: Harcourt, Brace and World, 1959.
This book represents the first authoritative work regarding the development of the nongraded school. The Park Forest, Ill., schools are featured. A 1963 revision is now available.

——— and Robert H. Anderson. "The Nongraded Elementary School," *N.E.A. Journal* 47:642–643, December, 1958.
An interesting survey involving 150 communities which were experimenting with some form of the ungraded program is described. A very helpful compilation of reasons for successful and unsuccessful experiences is included, as well as a listing of all the schools using an ungraded approach through 1958.

——— and others. "Readiness Levels Replace Grades in the Non-graded Plan," *Elementary School Journal* 57:253–256, February, 1957.
Here is an excellent discussion of how a nongraded primary may be organized according to readiness levels. The authors close with pertinent suggestions for initiating structural changes.

Gore, Lillian. "The Non-graded Primary Unit," *School Life* 44:9–12, March, 1962.
Dr. Gore reports on 10 ungraded schools out of the 28 she had visited and studied. She cites six features basic to all nongraded programs. Test results from Flint, Mich., Milwaukee, and Appleton, Wis., show

children's achievements favoring the nongraded school. Author warns against level standards that become more rigid than those of grades. Important questions are raised relative to (1) effect on curriculums, (2) effect on teachers, (3) effect on children.

Gran, Eldon E. "Why Not an Ungraded Intermediate Program?" *Instructor* 72:48 ff., January, 1963.

The Douglas School at Ellsworth Air Force Base is described.

Halliwell, Joseph W. "A Comparison of Pupil Achievement in Graded and Non-Graded Primary Classrooms," *The Journal of Experimental Education* 32:59–63, Fall, 1963.

Hart, Richard H. "The Non-graded Primary School and Arithmetic," *Arithmetic Teacher* 9:130–133, March, 1962.

Outlined in detail are the steps necessary for developing an ungraded arithmetic program including selection of materials to be used and a testing program.

Heathers, Glen. "Field Research on Elementary School Organization and Instruction," *Journal of Educational Sociology* 34:338–343, April, 1961.

A discussion of the increasing role educational r~search plays in the improvement of educational practices is given. Included are suggested ways that applied research may or may not operate. One significant statement is that pilot studies usually are needed to prepare the way for controlled studies.

Hillson, Maurie. *Change and Innovation in Elementary School Organization.* New York: Holt, Rinehart and Winston, 1966.

This is a book of selected readings in which various grouping plans, departmentalization, team teaching, and nongradedness are featured.

Imhoff, Myrtle, and Wayne Young. "School Organization," *Review of Educational Research* 29:155–164, April, 1959.

Here is an overview of the research in the areas of enrollment, size of classes and its effect, reorganization and grouping trends, promotion practices, length of the school day, and the control of the federal, state, and local governments. A very brief historical background is given for each area.

Ingram, Vivian. "Flint Evaluates Its Primary Cycle," *Elementary School Journal* 61:76–80, November, 1960.

An appraisal of Flint's initial work in nongrading is given. The author notes that both objective data and subjective responses helped substantiate the positive aspects of the evaluation.

Josephine, Sister, C.S.J. "Student Reaction to the Ungraded Primary," *Peabody Journal of Education* 40:291–295, March, 1963.

A summary review of organizational patterns for the elementary schools in the United States is broken down by regions. It is followed by a teacher poll citing reasons why a larger percentage of those primary teachers who responded preferred the ungraded primary unit.

Kauth, Priscilla, and B. Frank Brown. "The Non-graded High School in Melbourne, Fla.," *National Association of Secondary School Principals* 46:127–134, January, 1962.

Described is a report on nongrading procedures at the secondary level. Included are the philosophic presuppositions and implementation methods used to "provide educational experiences for a variety of talents." The authors also touch upon the need for a willing faculty as well as student transfer and a guidance program.

Kaya, Esin. "Problems in Evaluating Educational Plans in the School Setting," *Journal of Elementary Sociology* 34:355–359, April, 1961.

Here is a discussion of some of the fundamental problems in evaluating educational plans, with suggested ways for solving these problems. Kaya cites three areas which need closer scrutiny. They are establishing an operational definition of goals, establishing an effective research design, and using valid evaluation instruments.

Kelly, Florence C. "The Primary School in Milwaukee," *Childhood Education* 24:236–238, January, 1948.

Provided is an overview of the program of the children through the ungraded program as practiced at Milwaukee.

————. "Ungraded Primary Schools Make the Grade," *N.E.A. Journal* 40:645–646, December, 1951.

An evaluation of the success of the ungraded elementary program in Milwaukee is reported.

Lamers, William M. "Milwaukee's Ungraded Primary Plan," *American School Board Journal* 145:11–13, November, 1962.

Here is a thorough discussion of the ungraded primary plan in Milwaukee. The goals, levels of learning, process of "promotion" or "retention," parent orientation program, and reporting techniques are outlined. Lamers gives many practical hints for a more successful program.

Langer, Howard. "Melbourne Ungraded High," *Senior Scholastic* 83:18-T–19-T, October 4, 1963.

Described is a report of nongrading procedures used in the "first non-graded high school in the U. S." Included are detailed explanations of the "quest" and "remedial" phases of the Melbourne plan and programs as they functioned for two of Melbourne's students.

Manlove, Donald C., and David W. Beggs. *Flexible Scheduling: Bold New Venture.* Bloomington: Indiana University Press, 1965.

Complete details are provided for utilizing flexible scheduling at the high school level. Also included are the results of a survey of 33 schools using some form of flexible scheduling.

Mary Alice, Sister, R.S.M. "Administration of the Non-graded School," *Elementary School Journal* 61:148–152, December, 1960.

The author discusses the role of the administrator in initiating a non-graded primary.

————. "New Ventures in School Organization: The Ungraded School and Use of Teacher Aids," *Elementary School Journal* 57:268–271, February, 1957.

Described is a brief comparison of different organizational structures with special emphasis on the nongraded organization. Emphasized also are those factors necessary to ease transition from a graded to a nongraded organization. The use of teacher aids, as a solution to clerical, lunchroom and playground supervision, housekeeping, and other miscellaneous duties, is proposed.

Mercille, Margaret G. "The Primary School Unit," *Indiana University School of Education Bulletin*, No. 25, January, 1949, pp. 13–19.

A review of all of the more popular promotion and grouping practices used during the past fifty years, with an evaluation of their effectiveness and some of their drawbacks, is given.

Morse, Arthur D. *Schools of Tomorrow—Today.* New York: Doubleday, 1960.

The author describes many new educational innovations. Included are descriptions of nongraded schools.

National Council of Teachers of English Conference. "Topics of Current Interest," *Education* 84:313, January, 1964.

Here is a report of the 1964 activities of the N.C.T.E. and a brief description of a progressive learning program initiated in the Philadelphia Public Schools three years ago.

National Education Association Research Division. "Some Organizational Characteristics of Elementary Schools," *National Elementary Principal* 38:52–62, September, 1958.

A discussion of patterns and trends in school organization and supervision is reported.

O'Beirne, Gladys. "An Ungraded Early Elementary School Program," *Educational Method* 21:178–180, January, 1948.

The author describes an adaptation of ungradedness to the community's needs. She describes methods of evaluation, adaptations to individual differences, grouping, and records.

Patterson, G. J. "The Unit Promotion System in the Hamilton Public Schools," *Canadian Education and Research Digest* 3:48–53, March, 1963.

A clear description of nongraded grouping practices (unit system) is given. Considerable attention is devoted to promotion policies.

Peterson, D. L. "Non-graded High School," *School and Community* 49:20–21, September, 1962.

Here is more about the Melbourne High School. Peterson describes the concept of open-ended learning and some of its applications to curricular activities.

Polkinghorne, Ada R. "Parents and Teachers Appraise Primary-Grade Grouping," *Elementary School Journal* 51:271–279, January, 1951.

Here is an interesting survey conducted by a primary teacher in the

University of Chicago Laboratory School. It describes their ungraded program and gives tabulated responses from parents and intermediate grade teachers.

Prince, Thomas C. "Trends in Types of Elementary School Organization," *American School Board Journal* 106: 37–38, June, 1963.
This report on trends in elementary school organization was derived through 200 questionnaires. Analysis of practices and opinions about practice are included. Departmentalization also receives specific attention in the article.

Rollins, Sidney P. "High School Where No One Fails," *School Management* 5:77–79, May, 1962.
Described is the Middletown, R. I., High School, which is a six-year secondary school with no grade designations. It has a flexible-time schedule, achievement grouping, team teaching, and a unique pattern of curriculum organization.

Ryan, W. Carson. "The Ungraded Primary Schools," *Understanding the Child* 24:65, June, 1955.
The ungraded program is viewed as an answer to many of the mental health problems among pupils.

Shaplin, Judson T., and Henry F. Olds, eds. *Team Teaching.* New York: Harper and Row, 1964.
Team teaching and nongraded schools have many characteristics in common. These common elements are described and discussed.

Skapski, Mary King. "Ungraded Primary Reading Program: An Objective Evaluation," *Elementary School Journal* 61:41–45, October, 1960.
An excellent presentation of four objective comparisons between graded and nongraded achievement on the primary level is made. The results favor the ungraded.

Smith, Lois. "Continuous Progress Plan," *Childhood Education* 37:320–323, March, 1961.
The language arts consultant at Appleton, Wis., explains how the ungraded approach is better suited to the growth patterns of individual children's minds.

Snyder, Edith R. "A Community School Looks at Guidance," *Education* 74:483–487, April, 1954.
Here is a description of a school guidance program in a community where the schools had flexible organization.

Stoddard, George B. *The Dual Progress Plan.* New York: Harper and Row, 1961.
A program which is both graded and nongraded in organization is described in detail. In the latter, the following subjects are included: mathematics, science, physical education, and the creative arts. The public school programs in Long Beach and Ossining, New York, are described.

Story, M. L. "Let's Give Winnetka Another Chance," *Educational Forum* 27:99–102, November, 1962.

Described is the Winnetka Plan—an ungraded program of the 1920's which failed—and the reasons why it would be successful today. The author feels the theory followed by Winnetka is excellent and, with proper implementation, could be used very well in programs today.

Thompson, Ethel. "The Ungraded Plan,'" *N.E.A. Journal* 47:16–18, January, 1958.
A presentation of many of the problems involved in a graded approach led to acceptance and recognition of the ungraded concept. The author gives some insightful interpretations of pupil movement through an ungraded program.

Wagner, Guy. "What Schools Are Doing in Developing the Continuous Growth Program," *Education* 79:595–596, May, 1959.
A brief overview of the variety of names and approaches which have been used in developing the ungraded concept is given. Several recommended readings for further study in the area are also provided.

Washburne, Carleton, and Louis Edward Roths. "The High School Achievement of Children Trained under the Individual Technique," *Elementary School Journal* 28:214–224, November, 1957.
Reported is a careful study of the achievement attained in high school by pupils who progressed through elementary school under the "individual technique" of instruction as opposed to those who received traditional class instruction and mass promotions.

———— and Sidney P. Marland, Jr. *Winnetka: The History and Significance of an Educational Experiment.* Englewood Cliffs, N.J.: Prentice-Hall, 1963.
A complete account of the famous Winnetka school system, with its great emphasis on individualized instruction, is provided by the two educators who know it best.

Watson, Robert A. "People Not Projects Will Improve Education," *American School Board Journal* 147: 9–11, November, 1963.
Here is a critical look at the team teaching and dual-progress approaches to teaching, as well as some thought-provoking suggestions for improving the quality of teachers' education and pupil products.

Weaver, Fred J. "A Non-Grade-Level Sequence in Elementary Mathematics," *Arithmetic Teacher* 7:431, December, 1960.
The author describes the organization of a mathematics program for a nongraded school.

Notes

CHAPTER 1

1. John I. Goodlad and Robert H. Anderson, *The Nongraded Elementary School* (New York: Harcourt, Brace and World, 1959), pp. 44–60.

2. *Ibid.*, p. 204.

3. Henry J. Otto and Dwain M. Estes, "Accelerated and Retarded Progress," in *Encyclopedia of Educational Research*, ed. by Walter Scott Monroe (New York: Macmillan, 1960), p. 7.

4. Carleton W. Washburne and Sidney P. Malland, *Winnetka: The History and Significance of an Educational Experiment* (Englewood Cliffs, N.J.: Prentice-Hall, 1963).

5. John I. Goodlad, "More about the Ungraded Unit Plan," *N.E.A. Journal*, 44 (May, 1955), 295–97.

6. Eva M. Slater, *The Primary Unit*, Curriculum Bulletin No. 3 (Storrs, Conn.: School of Education, University of Connecticut, 1955), pp. 1–33.

7. Robert H. Anderson, "The Ungraded School as a Contribution to Improved School Practices," in *Frontiers of Elementary Education*, ed. by Vincent J. Glennon, II (Syracuse, N.Y.: Syracuse University Press, 1955), 28–29.

8. Kent C. Austin, "The Ungraded Primary School," *Childhood Education* 33 (Feb., 1957), 260–63.

9. John I. Goodlad and Robert H. Anderson, "The Nongraded Elementary School," *N.E.A. Journal*, 47 (Dec., 1958), 642–43.

10. Stuart E. Dean, *Elementary School Administration and Organization*, Bulletin No. 11 (Washington, D.C.: U.S. Department of Health, Education, and Welfare, Office of Education, 1960), pp. 1–126.

11. *Ibid.*, p. 23.

12. National Education Association Research Division, *Non-grading: A Modern Practice in Elementary School Organization*, NEA Research Memo (Washington, D.C., Oct., 1961), pp. 1–13.

13. B. Frank Brown, *The Nongraded High School* (Englewood Cliffs, N.J.: Prentice-Hall, 1963).

CHAPTER 2

1. Alexander Frazier, "Needed: A New Vocabulary for Individual Differences," *Elementary School Journal,* 61 (Feb., 1961), 263.

2. William H. Burton, "Basic Principles in a Good Teaching–Learning Situation," *Phi Delta Kappan,* 39 (March, 1958), 242–48.

3. Edgar A. Doll, "The Four I.Q.'s," *Exceptional Children,* 24 (Oct., 1957), 56–58.

4. John I. Goodlad and Robert H. Anderson, *The Nongraded Elementary School,* p. 20.

5. Lee J. Cronbach, *Educational Psychology* (New York: Harcourt, Brace and World, 1963), p. 263.

6. Jerome S. Bruner, *The Process of Education* (Cambridge, Mass.: Harvard University Press, 1962), p. 33.

7. Luella Cole, *Psychology of Elementary School Subjects* (New York: Farrar and Rinehart, 1934), pp. 6, 7.

8. William S. Gray, "The Teaching of Reading," in *Encyclopedia of Educational Research,* p. 1118.

9. Lee J. Cronbach, *Educational Psychology,* p. 262.

10. John I. Goodlad and Robert H. Anderson, *The Nongraded Elementary School,* p. 226.

11. Fred J. Weaver, "A Non-Grade-Level Sequence in Elementary Mathematics," *Arithmetic Teacher,* 7 (Dec., 1960), 431.

12. Maurie Hillson, et al., "A Controlled Experiment Evaluating the Effects of a Nongraded Organization on Pupil Achievement," *Journal of Educational Research,* 57 (July–August, 1964), 550.

13. Kimball Wiles and Franklin Patterson, *The High School We Need* (Washington, D.C.: Association for Supervision and Curriculum Development, National Education Association, 1959).

14. Jean D. Grambs, Clarence G. Noyce, Franklin Patterson, and John C. Robertson, *The Junior High School We Need* (Washington, D.C.: Association for Supervision and Curriculum Development, National Education Association, 1961).

15. B. Frank Brown, *The Nongraded High School, passim.*

CHAPTER 3

1. For a detailed discussion of the differences between a graded and nongraded secondary school, read B. Frank Brown, *The Appropriate Placement School: A Sophisticated Nongraded High School* (West Nyack, N.Y.: Parker Publishing Co., 1965), pp. 99–122.

2. The distribution of time students will spend in independent study and in assembly and inquiry groups will vary from student to student and from school to school. There will be wide deviation from the example of time distribution suggested here.

Chapter 4

1. Henry M. Brickell, *Organizing New York for Educational Change* (Albany, N.Y.: State Superintendent of Public Instruction, 1961), p. 24.

2. *Ibid.*, p. 23.

3. Francis Chase, "The Teacher and Policy Making," *Administrator's Notebook*, I (May, 1952), 1.

4. Frederick L. Ferris, "Testing in the New Curriculum: Numerology, 'Tyranny,' or Common Sense?" *School Review*, LXX, No. 1 (Spring, 1952), 342–47.

Chapter 5

1. N.E.A. Project on Instruction, *Planning and Organizing for Teaching* (Washington, D.C.: National Education Association, 1963), pp. 53–68.

2. David G. Ryans, *Evaluation and the Improvement of Instruction* (Santa Monica, Calif.: Systems Development Corporation, 1964), p. 1.

3. Vivian Ingram, "Flint Evaluates Its Primary Cycle," *Elementary School Journal*, 61 (Nov., 1960), 76–80.

4. Mary King Skapski, "Ungraded Primary Reading Program: An Objective Evaluation," *Elementary School Journal*, 61 (Oct., 1960), 41–45.

5. John Richard Zerby, "Comparison of Academic Achievement and Social Adjustment of Primary School Children in the Graded and Nongraded School Program," *Penn State Review of Educational Research* (May, 1961), 33.

6. Robert F. Carbone, "Achievement, Mental Health, and Instruction in Graded and Nongraded Elementary Schools." Unpublished Ph.D. dissertation, Department of Education, University of Chicago, 1961.

7. Boyd Aigner, "A Statistical Analysis of Achievement: Differences of Children in a Nongraded Primary Program and Traditional Classrooms," *Journal of Research Service*, 1, No. 1 (May, 1962), 43–46.

8. Edward G. Buffie, "A Comparison of Mental Health and Academic Achievement: The Nongraded School vs. the Graded School." Unpublished Ed.D. dissertation, School of Education, Indiana University, 1962.

9. John I. Goodlad and Robert H. Anderson, *The Nongraded Elementary School*, pp. 215–16.

10. Kent Austin, "The Ungraded Primary Unit in Public Schools of the United States." Unpublished Ed.D. dissertation, University of Colorado, 1957.

11. Cecilia R. Blackstock, "A Field Study to Initiate an Ungraded Primary School in Brazosport." Unpublished Ed.D. dissertation, University of Houston, 1961.

12. Richard H. Hart, "The Non-graded Primary School and Arithmetic," *Arithmetic Teacher*, IX, No. 3 (March, 1962), 130–33.

13. Abraham Kaplan, *The Conduct of Inquiry* (San Francisco, Calif.: Chandler Publishing Co., 1964), pp. 147–54.

14. Donald T. Campbell and Julian C. Stanley, "Experimental and Quasi-Experimental Designs for Research on Teaching," in *Handbook of Research on Teaching*, ed. by N. L. Gage (Chicago: Rand McNally, 1963), pp. 142–70.

15. David G. Ryans, *Evaluation and the Improvement of Instruction*, pp. 11–23.

CHAPTER 6

1. Stuart E. Dean, "Nongraded Schools," *Education Briefs*, No. 1, OE 20009 (July, 1964), 13–14.

2. Appendix A and Appendix B give examples of how two schools restructured their report cards.

3. Stuart E. Dean, *Elementary School Organization and Administration*, p. 24.

CHAPTER 13

1. Richard H. Hart, "The Effectiveness of an Approach to the Problem of Varying Abilities in Teaching Reading," in *Readings in Educational Psychology*, ed. by Victor H. Noll and Rachel P. Noll (New York: Macmillan, 1962), pp. 298–304.

2. Howard Smith, "A Comparison of Reading Achievement of Ungraded and Graded Primary Students." Unpublished Curriculum Report, School District No. 7, Hillsboro, Oregon, 1962.

3. Richard H. Hart, "The Non-graded Primary School and Arithmetic," pp. 130–33.

Index

Ability grouping, 9–10, 169

Accrediting agencies, and non-graded high schools, 70–71

Achievement, differences in, 24–27, 92–93; of graded vs. nongraded pupils, 101–2, 182; grouping by, 175–77, 179–80, 197; plans for continuous, 127–53, 159–63, 179–81, 209–11, 226–35; in reading as basis for nongraded grouping, 34–38, 175–80

Administrator of a nongraded school, Chicago assumptions about, 147; and future school policies, 112–113, 115; and high school problems, 69–70, 75, 223, 225; role in nongrading a school, 69–70, 80–83, 88–89

Age-grading, 31–32, 141

Anderson, Robert H., 5, 102, 151, 167; quoted, 7, 18–19, 34

Appleton, Wis., Continuous Progress Plan, 135–43, 239

Appraisal. See Evaluation

Arithmetic. See Mathematics

Ashmore, Myron L., quoted, 215

Assignment of pupils. See Grouping

Austin, Kent C., 18, 102

Automation, use in Nova School, 212

Batavia Plan, 9–10

Beatty, Willard W., 12

Beggs, David W., III, 53

Bellevue, Wash. Continuous Growth Program, 101, 127–34

Blackstock, Cecilia, 102

"Block program" of Webster School, 201–6

Board of education's role in nongrading a school, 83–84

Brickell, Henry M., quoted, 80

Brigham Young University's Continuous Progress School, 226–35

Broward County, Fla., Public School System, 207–16

Brown, B. Frank, 20, 50–51

Bruner, Jerome S., quoted, 32

Buffie, Edward G., 3, 101–2, 195

Buildings, new types for changing school needs, 87–88, 131

Burk, Frederick, 10–12

Burton, William H., 30

Cabool, Mo., Continuous Plan of Pupil Progress, 159–65, 240

Cambridge Plan, 9

Carbone, Robert F., 101–2

Carlson, Evelyn F., 144

Carrels, as individual study stations, 231, 233

Carter, James G., 6

Cedar Falls, Iowa, Primary Schools, 191–98

Chance, grouping by, 162, 202

Change in education, 77–78

Changing a school from graded to nongraded. See Development plan for nongrading a school

Chase, Francis, 80

Chicago's Continuous Development Program, 144–53

Child. See Pupil

Chronological age, grouping according to, 31–32, 141

City-school problems, Chicago's plan for, 144–53

Classrooms, children remain 3 years in same one in "block" program, 201–6; homelike, 203; self-contained, "little red schoolhouse" as, 5, 185; self-contained, in Monteith plan, 168

Cole, Luella, 32

Community involvement, in nongrading a school, 74–75, 83–84; parent education classes of Cabool, Mo., system, 163–64; in Peter Boscow School Plan, 177; *see also* Parents

Conferences, Monteith School's forms for, 241–43; parent-teacher-child, 205

Consultants, as valuable to nongraded school, 70–71

Content. *See* Curriculum

Continuous Development Program, Chicago's, 144–53

Continuous Growth Program of Bellevue, Wash., 127–34

Continuous Growth Program of Peter Boscow Nongraded Primary School, 179–81

Continuous Plan of Pupil Progress of Cabool, Mo., 159–65

Continuous Progress Plan of Appleton, Wis., 135–43

Continuous Progress Plan of Brigham Young University, 226–35

Cooperative Group Plan, 14

Costs of nongrading a school, 88, 212

Counselor's role in a nongraded project, 225

Cronbach, Lee J., quoted, 31–33

Culturally deprived children. *See* Disadvantaged children

Curriculum, changes needed for nongradedness, 170, 181; in child-centered school, 136–37; content selection for high school, 63–65; development and future of nongradedness, 118–20; of graded vs. nongraded schools, 113–15; materials, de-

velopment of, 86, 234; of Middletown High School, 221–22; Nova School's "hard core," 211; sequential elementary through secondary in Brigham Young Plan, 228–30

Dalton Plan, 11–12

Dame schools, 4–5

Dean, Stuart E., 107, quoted, 19

Decision making, as important to nongrading plan, 81–83, 110

Definition of a nongraded school, 21–23, 33–36

Departmentalization, 13–14, 16

Deprived children. *See* Disadvantaged children

Dessenberger, Dean, 208

Development plan for nongrading a school, 77–94; administrator's role, 80–81, 88–89; appraisal procedures, 88–91; community involvement, 83–84; decision making, 81–83, 110; orienting parents and pupils, 91–93; planning, 84–87; problems recognition, 79–80; programming, 87–88

Disadvantaged children, Cabool, Mo., plan for 160–61; Chicago's Tesla School for, 149–50; and nongraded schools, 114, 120–21

Discipline problems and nongraded schools, 164

District schools, 4–5

Doll, Edgar A., quoted, 30

Dual Progress Plan, 14

Education, changes needed in, 77–78; evaluation and measurement in, 100; tenets upon which nongraded movement rests, 29–33, 61

Elementary schools, in a big city, Chicago's plan for, 144–53; *Continuous Growth Program* for in Bellevue, Wash., 127–34; Continuous Progress Plan for in Appleton, Wis., 135–43; historical development of, 4–20; in lumber town of Southern Humbolt, Cal., 154–58; Monteith School in Grosse Pointe, Mich., 166–73; multi-graded in Torrance, Cal., 184–90; none truly nongraded, 166–67; nongradedness in, reviewed, 121–22; Peter Boscow Primary School in Hillsboro, Ore., 174–83; primary schools in Cedar Falls, Iowa, 191–98; and secondary combined in Continuous Progress Plan at Brigham Young University, 226–35; in small town of Cabool, Mo., 159–65; 3 years with one teacher "block" plan at Pontiac, Mich., Webster School, 199–206; see also Nongraded schools

Elizabeth, N.J., Plan, 8

Equipment, automation of, 212; Brigham Young Laboratory School's use of novel, 233; new products for changing needs, 87–88; Nova School's innovations in, 211–12; technological aids for high schools' use, 66–67

Evaluation, of Cedar Falls Primary Program, how structured, 195–96; of nongraded high school program, 74; of nongraded pupils vs. graded, 181–82; of nongraded schools, need for, 122–23; of nongraded schools defies measurement, 95–106, 172–73; procedures in nongrading a school, 88–91; of pupil progress, 130, 137–39, 146, 160, 163, 239–40

Examples of nongraded schools. See Plans of school organization

Experiments on value of nongraded schools, 102–6

Facilities, physical, buildings for nongraded schools, 131; carrels, 233; innovations at Nova School, 211–12; instructional materials center, 66–67, 233; laboratories,

233; new products for changing needs, 87–88; technological aids for high school use, 66–67

Faculty. See Teachers

Failure of students, as by-product of graded schools, 8; in graded school vs. Continuous Progress Plan, 139; none at Hillsboro, 181; nongradedness releases child from fear of, 173; as undesirable, eliminated in nongraded philosophy, 30–31, 35

Ferguson, D. A., 159

Flexible Progress Plan of Western Springs, Ill., 17

Flexible scheduling in nongraded high school, 60–61

Fort Lauderdale, Fla., Nova High School, 207–16

Frazier, Alexander, quoted, 29

Fund for the Advancement of Education, 217, 219

Future of nongraded schools, 107–24, 134

Garvue, Robert J., 95

Gaudet, Joseph H., 217

"Gifted" child, nongrading and, 23

Gilbert, Jerome H., 144

Goodlad, John I., 5, 18, 19, 102; quoted, 7, 31, 34

Goodrich, Lowell P., 17

Graded schools, compared with Continuous Progress Plan, 139; compared with nongraded, 101–2; disadvantages of, 15–16; early attempts to improve, 6–15; grouping in, 54–56; history of, 3–27; as outdated, 52; secondary, compared with nongraded, 53–59

Grambs, Jean D., 50

Gray, William S., quoted, 32

Grosse Pointe, Mich., Monteith School, 166–73

Grouping, by ability, 9–10, 169; by achievement, 175–77, 179–80, 197; by age, 31–32, 141; in Appleton Continuous Progress Plan, 137, 139, 142; by chance, 162,

Grouping, by ability (*Cont.*) 202; concept of, 35–36; considerations in elementary school, 38–41; criteria, 39–41; of differing age and achievement levels together in Torrance multigrade plan, 184–90; early innovations in, 9–13; in graded schools, 54–56; and mathematics continuum, 49–50; mixed or multi-class, 142; Monteith School plan for, 168–70; reading achievement as basis for, 175–77; reading readiness as basis for, 169; in secondary schools, 54–56; selective, in Cabool plan, 162

Growth, child's, as basis of Continuous Progress plans, 135–36

Guidance counselor's role in nongradedness, 225

Guidelines for the Primary Program of Continuous Development, 148–49

Hall, Samuel, 6

Hart, Richard H., 102, 174

Hartung, Dr., 151

Head Start program, 22

High schools, consultants to, 70–71; content selection for, 63–65; departmentalization in, 13–14; development plan for change to nongraded, 59–76, 122; and elementary school combined in Brigham Young University's Continuous Progress Plan, 226–35; evaluation of, 74; graded vs. nongraded, 53–59; individual learning in, 56–59; learning sequences for, 61–63; Middletown, R.I., 6-year secondary school, 217–25; nongrading movement in, 20–21, 50–51, 53–76, 122; Nova nongraded in Fort Lauderdale, Fla., 207–16; objectives of, 61–63; principal's role in, 69–70; Pueblo Plan pioneer attempt to individualize instruction in, 11; resource use in, 66–67; teaching changes in, 71–74

Hillsboro, Ore., Peter Boscow School, 174–83

Hillson, Maurie, 28, 111

History of schools in U.S., 3–27

Hull, John H., 184, 188

Hutchison, Gladys, 127

I.M.C. (Instructional Materials Center), 66–67, 233

Independent study, under Brigham Young Continuous Progress Plan, 231–32; in nongraded high school, 57, 64–65

Individualized instruction, as basis of Bellevue, Wash., program, 128; and culturally deprived, 120–21, 160–61; under multigrade plan, 184–90; and nongraded school, 24–27, 113–15; Pueblo Plan pioneer in, 11; in secondary schools, graded vs. nongraded, 54–59

Ingram, Vivian, 100

In-service programs, 69, 73–74, 141, 142

Instructional materials centers, in high schools, 66–67, 233

Instructional program. *See* Curriculum

Intermediate schools, in Chicago program, 153; and nongrading, 122; Peter Boscow School, 176–77; *see also* Elementary schools; High schools

I.Q. (intelligence quotient), and grouping, 38–39; theory of, 4, 30

Jameson, Marshall C., 166

Kaplan, Abraham, 103

Kurtz, Royce E., 135

Language arts program, nongraded, 176–78

Larmes, Roy A., 77

Learning, differences in, 30–33; level assignments adjusted to variations in, 42–43; sequences for nongraded high school, 61–63

LeFever, Welte, 188

"Levels" approach to school organization, 41–48, 110–11, 119

Libraries, instructional materials centers, 66–67, 233; replaced by several resource centers at Nova High School, 212

"Little red schoolhouse" concept, 5, 185

Linville, Warren, 154

Lumber country nongraded schools, 154–58

McDade, James E., 12

McGuffey Eclectic Reader, 6

Mann, Horace, 6

Mathematics, achievement as basis for nongrading, 34–35; achievement-levels program in, 180; programs, nongraded, 46–50, 148, 150

Median performance, as poor criterion for class judgment, 31

Middletown, R.I., Project, 217–25, 244–45

Milwaukee, Wis., nongraded school plan, 17–18

Miranda, Cal., Elementary School, 155

Monitorial system, 5

Monteith Plan, 166–73, 241–43

Morrison, Mr., 11

Motivation, as critical factor in student success, 224

Multi-Grade school plan, 151, 184–90

Multimedia teaching devices, Nova School's use of, 212

Myers Flat School, 155

National Education Association, 19–20

National Science Foundation's Course Content Improvement Programs, 90

NEA, 19–20

Neff, Neal, 159

The Nongraded High School, 20

Nongraded schools, concept of, 28–52; definition of, 21–23, 33–36; development plan for, 77–94; educational tenets upon which based, 29–33; evaluation of, 95–106, 122–23, 172–73; examples of, 127–235; future of, 107–24; high schools, 53–76; history of, 3–27; individualized instruction and, 24–27; levels assignments in, 41–46; "little red schoolhouse" as, 5, 185; operational problems of, 78–87; organizational plan for, 33–36; philosophy of, 29–33; primary units as, 17–19, 121–22; research on, 95–106, 122–23; success of, 51–52, 113–15; team teaching and, 116–18, 165

Nonpromotion of students. *See* Failure of students

Normal schools, as perpetuating graded structure, 6

North Denver Plan, 10

Nova High School, 207–16

Older teachers, and nongradedness, 168

Organization of schools. *See* Plans for school organization

Parents, acceptance of nongradedness by, 133; attitudes to experimentation, 85; cooperation with Appleton plan, 138; education classes for, 163–64; evaluation of nongraded primary unit by, 196–97; orientation to nongrading, 84–87, 91–94, 133, 171; responsibilities of, under Nova School system, 214; role in 3-year-block program, 204–5

Parent-Teacher Associations, of Brigham Young Laboratory School, 228; involvement in Cabool plan, 159–60, 164; role in nongrading a school, 84, 92

Parkhurst, Helen, 11

Passaic, N.J., nongradedness experiment, 114

Patterson, Franklin, 50

Peter Boscow Primary School, 174–83

Philosophy, of nongraded high school in Middletown's *Statement of Philosophy and Purposes,* 218–19, 225; of nongradedness, 29–33

Physical facilities. *See* Facilities, physical

Plans of school organization, Appleton, Wis., Continuous Progress Plan, 135–43; Bellevue, Wash., Continuous Growth Program, 127–34; Brigham Young University Continuous Progress Plan for elementary through secondary, 226–36; Cabool, Mo., Continuous Plan of Pupil Progress, 159–65; Cedar Falls, Iowa, primary schools, 191–98; Chicago's Continuous Development Program, 144–53; cyclical nature of, 108; and future of nongraded schools, 107–24; historical review of, 3–27, 108; Middletown's nongraded secondary school, 217–25; Monteith School nongraded, 166–73; need for research on, 97–100; nongraded, reviewed, 33–36; Nova High School, 207–16; Peter Boscow Primary School, 174–83; Southern Humboldt's nongraded elementary, 154–58; Torrance, Cal., multi-graded, 184–90; Webster School's 3-years-with-same-teacher block plan, 199–206

Platoon System, 13

Politics, and educational change, 96

Pontiac, Mich., Webster School, 199–206

Pope, Alexander S., quoted, 4

Portland Plan, 9

Pre-school movement, 22

Primary units, in Appleton plan, 137; in Cedar Falls schools, 191–98; nongraded, 17–19, 22, 121–22; Peter Boscow Primary School, 174–83; *see also* Elementary schools

Prince Edwards County, Va., schools, 114

Principal. *See* Administrator of a nongraded school

Program, school's. *See* Curriculum

Progress reports, as replacing report cards, 137–39; samples of, 239–40

Provo, Utah, Brigham Young University's Laboratory School, 226–35

Public's involvement in schools. *See* Community involvement

Pueblo Plan, 10–11

Pupils, achievement differences among, 24–27, 55–56, 92–93; assignment of, 152, 162, 193, 202; benefits of nongradedness to, 172–73; continuous development plans for, 127–53, 159–63, 179–81, 209–11, 226–35; development under nongradedness, 135–36, 139; failure of, 8, 30–31, 35, 139, 173, 181; "gifted" and nongrading, 23; in graded vs. nongraded schools, 54–56, 58–59, 101–2; interaction of older and younger in multigrade plan, 189–90; orientation for nongrading, 84–87, 93; progress in Hillsboro plan, 180–81; relationship with teachers in nongraded high school, 58; remain 3 years with same teacher under block plan, 201–6; slow-learning, 30–31, 224

Quincy Grammar School, 5, 6, 56

Read, Edwin A., 226

Reading, achievement as basis for grouping, 34–38, 175–80; achievement of graded vs. nongraded pupils, 182; Bellevue's program in, 129–30; Chicago's program in, 150–51; learning variations and, 42–45; level sequence for elementary school, example of, 156–58; Peter Boscow's program in, 174–82; readiness as basis for primary school grouping, 41–42, 169, 193; readiness and nongradedness, 33

Rehage, Kenneth, 151

Rehwoldt, Walter, 188

Reporting systems, cards being replaced by conferences and progress reports, 137–39; Chicago's, 146; diagnostic, 160, 163; Middletown's, 223; as problem of nongradedness, 112, 119; progress report of Appleton schools, 239; progress report of Cabool schools, 240; samples of, 239–40

Research on nongraded schools, need for more, 122–23; present status of, 95–106; by teachers, encouraged in Bellevue program, 131–32

Retention of students. See Failure of students

Retson, James N., 135

Rhode Island College, 219

Ryans, David, 106

St. Louis Plan, 8

Santa Barbara Concentric Plan, 10

Schedules, flexible, 60–61; as problem in nongraded high school, 220–21, 222; samples of student, 244–45

School day, lengthened, 209

School organization. See plans of school organization

School year, lengthened, 209

Schools, in Appleton, Wis., 135–43; in Bellevue, Wash., 127–34; Brigham Young University Laboratory, 226–36; in Cabool, Mo., 159–64; in Cedar Falls, Iowa, 191–98; in Chicago, 144–53; in Middletown, R.I., 217–25; Monteith in Grosse Pointe, Mich., 166–73; Nova High School in Fort Lauderdale, Fla., 207–16;

Peter Boscow in Hillsboro, Ore., 174–83; in Southern Humboldt, Cal., 154–58; in Torrance, Cal., 184–90; Webster School in Pontiac, Mich., 199–206; see also Elementary schools; Graded schools; High schools; Nongraded schools

Science grouping, in elementary school, 35, 36

Search, Preston W., 10–11

Secondary schools. See High schools

Shumaker, Clara, 154

Skapski, Mary K., 100

Skill cards, 137

Slater, Eva M., 18

Slow learners, as burden to Middletown Project, 224; nonpromotion of, 30–31

Smedstad, Alton O., 174

Snyder, Edith Roach, 199

Social changes, and future of nongradedness, 113–15, 120–21

Social growth, in multi grade classroom, 188–90

Social studies, how covered in multi-grade school, 186–87

South Florida Education Center, 208–16

Southern Humboldt, Cal., nongraded schools, 154–58

Sponsler, Verna, 191

Staff. See Teachers

State departments of education, and nongraded high schools, 70–71

Statement of Philosophy and Purposes of Middletown Project, 218–19, 225

Stoddard, George D., 14

Student. See Pupils

Study stations, individual, 231, 233

Study unit, at Nova High School, 210

Teachers, adjustment to change in nongrading a school, 60–61, 132, 168; adjustment to philosophy of Continuous Progress Plan,

Teachers (*Cont.*)
141–43; assignment of, 132; children's views on, 101; diagnostic skills needed by, 26; early innovations in role of, 13–15; individualized instruction by elementary as compared with secondary, 53–54; in-service programs for, 69, 73–74, 141–42; methodological problems of, 223–25; mobilized for change to nongradedness, 171; new role in Nova High School, 209–11, 213–14; in nongraded high schools, 53–54, 57–61, 75, 209–11, 213–14; older, as receptive to change, 168; remain 3 years with the same class under "block" plan, 201–6; relationship with students in nongraded high school, 58–59; role in Bellevue program, 131–32; role in developing a nongraded school, 80–83, 85, 157; team teaching by, 14–15, 60–61, 116–18, 165

Teaching devices, innovations in, 212

Teaching studios, 231–32

Team teaching, early attempts at, 14–15; in nongraded high school, 60–61; and nongradedness, 116–18, 165

Technological aids, 66–67, 87–88, 211–12, 233

Television, Nova High School's use of, 212

Tesla School, Chicago, 149–53

Testing procedures. *See* Evaluation

Testing room, high school's, 233

Textbooks, graded, 6; for nongraded reading plan, 37–38

Torrance, Cal., multi-grade plan, 184–90

Truancy, and nongraded school, 164

Trump, J. Lloyd, 20

Underpriviledged children. *See* Disadvantaged children

Ungraded schools. *See* Nongraded schools

United States Office of Education, 19

Wahle, Roy Patrick, 127

Walteria Elementary School, 188

Washburne, Carleton, 11–13

Weaver, Fred J., 35

Webster School, Pontiac, Mich., 199–206

Wiles, Kimball, 50

Wiley, Verna, 132

Winnetka Plan, 12–13

Wirt, William A., 13

Wolfe, Arthur B., 207

Woodruff, Asahel, 226

Zerby, John R., 100

Zieman, Marvin, 191